The Shambhala Dictionary of Taoism

For Reference

Not to be taken from this room

THE
Shambhala
Dictionary of
TAOISM✓

Ingrid Fischer-Schreiber

Translated by Werner Wünsche

Shambhala
Boston
1996

3/9?

Shambhala Publications, Inc.
Horticultural Hall
300 Massachusetts Avenue
Boston, Massachusetts 02115

©1996 by Shambhala Publications, Inc.

The Shambhala Dictionary of Taoism is based on material from
The Encyclopedia of Eastern Philosophy and Religion © 1989 by
Shambhala Publications, Inc., a translation of *Lexikon der östlichen
Weisheitslehren,* edited by Stephen Schuhmacher and Gert Woerner
© 1986 by Otto-Wilhelm-Barth Verlag, a division of Scherz Verlag,
Bern and Munich.

9 8 7 6 5 4 3 2 1

First Edition
Printed in Canada
∞ This edition is printed on acid-free paper that meets
the American National Standards Institute Z39.48 Standard.
Distributed in the United States by Random House, Inc.,
and in Canada by Random House of Canada Ltd

Library of Congress Cataloging-in-Publication Data
The Shambhala dictionary of Taoism.
     p.   cm.
  This edition based on the comprehensive Encyclopedia of Eastern
philosophy and religion: Shambhala, 1989.
   ISBN 1-57062-203-5 (alk. paper)
   1. Taoism—Dictionary.
BL1923.S48   1996
299'.514'03—dc20   95-25358
                                      CIP

Contents

Introduction

This dictionary presents the basic terminology and doctrinal systems of Taoism in a clearly understandable form. The entries do not cover the entire range of Taoist concepts, for they are not intended for the use of academic specialists, but rather to help general readers find their way through the thicket of unfamiliar terms and concepts that are frequently encountered today in widely varied fields of interest—in the sciences, in the media, in the health professions, in psychotherapy, in the study of meditation, and in psychophysical training.

Difficulties in the preparation of a work such as this arise from several sources. For one, the translation of the Chinese words is often a complex matter. The reader should keep in mind that a translation is an interpretation that reflects the translator's understanding, both in linguistic and substantive terms. Thus, many translations, but not *one single correct* translation, are possible. For this reason, the Bibliography includes several translations of basic texts as far as this has been possible.

Difficulties arise also and perhaps primarily from the subject matter of any wisdom teaching, "wisdom" being meant here not as a mere mental achievement but rather as immediately experienced intuitive wisdom whose essence is insight into the true nature of the world as well as eschatological matters. Thus, we are not dealing with an accumulation of factual knowledge in the form of the objective dates and measurements of natural science in the Western sense. This is true even though the research methods of Taoism are no less pragmatic than those of Western science; however, the essence of the insights that have been gained through their methods, as all wisdom teachings repeatedly stress, cannot be conveyed in a conceptual, rational manner. Thus the terms used always point to generally valid human experiences; yet their real content can be ultimately grasped only through immediate personal experience.

On this path, the spiritual researchers of the East have attained insight into areas and levels of consciousness that for the most part are completely unknown to the West and for which, therefore, the West has no concepts. This encyclopedia thus ventures into an area where, as far as the presentation of the material to Western readers is concerned, no fixed standards of form or content have yet been achieved—and indeed, perhaps none can be set. For this reason, there are bound to be criticisms. Such criticisms, it is hoped, will help to improve upon the pioneering attempt made in this volume to develop a unified terminology.

Guide to Using the Dictionary

The order of the entry titles is according to the letter-by-letter system of alphabetization, irrespective of word components: for example, *Ch'ang-sheng pu-ssu* . . . *Chang Tao-ling* . . . *Chang Tsung-yen,* and not, as in Chinese dictionaries, *Chang Tao-ling* . . . *Chang Tsung-yen* . . . *Ch'ang-sheng pu-ssu.*

The literal meaning of an entry title is given when it is different from the definition of the entry title or when a literal translation of the components of the entry title is an aid to understanding.

In Chinese there are many homonyms with different meanings. Since the transcriptions are based on pronunciation alone, one cannot tell that for each of these different words a different character is used in the original. Thus there are cases where the same entry title appears twice with a different literal meaning each time. In this case, it is not the *same* word with a different interpretation; rather these are different words (and characters) that are spelled the same way in the romanized form.

Transcription and Pronunciation

Although the Pinyin system for the romanization of Chinese was officially adopted by the People's Republic of China in 1979, the previously standard Wade-Giles system continues to be widely employed. Thus, in order to conform to the transcription most frequently encountered in scholarly literature, entry forms have been rendered in their familiar (Wade-Giles) form.

The following rules give approximate English equivalents for sounds as rendered in Wade-Giles:

ch	pronounced	j
ch'		ch
e		short *u* as in *fun*
j		like English *r* as in *ready*
k		g

k'	k
p	b
p'	p
t	d
t'	t
ts	dz
ts'	ts
hs	sh

Vowels are pronounced as in Italian or German.

Since readers may encounter Pinyin in publications issued after 1950, a conversion chart is provided below. (Note: Syllables whose transliteration is the same in Pinyin and Wade-Giles are not included.)

Pinyin to Wade-Giles

Pinyin	Wade-Giles	Pinyin	Wade-Giles
ba	pa	bin	pin
bai	pai	bing	ping
ban	pan	bo	po
bang	pang	bu	pu
bao	pao	ca	ts'a
bei	pei	cai	ts'ai
ben	pen	can	ts'an
beng	peng	cang	ts'ang
bi	pi	cao	ts'ao
bian	pien	ce	ts'e
biao	piao	cen	ts'en
bie	pieh	ceng	ts'eng

Pinyin	Wade-Giles	Pinyin	Wade-Giles
cha	ch'a	dao	tao
chai	ch'ai	de	te
chan	ch'an	deng	teng
chang	ch'ang	di	ti
chao	ch'ao	dian	tien
che	ch'e	diao	tiao
chen	ch'en	die	tieh
cheng	ch'eng	ding	ting
chi	ch'ih	diu	tiu
chong	ch'ung	dong	tung
chou	ch'ou	dou	tou
chu	ch'u	du	tu
chua	ch'ua	duan	tuan
chuai	ch'uai	dui	tui
chuan	ch'uan	dun	tun
chuang	ch'uang	duo	to
chui	ch'ui	e	eh
chun	ch'un	er	erh
chuo	ch'o	ga	ka
ci	tz'u (ts'u)	gai	kai
cong	ts'ung	gan	kan
cou	ts'ou	gang	kang
cu	ts'u	gao	kao
cuan	ts'uan	ge	ke, ko
cui	ts'ui	gei	kei
cun	ts'un	gen	ken
cuo	ts'o	geng	keng
da	ta	gong	kung
dai	tai	gou	kou
dan	tan	gu	ku
dang	tang	gua	kua

Pinyin	Wade-Giles	Pinyin	Wade-Giles
guai	kuai	ku	k'u
guan	kuan	kua	k'ua
quang	kuang	kuai	k'uai
gui	kui	kuan	k'uan
gun	kun	kuang	k'uang
quo	kuo	kui	k'ui
he	he, ho	kun	k'un
hong	hung	kuo	k'uo
ji	chi	le	le, lo
jia	chia	lian	lien
jian	chien	lie	lieh
jiang	chiang	long	lung
jiao	chiao		lüeh
jie	chieh	lüe	lüo
jin	chin		lio
jing	ching		
jiong	chiung	mian	mien
jiu	chiu	mie	mieh
ju	chü	nian	nien
juan	chüan	nie	nieh
jue	chüeh, chüo	nong	nung
jun	chün		nüeh
ka	k'a	nüe	nuö
kai	k'ai		nio
kan	k'an	nuo	no
kang	k'ang	pa	p'a
kao	k'ao	pai	p'ai
ke	k'e, k'o	pan	p'an
ken	k'en	pang	p'ang
keng	k'eng	pao	p'ao
kong	k'ung	pei	p'ei
kou	k'ou	pen	p'en
		peng	p'eng

Pinyin	Wade-Giles	Pinyin	Wade-Giles
pi	p'i	rou	jou
pian	p'ien	ru	ju
piao	p'iao	ruan	juan
pie	p'ieh	rui	jui
pin	p'in	run	jun
ping	p'ing	ruo	jo
po	p'o	shi	shih
pou	p'ou	shuo	sho
pu	p'u	si	su, szu, ssu
qi	ch'i	song	sung
qia	ch'ia	suo	so
qian	ch'ien	ta	t'a
qiang	ch'iang	tai	t'ai
qiao	ch'iao	tan	t'an
qie	ch'ieh	tang	t'ang
qin	ch'in	tao	t'ao
qing	ch'ing	te	t'e
qiong	ch'iung	teng	t'eng
qiu	ch'iu	ti	t'i
qu	ch'ü	tian	t'ien
quan	ch'üan	tiao	t'iao
que	{ ch'üeh ch'üo	tie	t'ieh
		ting	t'ing
qun	ch'ün	tong	t'ung
ran	jan	tou	t'ou
rang	jang	tu	t'u
rao	jao	tuan	t'uan
re	je	tui	t'ui
ren	jen	tun	t'un
reng	jeng	tuo	t'o
ri	jih	xi	hsi
rong	jung	xia	hsia

Pinyin	Wade-Giles	Pinyin	Wade-Giles
xian	hsien	zha	cha
xiang	hsiang	zhai	chai
xiao	hsiao	zhan	chan
xie	hsieh	zhang	chang
xin	hsin	zhao	chao
xing	hsing	zhe	che
xiong	hsiung	zhei	chei
xiu	hsiu	zhen	chen
xu	hsü	zheng	cheng
xuan	hsüan	zhi	chih
xue	hsüeh, hsüo	zhong	chung
xun	hsün	zhou	chou
yan	yen	zhu	chu
ye	yeh	zhua	chua
yong	yung	zhuai	chuai
you	yu	zhuan	chuan
yu	yü	zhuang	chuang
yuan	yüen	zhui	chui
yue	yüch	zhun	chun
yun	yün	zhuo	cho
za	tsa	zi	tzu (tsu)
tai	tsai	zong	tsung
zan	tsan	zou	tsou
zang	tsang	zu	tsu
zao	tsao	zuan	tsuan
ze	tse	zui	tsui
zei	tsei	zun	tsun
zen	tsen	zuo	tso
zeng	tseng		

The Shambhala Dictionary of Taoism

Alchemy, Taoist   → *wai-tan,* → *nei-tan*

✿   ✿   ✿

Chai   Chin., lit. "fasting"; one of the most important festivals of religious Taoism (→ *tao-chiao*), known since its beginnings. In the official state ritual *chai* designates a fast before sacrifices. In Taoism the term refers to feasts held under the direction of a master, at which a specific number of pupils (between six and thirty-eight) participate. These feasts serve mainly for the confession of sins, which are considered to be the cause of all illness.

Every school of religious Taoism celebrates its own fasts. These are particularly important in the → *t'ai-p'ing tao,* → *wu-tou-mi tao,* and the → *ling-pao p'ai.* One of the best-known ceremonies is the *t'u-t'an chai*—a fast during which the participants smear themselves with charcoal.

Chai ceremonies are very complicated, so that those participating at them require detailed instruction. They are usually held in the courtyards of Taoist monasteries and may extend over several days. After a platform of strictly prescribed dimensions—its sides limited by ropes—has been erected, the participants, holding hands, step onto it. Their hair is tousled and their faces are covered with coal dust and dirt to signify their remorse. To the accompaniment of a drum, the master of the ceremony implores various deities to attend the feast. There follows a recitation of sins and their possible consequences. At this point the religious ecstasy of the participants reaches its peak. They throw themselves to the ground and roll in the dust to demonstrate their repentance. As the twelve vows of repentance are recited, the participants touch their foreheads to the ground and ask for their sins to be forgiven. The ceremony ends with further rituals. These collective repentance sessions are held three times daily, but participants are allowed only one meal each day. The resultant physical exhaustion produces a psychic collapse, which effects an inner purification.

Ch'ang   Chin., lit. constant, enduring, eternal; concept of philosophical Taoism (→ *tao-chia*). *Ch'ang* designates the permanent, as opposed to the changeable, and is one of the symbols of the Tao. In the → *Tao-te ching* the term *ch'ang* is attributed to all laws that are universally applicable and not subject to change. Enlightenment (→ *ming*) consists in the realization of the unchangeable.

Chapter 1 of the *Tao-te ching* states "The Tao that can be expressed is not the eternal (*ch'ang*) Tao; the name that can be named is not the eternal name." And in Chapter 37, "The Tao abides (*ch'ang*) in nonaction [→ *wu-wei*], yet nothing is left undone" (Feng & English 1972). Concerning enlightenment as a realization of the nature of *ch'ang*, Chapter 16 says, "Things in all their multitude: each one returns to its root. Return to the root means stillness. Stillness means return to fate (its original state). Return to fate is the eternal (*ch'ang*) law." In a treatise on Lao-tzu, the philosopher Han Fei-tzu (3d century B.C.E.) describes *ch'ang* as follows:

"Things which now exist and then perish; which suddenly come into being and as suddenly die; which first bloom and then fade—such things are not *ch'ang*. Only that which was created simultaneously with the separation of Heaven and

Earth, and will not perish before Heaven and Earth, can be called *ch'ang*."

Chang Chüeh   d. 184 C.E., founder of the Taoist school of → *t'ai-p'ing tao* (Chin., lit. "Way of Supreme Peace"). His teachings are based on the doctrines of the → *T'ai-p'ing ching* and stem from the → *Huang-lao tao* (Way of Huang-ti and Lao-tzu). Chang Chüeh aimed at establishing supreme peace, with particular emphasis on the peaceful equality of all individuals. This ideal brought his teachings great popularity at a time when the people were plagued by famine and suppressed by their rulers. Within ten years Chang Chüeh attracted several hundred thousand followers. A further factor contributing to his success was the holding of collective rites for the healing of sicknesses, which he claimed to be a consequence of sinful actions. These ritual practices centered around collective ceremonies of repentance (→ *chai*).

Between 165 and 184 C.E. his teaching expanded over eight provinces. He organized his followers on a strictly hierarchical basis, with himself at their head as celestial duke-general. In 184 C.E. he led the rebellion of the → Yellow Turbans, which was ruthlessly put down and during which he and his brothers Chang Pao and Chang Liang, who enthusiastically fought by his side, were killed.

Chang Chüeh's religious activities were triggered by a revelation of an approaching age of supreme peace, of paradise on Earth. This age was to begin on the day the Han Dynasty was succeeded by that of the Yellow Heaven of the *t'ai-p'ing tao* (yellow being the color of → Huang-ti, the Yellow Emperor, whom the followers of Chang Chüeh venerated). This was expected to happen in 184 C.E.

Nevertheless, Chang Chüeh's enormous popularity was above all due to his capabilities as a healer. In addition to conducting fasting and healing ceremonies, he made use of magic formulae and sacred water (Chin. *fu-shui*), which he blessed by pronouncing magic spells over it, while holding a bamboo staff with nine knots (nine being the number of Heaven). He would command the sick to kneel, touch the earth with their foreheads, and contemplate their sins and omissions. After that they drank of his sacred water. If the patient was healed, he was considered to be a practitioner of the Tao. Similar ceremonies were held by other schools of religious Taoism (*wu-tou-mi tao*).

Chang Hsien   Chin., lit. "Chang the Immortal"; traditional immortal (→ *hsien*). In popular belief Chang Hsien bestows male offspring. He is usually depicted as an old man aiming a drawn bow at Heaven. Frequently the Hound of Heaven (*t'ien-kou*), against whom he protects children, is shown by his side. He is, as a rule, accompanied by his son, who carries in his arms the boy-child whom Chang Hsien bestows on those who believe in him. Sometimes he is in the company of Sung-tzu niang-niang, the "lady Who Bestows Children."

Chang Hsiu   general of the Han Dynasty and founder of a movement in religious Taoism (→ *tao-chiao*) similar to that of the → *t'ai-p'ing tao* and the → *wu-tou-mi tao* and widespread throughout the province of Szechwan. The central practices of this school consisted in healing ceremonies, during which sacrifices were made to the three rulers (→ *san-kuan*), i.e., Heaven, Earth, and Water. Chang Hsiu was murdered by Chang Lu in 190 C.E.

Like other leaders of early Taoist movements, Chang Hsiu was of the opinion that illnesses were a consequence of evil deeds. As part of his "therapy" the sick were locked up in "convalescent homes," there to contemplate their transgressions. However, a complete healing was possible only if the sufferer listed his sins on three separate strips of paper, which were then submitted to the three rulers (Heaven, Earth, and Water) by being respectively left on a mountaintop, buried, and thrown into a river. The family of a patient had to pay five pecks of rice for his treatment.

Chang Hsiu organized his followers on a strictly hierarchical basis, the most important functions being performed by the presenters of liquid sacrifices (the *chi-chiu*), whose task it was to determine whether all believers followed the teachings of the → *Tao-te ching*—the root text of the Chang Hsiu movement, albeit interpreted in a manner peculiar to that school. The religious hierarchy was based on a military model: the *chi-chiu* were "officers" and their subordinates "demon soldiers."

Chang Liang   d. 187 B.C.E.; high-ranking official of the early Han Dynasty and traditional founder of religious Taoism (→ *tao-chiao*). He is one of the first immortals (→ *hsien*) mentioned in Taoist literature. It is said that to attain immortality he performed physical exercises (→ *tao-yin*) and abstained from eating grain (→ *pi-ku*).

Chang Lu   2d century C.E.; one of the founders of the → *wu-tou-mi tao* ("Five-Pecks-of-Rice Taoism"). Chang Lu was a grandson of → Chang Tao-ling. In 190 C.E. he succeeded with the help of → Chang Hsiu in establishing a strictly hierarchical politico-religious state, which lasted for thirty years. As a leader he emerged from the circle of his later followers, who venerated him as a miraculous healer. His teachings were based on the view that external well-being is dependent on morality, so that illnesses are ordained by the spirits in retribution for sinful actions. He organized mass ceremonies during which believers repented of their transgressions and thereby were cured of their afflictions. For every such cure Chang Lu charged a fee of five pecks of rice, hence the name of the religious school founded by him. He called himself a celestial master (→ *t'ien-shih*)—a title passed on by his descendants to this day.

The state founded by Chang Lu was organized on a strictly military basis. Local communities were led by the presenters of liquid sacrifices, known as libationers (*chi-chiu*), who officiated at healing ceremonies for the sick, during which sacrifices were made to the three rulers (→ *san-kuan*), i.e., Heaven, Earth, and Water. Chang Lu adopted these ceremonies from Chang Hsiu. Public life centered on communal dwellings (*i-she*) in which everyone was provided with food free of charge. A further characteristic feature of Chang Lu's rule was the manner in which transgressions were punished: in the case of the first three transgressions the sinner simply had to regret his evil deeds. A fourth transgression, however, called for active repentance; i.e., the guilty person might be ordered to meet the cost of repairing a thousand paces of public road, or effect the repair in person.

Chang Po-tuan   984–1082 C.E.; well-known Taoist master who combined the teachings of Taoism with those of Zen Buddhism and Confucianism. Chang Po-tuan was one of the most important representatives of the alchemical School of the Inner Elixir (→ *nei-tan*), whose aim consisted in attaining spiritual immortality. The inner elixir is not produced by a method of chemical transmutation but rather is said to consist in spiritual enlightenment, in a return to the source (→ *fu*). Chang Po-tuan explains his teaching in his *Wu-chen p'ien* (*Essay on the Awakening to the Truth*).

According to the *Wu-chen p'ien*, which is couched in the language of the School of the Outer Elixir (→ *wai-tan*), the ingredients of the inner elixir are "true lead" and "true mercury," i.e., the essences of yang and yin. The latter has to be caught and absorbed by the yang; Chang Po-tuan calls this the "marriage of yin and yang." A commentary on the *Wu-chen p'ien* describes the essence of yang to be that which is real, and the essence of yin as that which is unreal.

By lying on his bed at midnight of the winter solstice and meditating, the alchemical practitioner marries these two essences within his body with the help of the life energy (→ *ch'i*), thereby giving birth to an embryo (→ *sheng-t'ai*), which increases in size proportionate to the growth of yang. By this method the alchemist can attain immortality. The embryo referred to is the new "I," which, being enlightened and knowing no difference between subject and object, is immortal.

Ch'ang-sheng pu-ssu Chin., lit. long-living, nondying; immortality, the goal of various Taoist practices. Immortality can be either physical or spiritual. The idea of physical immortality goes back to the very beginnings of Taoism and its attainment is the aim of most schools of religious Taoism (→ *tao-chiao*). The followers of the alchemical School of the Outer Elixir (→ *wai-tan*) strove to become immortals (→ *hsien*) by swallowing various life-prolonging substances. Other practices for attaining physical immortality were abstention from eating grain (*pi-ku*), various breathing exercises, gymnastics (→ *tao-yin*), meditation, and certain sexual practices (→ *fang-chung shu*). A person who is physically immortal ascends to Heaven (→ *fei-sheng*) in broad daylight or dies in ap-

7

pearance only; when his coffin is opened, it is found to be empty (→ *shih-chieh*).

The philosophical Taoism of → Lao-tzu and → Chuang-tzu strives for spiritual immortality, i.e., enlightenment and the attainment of oneness with the highest principle (→ Tao)—a state in which the distinction between life and death is dissolved and yin combines with yang. The followers of the inner elixir (→ *nei-tan*) also strive for spiritual immortality. Spiritual immortality implies not only freedom from life and death but also from time space and sexual identity; for that reason immortals may be depicted as either male or female.

Common immortality symbols found in Taoist-inspired art are a crane, a gnarled staff of wood, pine trees, peaches (→ Hsi wang-mu), the mushroom of immortality (→ *ling-chih*), the god of immortality (→ Shou-lao, → San-hsing), etc.

It may be difficult to determine which type of immortality a particular school or practice strives for, because many texts employ esoteric terminology that can be interpreted either way. Even some passages in texts of philosophical Taoists such as → Chuang-tzu and → Lieh-tzu can be taken as pointing toward physical immortality: descriptions of places such as → K'un-lun or the isles of the immortals (→ P'eng-lai, → Ying-chou, → Fang-chang), which are considered to be dwelling places of immortals, can be understood either abstractly or concretely. Ch'in Shih Huang-ti, the first Chinese emperor, organized several—albeit unsuccessful—expeditions with the aim of discovering the mysterious isles of the immortals and obtaining the draught of immortality. Some commentators consider such passages to be descriptive of a spiritual journey into the center or essence of man.

This ambiguity applies to alchemical texts in general; e.g., followers of the inner elixir (→ *nei-tan*) may employ the language of Outer Alchemy (→ *wai-tan*) to describe processes of consciousness. In the early stages of Chinese alchemy the inner and outer methods for achieving immortality were co-existent and of equal importance until ca. the 6th century C.E. when immortality increasingly came to be considered as being of a spiritual nature; instead of trying to manufacture a pill of immortality from gold, cinnabar, and other chemical substances, alchemists were almost exclusively concerned with developing the inner gold, the golden flower, the sacred embryo (→ *sheng-t'ai*). By the 13th century C.E. the Outer Elixir School had faded into insignificance, although its language continued to be used. The followers of the Inner Alchemy despised those who tried to attain immortality by the transmutation of chemical substances. The influence of Buddhism—above all, Zen—decisively contributed toward the spiritualization of the search for immortality, so that ancient alchemical texts were consistently interpreted in accordance with the teachings of the Inner Elixir School.

In the search for immortality specific sexual techniques played an important part in many schools of religious Taoism and were practiced in public (→ *ho-chi*) from the 2d to the 7th century, when they were forced to retreat to the private domain under the pressure of Confucianist morality but continued to be performed as a preliminary to Taoist meditation.

Chang Tao-ling also known as Chang Ling, 34-156 C.E.; founder of → *wu-tou-mi tao,* one of the most important schools of religious Taoism (→ *tao-chiao*). Toward the middle of the 2d century Chang Tao-ling practiced as a healer in Szechwan Province, curing the sick by the recitation of magical formulae and by serving them sacred water. His fee for each such treatment consisted of five pecks of rice, so that the school founded by him came to be known as Five-Pecks-of-Rice Taoism. His followers venerated him as a celestial master (→ *t'ien-shih*), a title borne by his descendants to this day.

According to legend, Chang Tao-ling carried out alchemical experiments over a period of many years and in the end even succeeded in producing a pill of immortality. Upon swallowing this pill, his face became as fresh and rosy as that of a young boy, despite the fact that he was sixty years old at the time. It is said that he received the instructions for producing such a pill and for healing the sick from → Lao-tzu in person, together with a book of spells for driving out demons. Chang worked as a healer to finance his expensive alchemical experiments and attracted a great number of followers. He died in Szechwan province at a ripe old age and allegedly ascended to Heaven in broad daylight (→ *fei-sheng*).

Chang Tsung-yen d. 1292 C.E.; celestial master (→ *t'ien-shih*) in the thirty-sixth generation. Chang was granted the title of celestial master in 1276 C.E. by the Emperor Khubilai, together with rulership over all Taoist believers south of the Yang-tse river. In 1288 C.E. the emperor again summoned him to court and demanded to see the jade seal and sword that, according to legend, had been passed from one celestial master to the next since the time of the Han Dynasty. The emperor considered the survival of these treasures to be a sign from Heaven and declared that the title and office of a *t'ien-shih* could be passed on by inheritance. The importance of the Chang family line in religious Taoism rests on this pronouncement (→ Chang Tao-ling).

Ch'eng-huang Chin.; protective deity of a city. In Taoist belief these deities ward off disasters and catastrophes and protect the inhabitants of cities under their care, who may also supplicate them. In periods of drought, the *ch'eng-huang* cause rain to fall and the sun to shine again after a thunderstorm. They grant a plentiful harvest and ensure the affluence of the citizens.

In addition, the *ch'eng-huang* act as guides of the souls of the departed. A Taoist priest who wishes to help the souls (→ *hun,* → *po*) of a dead person out of Hell, must inform the protective deity of the city by submitting a document.

The *ch'eng-huang* tradition dates back to ancient times and was adopted by Taoism, which admitted these city protectors to the ranks of its most important deities. As a rule, prominent citizens who devoted their energies to the public good were also venerated as *ch'eng-huang.* Toward the end of the 10th century it became the custom to accord to city deities the title *king* or *duke,* depending on the importance of the city in question. The feast day of a city deity was an important festival in the life of a city and was celebrated with parades, at which a statue of the *ch'eng-huang* was carried through the streets.

Cheng-i tao Chin., lit. "Way of Right Unity"; collective term for all Taoist schools that use talismans, amulets, etc. as part of their religious practice (→ *fu-lu p'ai*). Next to the → *ch'ün-chen tao* (Way of the Realization of Truth) the *cheng-i tao* was the most important branch of religious Taoism (→ *tao-chiao*) since the time of the Yuan Dynasty.

The beginnings of the *cheng-i tao* go back to the Five-Pecks-of-Rice Taoism (→ *wu-tou-mi tao*) founded by Chang Tao-ling during the Eastern Han Dynasty. During the T'ang and Sung dynasties the *cheng-i tao* school combined with the → *ling-pao p'ai* (School of the Magic Jewel) and several other schools. In 1304 C.E. one of Chang Taoling's descendants in the thirty-eighth generation was accorded the title *leader of right unity,* because he led several religious schools that made use of talismans. Since then all schools using talismans are considered to be part of the Way of Right Unity, in whose practices exorcisms, talismans, spells, and other magical elements play an important role. The priests of the *cheng-i tao,* unlike those of the *ch'üan-chen tao,* may marry. The *cheng-i tao* still has active followers in Taiwan and Hong Kong.

Cheng-i tao priests pass on their magical skills through inheritance. The believers visit the priests to obtain talismans, which protect the wearer against evil spirits, sorcery, sickness, fire, and other disasters. The → *tao-shih* of this school also officiate at various ceremonies, e.g., to cause the soul of a dead person to return into that person's body or to guide a dead person through Hell. Some *tao-shih* practice as spiritualists and soothsayers, basing their prophecies on astrology, physiognomy, or the *Book of Change(s)* (→ *I-ching*).

Chen-jen Chin., lit. "true [pure] human being"; ideal figure of philosophical and religious Taoism. The term was first employed by → Chuang-tzu and refers to a person who has realized the truth within himself and thus attained the → Tao. The true man is free of all limitations, has abandoned all concepts and attained total freedom.

Chuang-tzu (chap. 6) describes the true or pure men as follows:

"The pure men of old acted without calculation, not seeking to secure results. They laid no plans. Therefore, failing, they had no cause for regret; succeeding, no cause for congratulation. And thus they could scale heights without fear; enter water without becoming wet; fire without feeling hot. So far had their wisdom advanced toward Tao. The pure men of old slept without dreams, and waked without anxiety. They ate without discrimination, breathing deep breaths. For pure men draw breath from their innermost depths; the vulgar only from their throats. The pure men of old did not know what it was to love life or to hate death. They did not rejoice in birth, nor strive to put off dissolution. Quickly come, and quickly go— no more. They did not forget whence it was they had sprung, neither did they seek to hasten their return thither. Cheerfully they played their allotted parts, waiting patiently for the end. This is what is called not leading the heart astray from Tao, nor to let the human seek to supplement the divine. . . . Such men are in mind absolutely free; in demeanour, grave; in expression, cheerful. If it is freezing cold, it seems to them like autumn; if blazing hot, like spring. Their passions occur like the four seasons. They are in harmony with all creation, and none know the limits thereof." (*See* Giles 1961.)

The → *Huai-nan-tzu* says that the pure man is "neither born, nor does he die; he is not empty, nor is he full." The *Book of Supreme Peace* (→ *T'ai-p'ing ching*) places the *chen-jen* above the immortals (→ *hsien*) and below the gods (→ *shen*) in the Taoist hierarchy.

Since the T'ang Dynasty *chen-jen* has been an honorary title of historical personalities and Taoist masters. The Emperor T'ang Hsüan-tsung bestowed upon Chuang-tzu the title "Pure Man from the Southern Land of Blossoms" (*Nan-hua chen-jen*) from which the title of his collected writings (*Nan-hua chen-ching*) derives.

Chen-ta-tao chiao Chin., lit. "Teaching of the True Great Tao"; school of religious Taoism founded in 1142

13

C.E. by Liu Te-jen. Based on the concepts of the → *Tao-te ching,* this school stresses the ideals of unmotivated action (→ *wu-wei*), contentment, and altruism. The adherents of the *chen-ta-tao chiao* strive toward the good and endeavor to avoid evil. Life-prolonging and magical practices play no part in this school, in which a strong Confucianist influence can be felt. The *chen-ta-tao chiao* reached its peak in the 13th century but faded out soon after.

Chen-tsung   968-1022 C.E.; Sung Dynasty emperor who, in 1012 C.E., instituted the veneration of the Jade Emperor → Yü-huang after allegedly having received a letter from him. In 1016 C.E. Chen-tsung granted the use of a large area of land on Dragon-and-Tiger Mountain (→ Lung-hu-shan) to the then heavenly master (→ *t'ien-shih*). It is said that this mountain continued to be an abode of heavenly masters until the year 1949. In addition, Chen-tsung promoted the compilation of the Taoist canon (→ *Tao-tsang*), which first appeared in print in 1019 C.E.

Ch'en T'uan   ca. 906–89 C.E.; Taoist scholar well-versed in the teachings of both the inner and outer elixir (→ *nei-tan,* → *wai-tan*), Ch'en lived as a hermit on Hua-shan, one of the sacred Taoist mountains, where he is said to have carved the diagram of the ultimateless (*wu-chi-t'u*) into the rock face near where he meditated on the Inner Alchemy. Ch'en T'uan is also considered to be the creator of the diagram of primordial heaven (*hsien-t'ien-t'u*). These two diagrams influenced the neo-Confucian philosopher Chou I-tun as he worked on his diagram of the supreme ultimate (→ *t'ai-chi-t'u*).

Chang Chung-yüan interprets Ch'en T'uan's diagram of the ultimateless as follows:

"The diagram consisted of several tiers of circles describing the process of meditation. The first tier (bottom row in the illustration) was a circle labeled, in Lao-tzu's expression, 'The Gate of the Dark Femininity,' which is the Foundation of Heaven and Earth. The next tier is another circle, illustrating the process of compounding → Ching (essence) into → Ch'i (breath) and then into → Shen (spirit).

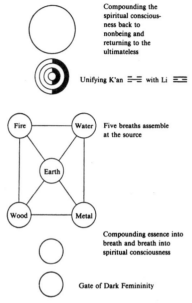

Compounding the spiritual consciousness back to nonbeing and returning to the ultimateless

Unifying K'an ☵ with Li ☲

Fire
Water

Earth

Wood
Metal

Five breaths assemble at the source

Compounding essence into breath and breath into spiritual consciousness

Gate of Dark Femininity

The Diagram of Ultimatelessness

Ching, ch'i and *shen* are the fundamental concepts of meditative breathing. . . . This tier [thus] shows how the energy from the lowest center of the body [→ *tan-t'ien*] is transformed into the circulation of breath and . . . further into spiritual consciousness. The following, or middle, tier of the diagram consists of the Five Elements [→ *wu-hsing*]: fire and wood on the left, metal and water on the right, and earth in the middle. They symbolise the five movers in the lesser circulation (of the breath), which ultimately reach the grand circulation. The fourth tier shows the unification of *k'an* and *li* in the form of a circle, which is divided into *yin* and *yang*. The fluctuation of *yin* and *yang* [represents] the grand circulation through the entire body. Both the five movers in the small circulation and *yin* and *yang* in the grand circulation lead to *shen*, or spiritual consciousness. The tier at the top of the diagram shows the compounding of *shen* back to *hsü*, or nonbeing.

"Thus all things return to ultimatelessness (*wu-chi*). The spiritual consciousness is the ultimate of the individual, and nonbeing is ultimatelessness. In other words: the spiritual consciousness is compounded back to absolute nonbeing, the origin of all things." (Chang 1963, p. 165)

Ch'i Chin., lit. air, vapor, breath, ether, energy; also "temperament, strength, atmosphere"; central concept in Taoism and Chinese medicine. In the Taoist view *ch'i* is the vital energy, the life force, the cosmic spirit that pervades and enlivens all things and is therefore synonymous with primordial energy (→ *yüan-ch'i*, → *nei-ch'i*). In the human body *ch'i* is accumulated in an area near the navel, known as the ocean of breath (→ *ch'i-hai*), and must be carefully tended to prevent it from being wasted, which results in sickness or death.

Ch'i as life energy is a central concept in Taoist breathing exercises aimed at strengthening and increasing this energy (→ *hsing-ch'i*, → *fu-ch'i*, *yen-ch'i*, *lien-ch'i*, → *t'ai-hsi*). By training his *ch'i* a Taoist adept can acquire extraordinary abilities, which, incidentally, play an important part in the various martial arts. The meditative breathing techniques of the Inner Alchemy (→ *nei-tan*) also work with the *ch'i*, with the aim of purifying and transmuting it.

In his *Pao-p'u-tzu* the great Taoist alchemist → Ko Hung says concerning the importance of *ch'i*, "Man is in *ch'i* and *ch'i* is within each human being. Heaven and Earth and the

ten thousand things all require *ch'i* to stay alive. A person
that knows how to allow his *ch'i* to circulate (→ *hsing-ch'i*)
will preserve himself and banish illnesses that might cause
him harm."

In addition to this understanding of *ch'i* as cosmic energy, *ch'i* also designates the breath—the air we breathe in
and out—and in this sense is known as outer *ch'i* (→ *wai-
ch'i*). *Ch'i* is moreover an important element in the teachings of the neo-Confucianist philosopher → Chu Hsi, who
distinguishes between *ch'i* as the material aspect of things
and *li* as their principle, or inner aspect. Only in combination with the form-giving power of *ch'i* can this principle
(*li*) manifest in the visible realm. In Chinese medicine *ch'i*
designates the general life energy that circulates through
the body along the so-called meridians and regulates the
body's maintenance and growth. Disruptions or blockages
in the circulation of *ch'i* are the cause of illness. In addition, *ch'i* designates the breath. In any case, these two aspects of *ch'i* are considered to be inseparable. Lastly, *ch'i*
refers to the emotions and—in a more modern view—to
the activity of the body's neurohormonal systems.

In the Taoist view the world is an expression of the Tao—
i.e., the One in which yin and yang intermingle with the primordial *ch'i* (→ *yüan-ch'i*). Heaven and Earth came into
being through the separation of yin and yang, and their re-
newed intermingling caused the ten thousand things—i.e., all
things and creatures—(→ *wan-wu*) to appear.

A Taoist text—*The Experience of the Golden Flower*—
contains the following passage: "Before Heaven and Earth
were separate, there was only the indefinable ONE. This ONE
was divided and yin and yang came into existence. That
which received *yang-ch'i* rose up bright and clear and became

Heaven; that which received *yin-ch'i* sank down heavy and obscure and became Earth; and that which received both *yin-ch'i* and *yang-ch'i* in right proportions became man." (Translated from Miyuki 1984, p. 185. *See also* Wilhelm 1938.)

Like human beings, Heaven and Earth breathe and as with human beings, the inhaled breath is clean, and the exhaled breath is stale. For that reason each day is divided into two periods. The period of the living *ch'i* (Chin. *sheng-ch'i*)—when Heaven and Earth inhale—runs from midnight to noon. The period of the dead *ch'i* (Chin. *ssu-ch'i*)—when Heaven and Earth exhale—from noon to midnight. According to the relevant Taoist teachings breathing exercises should only be performed during the living *ch'i* period, because only then can positive energy be absorbed.

Ch'ien and K'un   Chin.; the first and second hexagram of the → *I-ching* (*Book of Change* [*s*]) or two of the eight trigrams (→ *pa-kua*). The *ch'ien* hexagram consists of six yang (unbroken) lines and the *ch'ien* trigram of three yang lines, thus representing pure yang, Heaven and the creative principle. The *k'un* hexagram consists of six and the *k'un* trigram of three yin lines and symbolizes pure yin, the Earth and the receptive principle:

Ch'ien and *k'un* are the gateway to transformation and considered to be the parents of the remaining hexagrams, which are combinations of yin and yang lines. In the language of Taoist alchemy (→ *nei-tan, wei-tan*) *ch'ien* and *k'un* refer respectively to the furnace and cauldron (melting pot) or to the head and belly of the practitioner.

Ch'ien is furthermore associated with external features of the physical body such as the ears, eyes, nose, mouth, and tongue, whilst *K'un* is said to be related to the internal organs such as the heart, lungs, kidneys, and pancreas.

Ch'i-hai   Chin., lit. "ocean of breath"; a point situated two to three fingers' breadths below the navel near the lower cinnabar field (→ *tan-t'ien*), where → *ch'i,* the vital energy, is stored. The *ch'i-hai* is of special importance for a practice called embryonic breathing (→ *t'ai-hsi*), as well as in traditional Chinese medicine.

Chih-jen   Chin., lit. "perfected human being"; one of the names used by → Chuang-tzu to describe his ideal human being. *Chih-jen* is employed synonymously with → *chen-jen,* → *shen-jen* and → *sheng-jen.* A perfected human being has realized unity with the Tao and is free of all limitations and concepts.

The *Chuang-tzu* (chap. 2) describes the perfect man (through the words of Wang I) as follows: "The Perfect Man (*chih-jen*) is a spiritual being. Were the ocean itself scorched up, he would not feel hot. Were the Milky Way frozen hard, he would not feel cold. Were the mountains to be riven with thunder and the great deep to be thrown up by storm, he would not tremble. In such case, he would mount upon the clouds of heaven and, driving the sun and moon before him, would pass beyond the limits of this external world where death and life have no victory over man—how much less what is bad for him?" (Giles 1961).

Ch'i-kung   Chin., roughly "working the energy" (→ *ch'i*); physical exercises important in Chinese medicine. These health exercises combine Buddhist and Taoist elements and cover a wide range of practices, such as techniques for regulating the body, the mind (by reducing and quieting thought activity), and the breath (e.g. → *t'u-ku na-hsin*); movement exercises (e.g., → *t'ai chi chuan* and → *tao-yin*), self-massage, etc. In a wider sense the various martial arts (*wu-shu*) are also a form of *ch'i-kung*. Instructions for performing certain basic *ch'i-kung* exercises can be found in Zöller 1984.

Ch'i-kung exercises are usually classified as either active (*tung-kung*) or passive (*ching-kung*). The former are performed while standing, sitting, or lying down and are aimed at relaxing the body, regulating the breath, and turning the mind inward. They are also known as inner exercises (*nei-kung*). The active exercises consist of sequences of physical movements of the body and with which the consciousness and breath of the practitioner have to be coordinated. They are also known as outer exercises (*wai-kung*).

Ching Chin., lit. "semen, spermatozoa"; one of three life forces, the intermingling of which—according to Taoist teachings—is essential for the preservation of life. The other two are the breath, or vital energy (→ *ch'i*), and the mind, or consciousness (→ *shen*). *Ching* literally designates the semen of a man or the menstrual flow of a woman. In Taoist texts, however, it is not used in such a concrete sense but rather describes a subtle substance or essence, capable of combining with → *ch'i*.

Ching is produced in the abode of ching (*ching-she*) near the lower cinnabar field (→ *tan-t'ien*). If *ching* is present only in small quantities within the body, the person concerned will become ill; when the *ching* is exhausted, death ensues. For that reason, Taoist adepts strive to restrict the loss of *ching* by means of various sexual practices and techniques essentially based on avoiding ejaculation and to strengthen the *ching* (→ *fang-chung shu,* → *huan-ching pu-nao*) with the help of the female yin essence (→ yin-yang).

According to the most ancient Chinese dictionary, *ching* designates cleaned rice; it is additionally defined as "seed," and "source of life." The → *Huang-ti nei-ching* defines *ching* not only as "seed essence" but also as "essence of the [bodily] organs" and "germ of life." It is said that after conception the first to form is the *ching,* and only after that the brain and spinal cord.

Taoist practice knows several methods to strengthen and increase *ching.* The simplest of these states that a man should, as often as possible, have successive sexual intercourse with different—and preferably young and beautiful—female partners but not allow himself to ejaculate until the end of the final copulation. By this practice his essence is strengthened under the influence of the female yin, any illnesses are healed and the life force increases. The practice of allowing the semen to return to nourish the brain (*huan-ching pu-nao*) is considered to be more effective.

Ch'ing-lung   Chin. → *k'an* and *li*

Ch'ing-t'an   Chin., lit. "pure conversation"; neo-Taoist school (→ *hsüan-hsüeh*) that originated in the 3d century C.E. *Ch'ing-t'an* refers to a refined form of conversation on the teachings of philosophical Taoism (→ *tao-chia*), particularly those of Lao-tzu and Chuang-tzu. In this way the followers of the *ch'ing-t'an* formed a basis for reinterpreting the Confucianist classics from a neo-Taoist point of

21

view. The most important representatives of the school were → Wang Pi (226–49 C.E.), Kou Hsiang (?–ca. 312 C.E.), and Hsiang Hsiu (221–300 C.E.).

Wang Pi and several others held that Confucius (→ K'ung-tzu) was a greater Taoist than either Lao-tzu or Chuang-tzu, because he actually attained a state of nonbeing (→ *wu*), while Lao-tzu and Chuang-tzu contented themselves with talking about such a state. The *Ch'ing-t'an* School also shows Buddhist influences.

Chin-lien   Chin., lit. "golden lotus"; → *ch'üan-chen tao*

Chin-tan   Chin., lit. "golden cinnabar"; the golden elixir, a variously interpreted concept in Taoist alchemy (→ *nei-tan*, → *wai-tan*). In texts predating the T'ang and Sung dynasties, *chin-tan* usually refers to the outer elixir. The adherents of the Outer Alchemy strove to produce gold from various chemical substances, which was to bestow immortality on those who swallowed it. In later texts *chin-tan* usually designates the inner elixir, and in this sense is synonymous with the sacred embryo (→ *sheng-t'ai*) and the golden flower of Inner Alchemy (→ *nei-tan*).

Ch'iu Ch'u-chi   → *ch'üan-chen tao*

Chiu-kung   Chin., lit. "nine palaces"; according to the teachings of the → Inner Deity Hygiene School, the human brain is divided into nine palaces, which are inhabited by different deities (→ *shen*) and arranged between the forehead and the nape of the neck in two rows, of four and five compartments. The most important of these are the first three palaces of the lower row, where → Huang-lao-chün and his assistants reside. The palace found at the center of the head is called → *ni-huan* (after the Buddhist term *nirvana*) and is the seat of the highest body deity, the Supreme One (T'ai-i).

In some Taoist texts *chiu-kung* refers to nine bodily organs, namely the heart, kidneys, liver, lungs, pancreas, gall bladder, small intestine, large intestine, and bladder.

Chou-i   Chin., lit. *"Change(s) of the Chou Dynasty"*; a designation found in Chinese texts for the *Book of Change(s)* (→ *I-ching*), referring to both the root text and the commentaries (→ *Shih-i*).

Chou-i ts'an-t'ung-ch'i   Chin., → Wei P'o-yang

Chou Tun-i   → *t'ai-chi-t'u*

Ch'u   Chin., lit. "kitchen," banquet; feasts held by followers of the → *t'ai-p'ing tao* and → *wu-tou-mi tao* schools to honor and thank priests for their help and ministrations in important family matters.

At these banquets the members of the community give the → *tao-shih* presents, the value of which varies with the nature of the occasion. The most lavish of these ceremonies is held to celebrate the birth of a son. It is attended by ten members of the community, and the present given to the priest consists of a hundred sheets of paper, several writing brushes, ink, etc.

Only five guests are invited to celebrate the birth of a daughter and the *tao-shih* is offered a straw mat, a broom, and a waste basket. These presents have to be handed to the priest within a month of the birth of a child if the family concerned does not wish to run the risk of losing merit. Similar feasts are held after the death of a relative and at the beginning of the new year. The believers ask to be blessed with wealth and children or even good fortune in general or promotion to a higher post. *Ch'u* are furthermore thought to be a way of curing illnesses and warding off misfortunes and disasters.

Ch'üan-chen tao Chin., lit. "Way of the Realization of Truth"; one of two main streams of religious Taoism (→ *tao-chiao*), the other being the "Way of Right Unity" (→ *cheng-i tao*). The *ch'üan-chen tao* is also known as *chung-yang* (pure yang) and *chin-lien* (golden lotus).

The Way of the Realization of Truth is said to have been founded by Wang Ch'un-yang (1112-70 C.E.), who, according to tradition, in 1159 C.E. met a hermit who was a reincarnation of two immortals, Lü Tung-pin and Chung Li-ch'üan (→ *pa-hsien*), and from this hermit received secret verbal teachings, which came to form the basis of the school founded by him. In 1167 C.E. he established a monastery on Shantung peninsula, known as the Monastery for the Realization of Truth. According to Wang Ch'un-yang a Taoist realizes the truth by understanding his mind and realizing his true nature.

Ch'üan-chen tao is a synthesis of the basic tenets of the three great religions of China—Confucianism, Buddhism, and Taoism—with Zen Buddhist elements predominating. In his *Treatise on the Foundation of the Way for the Realization of Truth* (*Li-chiao shih wu-lun*), which outlines the practices of the school founded by him, Wang Ch'un-yang combines the teachings of the *Prajñāpāramitā sūtra* with those of the Inner Elixir School (→ *nei-tan*). Seven of his pupils—known as the seven enlightened ones of the North—initiated separate movements within the *ch'üan-chen tao*. One of them—Ch'iu Ch'u-chi—is said to have been well connected to the imperial court. He was a protégé of the Emperor T'ai-tzu (1206-27 C.E.), who founded the Yüan Dynasty and bestowed on Ch'iu the title *divine immortal* (*shen-hsien*). The wide dissemination of the *ch'üan-chen tao* was largely due to this imperial patronage.

In time, two movements within the *ch'üan-chen tao* gained special importance. The first of these was the *Lung-men* (lit. Dragon Gate) School, founded by Ch'iu and also known as the Northern School. One of its best-known texts is *The Secret of the Golden Flower* (→ *T'ai-i chin-hua tsung-chih*). Its main seat is the Monastery of the White Clouds (→ Pai-yün kuan). The second is the Southern School, which was founded by → Chang Po-tuan and died out near the beginning of the 18th century.

The followers of the *ch'üan-chen tao* aim at transcending the mundane world through experiencing the Tao. To this end they practice meditation without the use of external objects of faith, such as talismans (→ *fu-lu*) or methods employed by the followers of Outer Alchemy (→ *wai-tan*). The → *tao-shih* of the *ch'üan-chen tao* remain throughout their lives in strict celibacy.

The *ch'üan-chen tao* lays claim to five patriarchs: Wang Hsiao-yang (to whom the teachings were transmitted by → Lao-chün, a pupil of Lao-tzu); Chung Li-chüan; Lü Ch'un-yang; Liu Hai-shan (who is said to have initiated Chang Po-tuan, the founder of the Southern School); and lastly the actual founder of the *ch'üan-chen tao,* Wang Ch'un-yang.

The teaching and practice of the school are based on the following fifteen points of Wang Ch'un-yang's *Treatise on the Foundation of the Ch'üan-chen tao:*

(1) to live in a hermitage, where mind and body can find rest and peace and where →*ch'i* and → *shen* are brought into balance and harmony; (2) to follow the path of the clouds, i.e., to be untiring in the search for the Tao; (3) the study of books, letting their meaning deeply penetrate into oneself, as

a result of which spontaneous insight arises and the "wisdom mind" manifests; (4) on the coagulation of elixir materials; (5) on the construction of a hermitage; (6) on winning Tao friends; (7) on correct sitting meditation; (8) on keeping one's soul in check and cultivating the mind of stillness; (9) on keeping one's nature in balance; (10) on fusing the five elements [→ *wu-hsing*]; (11) on the manifestation of spirit nature in life; (12) on sacredness; (13) on transcending the threefold world (i.e., the world of desire, the world of appearances, and the world of the unformed); (14) on nourishing the spirit; (15) on leaving the world. (Miyuki 1984, p. 62ff.)

Chuang chou   → Chuang-tzu

Chuang-tzu   1. Taoist sage, ca. 369-286 B.C.E., also known as Chuang Chou; author of the Taoist classic, *Chuang-tzu*. He and → Lao-tzu are considered the founders of philosophical Taoism (→ *tao-chia*). Little is known about his life apart from the fact that he was born in what is now Ho-nan province, was married and held a minor administrative post in Ch'i-yüan. Being unwilling to serve under a prince or ruler, he lived in humble circumstances. His philosophy owes much to the teachings of Lao-tzu. He was a relentless critic of Confucianism.

A historical work dating from the Western Han Dynasty contains an anecdote that may serve as evidence of Chuang-tzu's strong sense of independence: "King Wen of Chou, having heard about Chuang Chou's talents, sent a messenger laden with expensive presents to invite him to join his court and offer him a post as minister. Chuang Chou laughed at the offer and said, 'A thousand pieces of gold is no mean sum, I readily admit, and the office of minister is no doubt an honorable one. But have you ever seen an ox on its way to be slaughtered? Having been carefully fattened over a number of years, it is bedecked with richly embroidered ribbons and led to a great temple. At that moment, that ox would dearly love to be a little pig to which no one pays any heed, but it is too late then. Leave me! Do not sully me! I would rather wallow joyfully in a dirty puddle than be led on a rope by the ruler of a kingdom. I live as I please and so shall never accept an official post'" (Kaltenmark 1981, p. 125ff.).

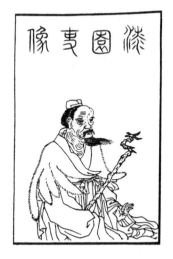

Chuang-tzu

2. A Taoist classic by Chuang-tzu (see 1 above), also known as *The Divine Classic of Nan-hua* (Chin. *Nan-hua chen-ching*). The *Chuang-tzu* consists of thirty-three chapters, the first seven of which are called the "inner" books and were actually written by Chuang-tzu. The fifteen "outer" and eleven "mixed" books, on the other hand, are believed to be the work of his disciples.

The themes dealt with by Chuang-tzu are in part identical with those to which Lao-tzu addresses himself in the → *Tao-te ching,* and the views of both authors on such matters as the nature of the → Tao and the → *te* essentially coincide. The *Chuang-tzu* furthermore attaches central importance to unmotivated action (→ *wu-wei*), stresses the relativity of all opposites, the identity of life and death, and the importance of meditation as a means of becoming one

27

with the Tao. Nature herself is seen by Chuang-tzu as a never-ending transformation of appearances. He was thus one of the first to point to the illusory nature of the world.

However, the *Chuang-tzu* also shows the influence of non-Taoist movements, and → Hui Shih, Chuang-tzu's closest friend, played an important part in the development of its philosophy. The book contains numerous attacks on Confucius (→ K'ung-tzu) and his teachings. For example, Chuang-tzu rejected the Confucianist cardinal virtues of fellow-feeling (→ *jen*) and uprightness (→ *i*) as artificial concepts that could easily become no more than mere ideas without any correspondence to living reality.

The *Chuang-tzu* is valued both for its philosophical insights and as a work of great literary merit.

Chuang-tzu considers the harmony and freedom attainable by following our own nature the highest good a human being is capable of realizing. He further considers the egalitarianism of institutions that ignore the originality and uniqueness of people to be a major cause of human suffering. For that reason he is categorically opposed to "government by government," arguing instead that the world can only be kept in order by nongoverning, i.e., by a ruler adhering to the principle of unmotivated action. Book 7 of the *Chuang-tzu* gives the following description of an ideal ruler:

"The goodness of a wise ruler covers the whole empire, yet he himself seems to know it not. It influences all creation, yet none is conscious thereof. It appears under countless forms, bringing joy to all things. It is based upon the baseless and travels through the realms of Nowhere." Book 3 gives the following advice: "Resolve your mental energy into abstraction, your physical energy into inaction. Allow yourself to fall in with the natural order of phenomena, without admitting the element of self,—and the empire will be governed." Chuang-tzu rejects all distinctions between good and evil, claiming that there are no universally valid criteria by which to judge such matters. This view is reflected by the title of Book 2. "The Identity of Contrasts." He even considers life and death to be essentially identical, because they are part of the flow of ever-lasting change and transformation, rather than a beginning or end. This helps to explain his–in the Confucianist view—frivolous reaction to the death of his wife. He came to realize "that she had already existed in a previous state before birth, without form, or even substance; that, while in that uncondi-tioned state, substance was added to spirit; that this substance then assumed form; and that the next stage was birth. And now, by virtue of further change, she is dead, passing from one phase to another, like the sequence of spring, summer, autumn and winter. And while she thus lies asleep in Eternity, for me to go about weeping and wailing would be to proclaim myself ig-norant of these natural laws. Therefore I refrain."

Again and again the *Chuang-tzu* returns to the subject of longevity. It mentions a Master Kuang Ch'eng, who lived for twelve hundred years, and one called Kui who had in his pos-session a prescription that enabled him to gain the appearance of a child. Indeed, Chuang-tzu describes various methods for attaining immortality that came to be of paramount impor-tance in later religious Taoism (→*tao-chiao*). Book 1, for in-stance, tells of a divine sage living on Miao-ku-she mountain, "whose flesh is like ice or snow, whose demeanour is that of a virgin, who eats no fruit of the earth [→*pi-ku*] but lives on air and dew [an allusion to various breathing techniques: → *hsing-ch'i*,→*fu-ch'i*] and, riding on clouds with flying dragons for a team [→*fei-sheng*], roams beyond the limits of mortality. His being is absolutely inert. Yet he wards off cor-ruption from all things, and causes the crops to thrive."

29

Although Chuang-tzu would not appear to attach particular importance to either physical (→ *tao-yin*) or breathing exercises, Book 1 points out that the pure men of old draw breath "from their uttermost parts" (lit. "with their heels"). This might be an oblique reference to the practice known as embryonic breathing (→ *t'ai-hsi*).

The *Chuang-tzu* moreover contains descriptions of such meditative practices as → *tso-wang* (in Book 6); and the dialogue (in Book 11) between the Yellow Emperor (→ Huang-ti) and Master Kuang Ch'eng-tzu can be seen as a complete instruction in a Taoist meditation technique that employs visualizations.

All such practices are said to result in the acquisition of supernormal powers. Those fully skilled in them are said to be immune against fire and water and capable of ascending to the clouds, riding through the air on dragons, healing the sick, and ensuring a rich harvest. With these teachings Chuang-tzu contributed toward the development of the cult of the immortals (→ *hsien*). (Quotes from Giles 1961.)

Chu Hsi   1130-1200 C.E.; one of the most important philosophers in the history of China. He was a representative of neo-Confucianism, which predominantly concerned itself with metaphysical problems and was influenced by both Buddhism and philosophical Taoism (→ *tao-chia*). Under Chu Hsi the philosophical analysis of → *li* reached its highest level. He specifically investigated the relationship between *li* (the principle, or formal, aspect of a thing) and → *ch'i* (its material aspect) and considered the highest reality to be → *t'ai-ch'i,* the supreme ultimate.

Chu Hsi's philosophy is based on two concepts: *li,* the principle, and *ch'i,* the material. Anything beyond form he categorized as *li*, which in this sense can be taken as synonymous with the term *Tao*. *Ch'i*, on the other hand, is capable of bringing form into being. *Li* and *ch'i* are inseparable: wherever there is matter, *ch'i*, there must also be *li*, because without *li* the thing in question could not exist. Things are thus the instruments through which *li* finds expression. The specific *li* of a thing exists prior to that thing coming into being in the physical realm. The highest reality is *t'ai-ch'i*, which embraces the *li* of Heaven and the *li* of Earth. Thus each thing, apart from its own specific *li*, partakes of this ultimate reality.

For Chu Hsi the universe is the result of *ch'i*'s continually alternating phases of rest and movement. *Ch'i* at rest is *yin*, *ch'i* in motion is *yang* (→ yin-yang). Out of this the five elements (→ *wu-hsing*) arise, which, by their infinite combinations, give rise to the material world.

Chu-i   Chin. → Wen-ch'ang

Chu-lin ch'i-hsien   Chin., lit. "The Seven Sages of the Bamboo Grove"; a group of seven Taoist scholars and artists who lived during the 3d century C.E., the most important of them being the poet and musician Hsi K'ang (224-263 C.E.). His companions were Juan Chi (210-263 C.E.) and his nephew Juan Hsien, both of whom were also poets and musicians; Liu Ling (221-300 C.E.), a great lover of wine; and Hsiang Hsiu, Wang Jung, and Shan Tao. The seven gathered in a bamboo grove near Hsi K'ang's house to practice pure conversation (→ *ch'ing-t'an*). They sought harmony with the universe and oneness with the Tao by drinking wine. Their ideal consisted in following their impulses and acting spontaneously. Their outstanding collective characteristic was their sensitivity to the beauties of nature.

Hsi K'ang was born into a wealthy family and brought up in accordance with Confucian principles but felt strongly drawn toward Taoism. He practiced the technique, "nourishing the life principle" (→ *yang-hsing*). After extensive travels, during which he made the acquaintance of immortals (→ *hsien*), he and his wife settled in what is now Ho-nan and gathered a group of friends. A collection of anecdotes that conveys an idea of their life style is extant.

The two Juans were known for drinking wine from a large bowl, which they would occasionally share with the neighbors' pigs. Of Juan Hsien it is related that as a host, he offended against all principles of etiquette by leaving his guests and riding after his eloping mistress.

Liu Ling is said to have traveled in the company of a servant who always carried a bottle of wine and a spade so that he could instantly supply his master with drink or bury him without delay, if worst came to worst. Liu Ling would normally wear no clothes at home. To a somewhat dumbfounded Confucian visitor he explained that he considered the whole universe his home, and his room his trousers. He then asked the visitor what business he had in his trousers.

Chung Li-ch'üan   → *pa-hsien*, → *ch'üan-chen tao*

Ch'ung-yang   Chin., lit. "pure yang"; → *ch'üan-chen tao*

Chün-tzu   Chin., → K'ung-tzu, → *jen*

Cinnabar field   → *tan-t'ien*

Confucianism   (*ru-chia*, Chin., roughly "School of Scholars"); a state doctrine combining philosophical, religious, and sociopolitical aspects reflected in the teachings of Confucius (→ K'ung-tzu). The original basis of Confucianism was the classical writings attributed to Confucius. The further development of the doctrine was decisively influenced by → Meng-tzu (ca. 372–289 B.C.E.), also known as Mencius, and Hsün-tzu (ca. 313–238 B.C.E.). Central to Meng-tzu's teaching is the belief in inherent goodness of human nature, bestowed by Heaven (→ *t'ien*) and reaching its ultimate perfection in Confucianist saints who, according to Meng-tzu, play an important role in maintaining and defending the so-called royal path (*wang-tao*) against erroneous views and moral decay. Hsün-tzu, on the other hand, argued that man was not inherently good and therefore had to be taught goodness. In addition he stressed the role of → *li* as a principle of cosmic order. The ritualistic practices of Confucianism are mainly based on two sections of the *Book of Rites* (*Li-chi,* → K'ung-tzu): the *Great Teaching* (*Ta-hsüeh*), which stresses the relationship between the individual and the cosmos, and the *Application of the Center* (*Chung-yung*), which describes the role of the saint as a mediator between Heaven and Earth.

Confucianism suffered for some time under the excesses of legalism, but reestablished its influence during the Han Dynasty. Under the emperor Han Wu-ti philosophical Confucianism was extended by the addition of various legalistic elements of considerable political significance and proclaimed an orthodox doctrine. The imperial academy began to employ scholars, who were responsible for the study and interpretation of the Confucianist classics. This development marked the beginning of the selection of state officials by conducting state examinations on Confucianist teachings.

An essential contribution to the development of a Confucianist state doctrine was made by T'ung Chung-shu, who combined the cosmological speculations of the → *yin-yang chia* and the teachings concerning the five elements

(→ *wu-hsing*) with the political and socioethical elements of the Confucianist classics.

Between the 3d and 8th centuries Confucianism was penetrated by the teachings of other philosophical schools, mainly of Taoist and Buddhist origin. This led to a revival of mystical traditions within the proclaimed doctrine. The → *I-ching*, in particular, acquired its mystical significance during this period. In philosophy, the prevailing mechanistical correspondences between man and nature were replaced by a search for an inner connection with the → Tao, the primordial principle of the universe. In Western philosophical terminology this phase, marked by the revival of mystical traditions and their incorporation into the Confucianist canon, is known as neo-Confucianism. The so-called *Four Books* (*Ssu-chu*), i.e., the *Analects* of Confucius, the *Meng-tzu,* the *Ta-hsüeh,* and the *Chung-yung* came to be considered more important than the *Five Classics* of early Confucianism. The most significant neo-Confucianist innovation consisted in providing a metaphysical rationale for traditional ethics. In this context *li,* the cosmic principle, is of special importance and central to the teachings of → Chu Hsi, perhaps the most important representative of neo-Confucianism.

In the course of time philosophical speculations became increasingly predominant. The first openly critical writings date from the end of the Ming Dynasty, but it was not until the 19th century that the hollowness of orthodox Confucianist thought was clearly exposed under the scrutiny of Western philosophy.

Various reforms were followed by conservative reversals. The official state examinations were abolished in

1905; and with this Confucianism, as an orthodox state doctrine, came to an end.

After the proclamation of a republic it was recognized that Confucianism had exerted a significant influence on the way the Chinese, as a people, see themselves. It continues to be important as a personal philosophy of life.

Confucius → K'ung-tzu

＊　＊　＊

Dragon King → *lung-wang*

＊　＊　＊

Fan Chin. → *fu*

Fang-chang Chin., lit. "Square Fathom," also called Fang-hu ("Square Urn"); one of the three isles of the immortals off the east coast of China. They are the home of the immortals and the epitome of ultimate bliss. The search for these islands (→ P'eng-lai, → Ying-chou) is an important feature of religious Taoism (→ *tao-chiao*).

A Taoist text dating from the 4th or 5th century gives the following description of Fang-chang:

"The island of Fang-chang is in the exact center of the eastern ocean. Its four coasts, facing west, south, east, and north, form a perfect square, each side of which is five thousand miles long. The island is a favorite dwelling place of dragons. On it there are palaces of gold, jade, and crystal. . . . Immortals who do not wish to ascend to Heaven travel to this continent, where they receive their 'certificate of the primordial source of life.' Several hundred thousand immortals live there.

They till the fields and plant the herb of immortality. . . . There are also rocks of jade and many springs, among them the 'Nine [life-giving] Springs.' The rulers of the land are married to princesses, who rule over water spirits, dragons, sea snakes, whales, and all other marine animals" (Bauer 1974, p.151).

Fang-chung shu Chin., lit. "arts of the inner chamber"; collective term for all sexual techniques said to lead to the realization of the → Tao and to the attainment of immortality (→ *ch'ang-sheng pu-ssu*).

The various Taoist sexual techniques aim at nourishing and strengthening the semen or essence (→ *ching*). For this the adept requires the energy of a sexual partner of the opposite sex, because a man can strengthen his yang only with the help of the feminine yin and vice versa. The most important methods for strengthening the *ching* are prevention of ejaculation and allowing the *ching* to return, in order to strengthen the brain (→ *huan-ching pu-nao*). There is historical evidence of collective sexual practices in early Taoist schools. The followers of Five-Pecks-of-Rice Taoism (→ *wu-tou-mi tao*) and of the Way of Supreme Peace (→ *t'ai-p'ing tao*) practiced the so-called unification of the breaths (→ *ho-ch'i*). These *fang-chung shu* have been known since the Han dynasty and were practiced both privately and publicly until about the 7th century, when they were forced to withdraw to the private sphere under the pressure of Confucianist morality. There is no mention of such practices in Taoist texts dated later than the Sung Dynasty, but it may be assumed that they continued up to the very recent past.

The philosophical foundation of the *fang-chung shu* is the widespread idea that the world came into being as a result of the marriage of Heaven and Earth—of yin and yang—a process that continually repeats itself in nature. Human sexual intercourse was seen as an opportunity to participate in this creative process both physically and psychologically and thereby experience the Tao.

An essential feature of these sexual practices is the exchange of energy. To strengthen his yang a man may—for example, during foreplay to sexual intercourse—partake of the special yin essence of the woman from the saliva under her tongue and from her breasts, thereby strengthening his own energy. The most powerful essences, however, are liberated during orgasm. The man absorbs these energies through his penis from the vagina of the woman, and the woman through her vagina from the penis of the man. This exchange of yin and yang produces good health and longevity.

In most cases, however, the aim of such practices goes further in that it consists in the accumulation of energy rather than its mere exchange. The Taoist adept must learn to prevent ejaculation of his semen in order to preserve all the *ching* within his body. At the same time, however, he endeavors to produce as many sexual climaxes as possible in his female partner with the aim of absorbing the female yin energy thereby liberated. A man may increase the effectiveness of this technique by having successive sexual intercourse with as many partners as possible. These partners, ideally, should be young and beautiful. The legendary Yellow Emperor (→ Huang-ti) is said to have had intercourse with twelve hundred concubines without any damage to his health, because he knew how to inhibit ejaculation.

A more advanced technique is described as "allowing the essence to return, in order to strengthen the brain." This technique was also used as a preliminary to meditative Taoist breathing exercises aimed at developing the sacred embryo (→ *sheng-t'ai*).

It cannot be denied, however, that in most cases these techniques constituted an exploitation of the female partners involved. For that reason a further tradition states that both partners should suppress orgasm and instead strive to unite at a higher level. We quote a relevant Taoist tract: "To live for a long time without aging, a man should indulge in amorous play with his female partner. He should drink the 'jade fluid,' i.e., swallow her saliva; in this way passion will be aroused in both the man and the woman. Then the man should press the *p'ing-i* spot with the finger of his left hand. (This spot is situated approximately 2.5 cm above the nipple of the right breast and is also referred to as 'yin present in yang.') Then the man should visualize in his (lower) cinnabar field (→ *tan-t'ien*) a bright essence, yellow within and red and white without. He should then imagine that this liquid separates into a sun and a moon, which move about in his abdomen and then rise within him until they reach the → Ni-huan point in his brain, where the two halves are once again united" (trans. from Colegrave 1980). This symbolic gathering back of the semen thus culminates in the fusion of the male and female principles represented by the sun and moon respectively.

The detailed instructions for practicing these sexual techniques were mostly kept secret or revealed in a language reminiscent of that employed by the Outer Alchemy (→ *wai-tan*), which could only be understood by initiates.

Not all Taoist schools approved of sexual practices as means of attaining enlightenment. The Way for the Realization of Truth (→ *ch'üan-chen tao*), among others, rejects them and teaches that sexuality has to become an exclusively inner experience. Chinese art is replete with sexual symbols. The peach, because of its clearly discernible notch, represents the female vulva; further symbols for the feminine are vases, clouds, open peony blossoms, mushrooms, the white tiger, kidney-shaped stones, etc. Masculine symbols are jade, sheep, phallus-shaped rock formations, the green dragon, the color green, and the phoenix bird.

Fang-hu   Chin. → Fang-chang

Fang-shih   Chin., lit. "master of prescriptions"; magician; precursor of Taoist sages and priests (→ *tao-shih*). The earliest reports about *fang-shih* date from the 3d century B.C.E. These magicians (shamans) lived mainly on the northeastern coast of China and were proficient in a great variety of arts (Chin., *fang-shu*) such as astrology, astronomy, spirit healing, prophecy, geomancy, sexual practices, the science of calendars, etc. They were in the possession of prescriptions for attaining immortality and were believed to be experts in the search for the isles of the immortals (→ P'eng-lai, → Fang-chang, → Ying-chou), which secured them the patronage of rulers. They made use of drugs and talismans (→ *fu-lu*), developed physical exercises and breathing techniques aimed at the prolongation of life, and enlisted the help of gods. For all these reasons they played an important part in the creation of religious Taoism (→ *tao-chiao*), their knowledge and proficiencies forming the basis of various streams within the *tao-chiao*. One of the most famous and influential *fang-shih* was → Li Shao-chün.

Fei-sheng   Chin., roughly "ascending to Heaven in broad daylight"; a metaphor descriptive of the ultimate apotheosis of a follower of religious Taoism (→ *tao-chiao*) who has succeeded in transforming his nature by the performance of various exercises, and thus become an immortal (→ *hsien*).

Five elements   → *wu-hsing*

Five-Pecks-of-Rice Taoism → *wu-tou-mi tao*

Five phases of transformation → *wu-hsing*

Fu also *fan,* Chin., lit. "return"; a concept in the *Tao-te ching* to describe the natural movement of the Tao: "Returning (recurrence) is the motion of the Tao" (Chapter 40). The law underlying all appearances is that all things return to their origin. All things arise from the Tao and must return to it. In Taoist meditation practice, "returning to the root or source" is synonymous with attaining enlightenment.

This idea is expressed in Chapter 16 of the *Tao-te ching:* "Empty yourself of everything. Let the mind rest at peace. The ten thousand things rise and fall while the Self watches their return. They grow and flourish and then return to the source. Returning to the source is stillness, which is the way of nature. The way of nature is unchanging. Knowing constancy is insight. Not knowing constancy leads to disaster" (Feng & English 1972). The *Tao-te ching* describes the destination of this return in a number of ways: most frequently it is simply referred to as the Tao, but in some passages it is related to the idea of the homeland, the mother, or the root. In yet other passages it is seen as original simplicity (→ *p'u*), the limitless (→ *wu-chi*) or as an ideal primordial state of society (golden age). If the notion of a return refers to the Tao itself, what is meant is the return of the Tao to its primordial state of nonbeing, nonaction (→ *wu-wei*), and namelessness.

In the *Book of Change(s)* (→ *I-ching*) *fu* describes the process of a quality changing or being transformed into its opposite: when the yin (→ yin-yang) has reached its peak, the yang returns. This motion is symbolized by the hexagram *fu,* which consists of an unbroken yang line below five broken yin lines. In Chinese thought in general *fu* may symbolize the recurrence of the seasons and/or the succession of life and death.

Fu-ch'i Chin., lit. "nourishing oneself by the breath"; Taoist breathing technique, in which the practitioner focuses his attention on the breath and allows it to penetrate and circulate in the five internal organs (→ *wu-tsang*). From there the breath is directed to flow through the feet, heart, neck, joints, and nine bodily orifices. In this way the body is nourished. This technique is a preliminary for embryonic breathing (→ *t'ai-hsi*).

A special form of *fu-ch'i* consists in absorbing the breaths of the five shoots, or sprouts (*wu-ya*): the → *ch'i* of the five elements (→ *wu-hsing*) is allowed to enter the corresponding internal organs by absorbing the breaths of the five heavenly directions (the fifth being the center). During this exercise the Taoist adept follows the breath with his mind and sees it enter the organs in question, where it mingles with the secretion or essence of that particular organ. In this way the breath is circulated through the body and can release its healing powers. The absorption of the breath of the five shoots results in a strengthening of the five internal organs.

Fu Hsi figure in Chinese mythology and husband of → Nü-kua. Fu Hsi is the first of China's three noble emperors. According to tradition he ruled either from 2852 to 2737 B.C.E. or from 2952 to 2836 B.C.E. Mankind is said to owe many inventions to him. He taught the use of the fishing net as well as ways of taming wild animals and the breeding of silkworms. He invented the set square, which became his emblem and with which Great Yü (→ Ta-yü) later measured the world. His most important creations, however, were music and the eight trigrams (→ *pa-kua*, → *I-ching*), said to be the basis of Chinese writing. Tradition furthermore ascribes to him the invention of casting oracles by the use of yarrow stalks. He is also said to have invented the one hundred Chinese family names and decreed that marriages may only take place between persons bearing differing family names. Fu Hsi is represented as a human being with the body of a snake. In Taoist temples he is usually portrayed holding a panel on which the eight trigrams are inscribed.

Fu jih-hsiang Chin., lit. "absorbing the image of the sun into oneself"; Taoist heliotherapeutic technique practiced in combination with breathing exercises. The technique is confined to men; women absorb the image of the moon.

The Taoist adept practicing *fu jih-hsiang* writes the Chinese character depicting the sun in vermilion ink on a rectangular piece of green paper. Every morning thereafter, holding the paper in his left hand and facing east, he concentrates on this image until it is transformed into the sun itself. He then dissolves the green paper in water, which he drinks, knocking his teeth together nine times (→ *k'ou-ch'ih*), and swallows his saliva (→ *yü-chiang*).

Fu-lu Chin.; magical talismans used by many schools of religious Taoism (→ *tao-chiao*). According to tradition, the first to use *fu-lu* was → Chang Tao-ling, to whom they were revealed by → Lao-tzu.

Fu-lu are strips of paper, metal, or bamboo, inscribed with lines that resemble Chinese writing, and are said to protect the wearer against illness and ward off demons. The use of such talismans was most widespread in the school of the → *cheng-i tao*.

Originally *fu-lu* were contracts written on small pieces of paper or metal and then split in two, so that each party would hold half of such a contract. The *fu-lu* employed by celestial masters (→ *t'ien-shih*) were magic formulae to guarantee that contracts entered into with deities would be honored. Taoist believers promised the deities to abstain from sinful actions, and the deities in return undertook to ensure that a believer making such a promise does not fall ill. The *fu-lu* symbolized these contracts. Later, however, they were used as contracts for all important transactions. According to → Ko Hung the

Talisman (fu-lu) for establishing contact with spirits and achieving unity.

wearing of *fu-lu,* when engaged in a special project such as a search for the draught of longevity, was of paramount importance. Without such a talisman one would be in danger of falling prey to the spirits, and the genies ruling the mountains would conceal the desired substances (herbs or minerals) from the seeker.

Nowadays *fu-lu* are mainly of psychological significance. They are believed to heal sicknesses, facilitate giving birth, and ward off misfortunes and disasters.

Fu-lu p'ai Chin., lit. "School of Talismans" (→ *fu-lu*); collective term descriptive of all streams of religious

Taoism (→ *tao-chiao*) in which the use of talismans for the purpose of curing illnesses and casting out demons has a central place. Among these movements are the Way of Supreme Peace (→ *t'ai-p'ing tao*), Five-Pecks-of-Rice Taoism (→ *wu-tou-mi tao*), and the Way of Right Unity (→ *cheng-i tao*).

All these schools had their origin in shamanic practices—the veneration of various deities, the use of spells, and the casting out of demons or evil spirits being common features. They were most widespread among the simple people and played an important part in several peasant uprisings.

Fu-mo ta-ti   → Kuan-ti

    ✢   ✢   ✢

Golden elixir   → *chin-tan*

    ✢   ✢   ✢

Heng O   also known as Ch'ang O; the lunar goddess of Chinese mythology and wife of the celestial archer, Shen I, who received the draught of immortality (→ *ch'ang-sheng pu-ssu,* → *hsien*) from the Royal Mother of the West (→ Hsi wang-mu). Heng O tried to abduct this draught from her husband, but he caught her before she could drink all of it. The draught gave her the power to ascend to Heaven, but, as she had not consumed all of it, she had to halt halfway up and settle on the moon. Shen I himself went to the abode of the immortals and became ruler of the sun. Heng O is usually portrayed sitting on a three-legged toad.

Ho   Chin., lit. "crane"; Taoist symbol of immortality (→ *Ch'ang-sheng pu-ssu,* → *shou*) and wisdom. Frequently, the crane is shown together with a pine tree and a rock, both of which are symbols of longevity. Taoist adepts who have attained immortality (→ *hsien*) ascend to Heaven riding on a crane (→ *fei-sheng*). The crane's red head is taken as a sign that it has preserved its vital energy and thus consists of pure yang (→ yin-yang).

Representations that show a crane flying towards a pavilion situated on a rock above the sea are symbols for the isles of the immortals (→ P'eng-lai, → Ying-chou, → Fang-chang). Pairs of cranes, on the other hand, are symbols of good fortune and an elegant literary style and thus repre-sent the Lucky Star (→ *san-hsing*) and the deity of literature (→ Wen-ch'ang).

Ho-ch'i   Chin., lit. "unification of the breaths"; collective sexual orgies practiced since the time of the Han Dynasty by the Taoist school of the Way of Supreme Peace (→ *t'ai-p'ing tao*) and by Five-Pecks-of-Rice Taoism (→ *wu-tou-mi tao*). These practices continued until the time of the Sung Dynasty. *Ho-ch'i* aims at the unification of yin and yang (→ yin-yang), the female and male essence, respectively, thereby nourishing the life principle (→ *yang-hsing*). It is said that the practice of *ho-ch'i* can enable the practitioner to attain immortality.

Ho-ch'i ceremonies were held on the days of the new moon and the full moon. After performing the dances of the dragon (a symbol for yang) and of the tiger (symbol for yin) the participants withdrew to private chambers, where they endeavored to have sexual intercourse with as many different partners as possible.

We have no details of the precise *ho-ch'i* ritual, because all descriptions of it were deleted from the Taoist canon (→ *Tao-*

tsang) under the pressure of Confucianist morality. The practice of *ho-ch'i* is based on the idea that male semen (→ *ching*), the essence of yang, can best be nourished by the female orgasm (yin). If a man has intercourse with many female partners, each of whom experiences an orgasm, but does not allow himself to ejaculate until the final copulation, he will accumulate a large quantity of yang. This has a positive effect on the duration of his life. It is said that the legendary Yellow Emperor (→ Huang-ti) had sexual intercourse with twelve hundred concubines yet suffered no damage to his health, because he was acquainted with the technique of *ho-ch'i*.

Ho-shang kung   Chin., lit. "Venerable of the River"; commentator of the *Tao-te ching* who, according to tradition, lived during the early period of the Han Dynasty at the time of the Emperor Wen (180–157 B.C.E.). Recent research, however, has shown that the commentary bearing his name dates from the end of the Han Dynasty (2d century C.E.). The reason for his name is that he lived in a hut on the bank of a river. In Taoism he is venerated as an immortal (→ *hsien*).

About Ho-shang kung's life there is only one well-known legend, which is quoted at the beginning of the commentary attributed to him: "Emperor Wen was fond of the writings of Lao-tzu, but there were many passages he was unable to understand, and he knew of no-one that might explain them to him. One day he heard reports of a venerable Taoist sage said to live in a straw-covered hut by a river, who devoted all his time to the study of the *Tao-te ching*. The emperor despatched a messenger to question him about the difficult passages in Lao-tzu's writings. Ho-shang kung, however, insisted that the emperor come to see him in person. Thereupon the emperor went to Ho-shang kung, but before questioning him about the incomprehensible passages berated him for his arrogance, saying: 'There is no place below heaven that does not belong to the king, and all who dwell upon this earth are vassals of the king. . . . You may possess the Tao but nevertheless are one of my subjects. . . . Could it be that by refusing to bow to my wishes you are overestimating your own status? Consider that I have the power to make anyone rich or poor, mighty or miserable.' At this Ho-shang kung rose from his seat and ascended high into the air, from where he addressed the emperor as follows: 'Since I am neither in heaven, nor among the people or on earth, am I still your subject?' Emperor Wen then realised that he was dealing with a supernatural being. He apologised most humbly and thereupon received from Ho-shang kung the *Tao-te ching* and Ho-shang kung's commentary" (trans. from Kaltenmark, *Lao-tzu und der Taoismus;* see Kaltenmark 1969).

Ho-t'u and Lo-shu   Chin., lit. "diagram from the [Yellow] River and diagram from the River Lo"; two magical diagrams by which Confucianism explains the origin of the *Book of Change(s)* (→ *I-ching*) and the → *Hung-fan.* In all probability the two diagrams are the result of combining numerological speculations with the → yin-yang teachings of the *I-ching,* and they are in fact mentioned in a commentary known as *Hsi-tz'u* (→ *Shih-i*).

The *Ho-t'u* is so constructed that its odd numbers as well as its even numbers add up to twenty, if the central five

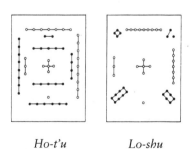

Ho-t'u   *Lo-shu*

and ten are ignored. In the *Lo-shu,* on the other hand, the sum of its horizontal and vertical rows, as well as its diagonals, is always fifteen. In both diagrams, even (yin) numbers are indicated by white and odd (yang) numbers by black circles.

In ancient times both diagrams were used for purposes of prophecy. In the Inner Alchemy (→ *nei-tan*) they serve to explain processes occurring within the body under the influence of the inner elixir.

There are conflicting reports about the origin of these diagrams. According to one tradition, Yü the Great (→ Ta-yü) received them from two fabulous animals. The *Ho-t'u* appeared on the back of a dragon-horse emerging from the Yellow River, and the *Lo-shu* on the back of a turtle from the River Lo.

Another tradition states that → Fu Hsi acquired the diagrams in the same manner and then derived the eight tri-grams (→ *pa-kua*) from the *Ho-t'u.* According to yet another version, the *Lo-shu* originated with Yü and the *Ho-t'u* with Fu Hsi.

Until the 12th century the names of the two diagams were reversed, i.e., the present *Lo-shu* was known as *Ho-t'u* and vice versa. They were given their present designations by → Chu Hsi and have retained them to this day.

Hou-t'ien   Chin., lit. after Heaven, post-celestial, after time; a concept occurring in the *Book of Change(s)* (→ *I-ching*) to describe the phenomenal, i.e., the state following the creation of Heaven. *Hou-t'ien* can also refer to "form" or to that which is after birth.

In the *hou-t'ien* ordering of Emperor Wen's eight tri-grams (→ *pa-kua*), these are not arranged according to their polar correspondences, i.e., in a precelestial order, but in accordance with their periodical return. In the Inner

Alchemy (→ *nei-tan*) the physical forms of the three life forces (→ *ching*, → *ch'i*, → *shen*) are said to be postcelestial.

Hsiang Hsiu   → *Chu-lin ch'i-hsien*, → *hsüan-hsüeh*

Hsiang-sheng hsiang-k'o   Chin., → *wu-hsing*

Hsien   Chin., immortal; ideal of religious Taoism (→ *tao-chiao*). *Hsien* designates a being who has attained physical immortality, is no longer subject to the "world of dust" and is a master of various magical skills.

Taoism teaches various ways of restoring to the body pure energies it possessed at birth and thereby attaining immortality (→ *ch'ang-sheng pu-ssu*). Some Taoists follow the alchemical path and strive to produce an elixir of immortality (→ *wai-tan*); others endeavor to reach their aim by special hygiene exercises (→ Inner Deity Hygiene School), breathing exercises (→ *hsing-ch'i*, → *fu-ch'i*, → *t'ai-hsi*, etc.), gymnastics (→ *tao-yin*), sexual techniques (→ *fang-chung shu*), fasting (→ *chai*) or meditation (→ *tso-wang*, → *shou-i*, → *ts'un-ssu*).

Taoist literature mentions various categories of immortals. The great alchemist → Ko Hung speaks of three such categories, namely celestial immortals, terrestrial immortals, and immortals who have separated from their dead body (→ *shih-chieh*). Terrestrial immortals live in forests or in the mountains, whereas celestial immortals dwell either in the Taoist Heaven (→ *t'ien*); on the isles of the immortals (→ P'eng-lai, → Ying-chou, → Fang-chang), which are situated in the eastern sea; or in the → K'un-lun Mountains toward the West.

Immortals are often portrayed riding on a crane, because according to an ancient belief cranes may live for a thousand years or longer. The vermilion red color of the crane's head is considered to be proof that the crane has preserved his life energy and consists of pure yang (→ yin-yang). That is why immortals are said to ascend to Heaven riding on the back of a crane (→ *fei-sheng*).

In the course of time famous and venerated historical personalities came to be admitted to the ranks of the immortals. The best-known *hsien* are the eight immortals (→ *pa-hsien*).

Immortals have for centuries been a favorite subject in Chinese art. Frequently they are portrayed as having a body covered with feathers. This points to an earlier interpretation of the word *hsien*, related to the development of the relevant Chinese pictogram: originally the pictogram for *hsien* was a sign that signified rising, ascending into the air. The present pictogram for "immortal" (consisting of the signs for "man" and "mountain") was not introduced until later, when immortals came to be seen as seeking the seclusion of the mountains or withdrawing to a paradisical island.

In Ko Hung's classification celestial immortals are accorded the highest stage of realization. He describes them as follows: "Some immortals ascend to the clouds, their body upright, and they fly among the clouds without the beating of wings; some glide across the cloudy vapor by harnessing a dragon and ascend up to the very steps of Heaven; some transform themselves into animals and roam through the azure clouds; yet others dive deep into rivers and oceans or flutter on wings to the peaks of famous mountains. . . . Their kind has attained an eternal life, free from death; but before they reach their goal they have to shed all human emotions and all ambitions about fame and glory. . . . They have abandoned their former nature and are pervaded by a new life energy" (trans. from W. Bauer, *China und die Hoffnung auf*

Glück [Munich, 1974], 157). The terrestrial immortals prefer to live in the seclusion of the mountains. They are masters of various supernatural skills; e.g., they are able to conquer demons, walk through forests without being attacked by wild animals, make themselves invisible in moments of danger, etc. They are saints and retain their youthful appearance despite their great age. Occasionally they mingle with ordinary mortals to astonish them by their magical abilities and transmit to them long-forgotten knowledge. They have decided not to die and thus had to forgo the possibility of ascending to Heaven.

Hsien-t'ien   Chin., lit. "before Heaven, precelestial, before time"; a concept found in the *Book of Change(s)* (→ *I-ching*), describing the state that existed before the creation of Heaven, i.e., the absolute. *Hsien-t'ien* can also be understood to refer to the formless, i.e., that which exists before birth.

→ Fu Hsi's arrangement of the eight trigrams (→ *pa-kua*) is said to be precelestial. In his ordering of the trigrams, pairs of forces with a polar relationship face each other and hold each other in balance. The later ordering of the trigrams by the Emperor Wen is described as postcelestial (→ *hou-t'ien*).

In the Inner Alchemy (→ *nei-tan*) the purified cosmic state of the three life forces (→ *ching*, → *ch'i*, → *shen*) is described as precelestial.

Hsien-t'ien-t'u   Chin. → Ch'en T'uan

Hsi K'ang   Chin. → *chu-lin ch'i-hsien*

Hsin-chai   Chin., lit. "fasting or abstinence of the heart"; a concept found in the writings of → Chuang-tzu to describe the purification of the mind, thereby making it possible to experience the Tao. Chuang-tzu describes this

51

fasting of the heart as follows: "Unify your will. No longer hear with your ears, but with your heart. Nay, hear no longer with the heart but with the → *ch'i*. Auditory perception is limited by the ears, and even the heart [i.e., (self)-consciousness] is restricted by its attachments to certain external things; the *ch'i,* however, perceives through emptiness, and the Tao arises from emptiness. This emptiness is attained by [what I call] fasting of the heart" (trans. from Kaltenmark, *Lao-tzu und der Taoismus;* see Kaltenmark 1969).

In the official state religion *chai* denotes ritual fasting before sacrifices are offered. Chuang-tzu explains this to Hsing-ch'i by referring to a conversation between Confucius and his pupil Yen Hui, who is planning to civilize a tyrant. Confucius—here presented as a Taoist—points out the pitfalls and dangers of [self]-conscious will and action to Yen Hui and advises him to practice *hsin-chai* and thereby purify his mind. Only then would Yen Hui be able to influence the tyrant constructively: "Then you may enter the cage [i.e., enter the tyrant's service] and move therein without causing undue offence. If people are willing to listen, sing your song; if not, keep silent. You cannot influence men by force or guile. You are in the same cage with them and should live among them quite naturally. In this way you may be able to achieve something" (trans. from Wilhelm 1969).

Hsing-ch'i   Chin., lit. "allowing the breath to circulate"; Taoist breathing technique by which the practitioner allows the breath to circulate through all parts of the body. *Hsing-ch'i* forms part of embryonic breathing (→ *t'ai-hsi*) as well as the practices of → *tao-yin,* → *t'u-ku na-hsin* and other methods of nourishing the body (→ *yang-sheng*). The *hsing-ch'i* practitioner directs his breath by the power of his mind. Each practitioner develops his own method of doing this: some see the breath as two white lines (it enters through the nostrils and circulates through the body in two separate and independent streams); others prefer to imagine that the breath is led by a small figure whose progress they follow in their mind. The breath is circulated within the body as slowly as possible, endeavoring to dispatch it to all parts of the body. By this method sicknesses may be cured and blockages dissolved.

Concerning *hsing-ch'i* practices → Ko Hung writes, "The absorption of medicaments and draughts is a basic requirement for attaining immortality. However, by practicing the circulation of the breath, the process can be accelerated. Even without medicaments or draughts a person can reach the age of a hundred years by just practicing *hsing-ch'i*. It nourishes the body within and helps to ward off external evils."

The *hsing-ch'i* practitioner should retire to a quiet room, lie on the floor, place a flat cushion under his head, and close his eyes. The practitioner should eliminate thoughts and sense perceptions, as well as all feelings and emotions. Then he should inhale and hold the breath for several heartbeats. A practitioner will not approach the state of immortality until he is able to let his breath circulate through his body for a thousand heartbeats.

Hsing-ming Chin., lit. "nature and life"; the spiritual nature and the life or fate of a human being. *Ming* stands for the substance of life and death, *hsing* for the root of spiritual consciousness. *Ming* is seen as the source of life-giving breath (→ *ch'i*), and *hsing* as the source of the mind (→ *shen*).

Both *hsing* and *ming* arise from the void (*hsü*) existing before birth: at the moment of birth this primordial energy sep-

53

arates into the two components *hsing* and *ming*. The aim of the Inner Alchemy School (→ *nei-tan*) consists in purifying the mind so as to be able to return to the void (*lien-shen fu-hsü*). In the symbolic language of the alchemists this process is described as the uniting of → *k'an* and *li,* or the heart and kidneys.

Hsi Wang-mu Chin., lit. "Royal Mother of the West"; Taoist figure that rules over the western paradise (of the immortals) in the K'un-lun Mountains. As the ruler of the immortals (→ *hsien*) she is portrayed as a young beautiful woman wearing a royal gown, sometimes also riding on a peacock. She lives in a nine-storied palace of jade, which is surrounded by a wall over a thousand miles long and of pure gold. The male immortals reside in the right wing of this palace, the female immortals in the left wing.

In her garden Hsi Wang-mu cultivates the peach of immortality; whoever partakes of this fruit is no longer subject to death. However, her miraculous peach tree forms only one peach every three thousand years, which then takes a further three thousand years to ripen. When it is ripe, the Royal Mother of the West invites all the immortals to a feast to celebrate their birthday and to partake of the miraculous peach, which bestows another lease of immortality. The feast has often been described in Chinese literature.

In the course of history the figure of Hsi Wang-mu has undergone considerable changes of meaning. In ancient texts, such as the *Shan-hai ching* (*Book of Mountains and Oceans*) she is described as a monster with a human face, the teeth of a tiger, and a leopard's tail. She was the goddess of epidemics, who lived in the West and ruled over the demons of the plague.

By the beginning of the Christian era, however, she had become a noble lady. According to legend she presented gifts to several ancient Chinese rulers, at first of jade and later of the life-prolonging peach, which has ever since been her symbol.

In the Taoist view, the Royal Mother of the West arose from the purest air of the West and is representative of yin, the passive feminine principle, whereas Tung Wang-kung, her male consort—known as the Prince of the East—was born of the pure breath of the East and represents yang, the active male principle (→ yin-yang).

Hsü   Chin., → *hsing-ming*

Hsüan-hsüeh   Chin., lit. "secret mystical teaching"; a philosophical movement of the 3d and 4th centuries C.E., known as neo-Taoism, and based on the philosophical Taoism (→ *tao-chia*) of Lao-tzu and Chuang-tzu. The term *hsüan-hsüeh* as a concept goes back to the *Tao-te ching*, which describes the → Tao as the "secret of secrets."

The followers of the *hsüan-hsüeh* movement combine Taoist ideas with Confucianist principles. They consider Confucius (→ K'ung-tzu) to be the greater sage because he attained a higher level of insight than either Lao-tzu or Chuang-tzu.

The neo-Taoists developed and refined a special form of converse known as pure conversation (→ *ch'ing-t'an*). The most important representatives of the *hsüan-hsüeh* movement were → Wang Pi (226–49 C.E.), Hsiang Hsiu (221–300 C.E.), and Kuo Hsiang (?–ca. 312 C.E.), all of whom wrote important commentaries on the *Tao-te ching*.

Neo-Taoists see the Tao as literally nothingness, whereas Lao-tzu holds that the true Tao cannot be named. It follows from this that the Tao cannot be the cause of anything: to say that something was caused by the Tao would amount to saying that it was caused by itself. The *hsüan-hsüeh* philosophers thus refute the view that nonbeing (→ *wu*) can give rise to being (*you*).

Thus in neo-Taoism the Tao—the central concept of original Taoism—was increasingly replaced by the idea of Heaven (→ *t'ien*), which is said to be the totality of all that exists. To see the world from the point of view of Heaven means to transcend phenomena and differentiations. The identity of things is therefore a central tenet of neo-Taoism. To realize this identity, it is necessary to abandon all likes and dislikes and live in complete harmony with one's true self, uninfluenced by external factors. Such an attitude is said to lead to complete freedom and happiness.

Unlike Lao-tzu, the supporters of neo-Taoism do not condemn institutions and customs, providing these adapt themselves to social change and to the requirements of the times. They see change as a mighty force, which man is unable to perceive directly but to which everything is subject. Voluntary submission to this principle is known as → *wu-wei*, i.e., to let things take their course by not opposing or resisting the process of natural change.

Since the 5th century C.E. neo-Taoism has been strongly influenced by Buddhism and in consequence lost a great deal of its earlier importance.

Hsün-tzu   Chin. → Confucianism

Hua-hu ching   Chin., lit. *"Classic [Treatise] on the Conversion of Barbarians";* Taoist work, dating from ca. 300 C.E., in which the missionary activities of → Lao-tzu "in the West of China" (i.e., India) are described. The *Hua-hu ching* claims that the Buddha was a pupil of Lao-tzu and Buddhism therefore a variant of Taoism.

The *Hua-hu ching* figures prominently in the early contro-versies between Taoists and Buddhists, the Taoists citing it as proof of their superiority over the followers of Buddhism and demanding that Taoism be accorded the status of an official religion. The Buddhists countered by moving the Buddha's date of birth back to the 11th century B.C.E.: Lao-tzu could not possibly have converted a person that lived several cen-turies before him.

Huai-nan-tzu   Chin., philosophical treatise dating from the 2d century B.C.E.; more specifically, a collection of writings by scholars gathered around Liu An, the prince of Huai-nan, who later became involved in a conspiracy against the ruler and committed suicide in 122 B.C.E.

Like the → *Lü-shih ch'un-ch'iu*, the *Huai-nan-tzu* is an analytical compilation of the teachings of philosophical schools prevalent during the 2d century. It accords special emphasis to Taoist ideas. Of particular importance are its chapters on the origin of the cosmos, because they are clearer and more lucid than relevant passages in other works. In addition, the *Huai-nan-tzu* deals with the doctrine of the five elements (→ *wu-hsing*) and with the → yin-yang.

The *Huai-nan-tzu* originally consisted of twenty-one "inner" chapters, which contain Taoist teachings, and thirty-three "outer" chapters devoted to the philosophies of other schools. The thirty-three "outer" chapters are lost. The third of the "inner" chapters describes the genesis of the universe as follows:

"Before Heaven and Earth took on form, there was a state of amorphous formlessness. This is known as the great begin-ning [→ *t'ai-shih*], which gave rise to an empty expanse, from which emerged the cosmos, which produced the (no longer unlimited or infinite) primordial breath [→ *yüan-ch'i*]. That which was lucid and light gathered to form Heaven, and that which was heavy and opaque combined to form Earth. The joining of the light and the opaque was effortless, whereas the fusion of the heavy and opaque was difficult. That is why Heaven was formed before Earth.

"The essences of Heaven and Earth formed yin and yang, and their concentrated essences in turn gave rise to the four seasons. The scattered essences of the four seasons produced the ten thousand things. The hot yang energy, having accumulated over a long period of time, produced fire, the essence of which became the sun. The cold yin energy, similarly accumulated over a long period of time, produced water, the essence of which became the moon. The purified essences of sun and moon gave rise to the stars and planets. Heaven received the sun, moon, stars and planets, while Earth received water, rivers, soil, and dust."

Huan-ching Chin., lit. "allowing the semen to return"; Taoist sexual practice aimed at prolonging life, in which the practitioner causes his essence (→ *ching*) to intermingle with his breath (→ *ch'i*) and then to circulate through his body, dispatching it from the lower to the upper cinnabar field (→ *tan-t'ien*), with the aim of nourishing the brain (*pu-nao*). Before *huan-ching* can be practiced the adept must increase and strengthen his *ching* by refraining from ejaculation during sexual intercourse (see next entry).

Huan-ching pu-nao Chin., lit. "allowing the semen to return [in order to] strengthen the brain"; Taoist sexual technique (→ *fang-chung shu*) for strengthening the *ching* essence and prolonging life.

When practicing *huang-ching pu-nao* the man firmly grips the root of his penis between two fingers prior to ejaculation, while deeply exhaling through the mouth and grinding his teeth (→ *k'ou-ch'ih*). This causes the semen to ascend to the upper cinnabar field (→ *tan-t'ien*) in the brain. *Huang-ching pu-nao* should only be practiced on certain days and at certain hours of the day. In addition, the practitioner should be in a state of meditative absorption.

The alleged reason for the rejuvenating effect of this practice is that the semen (*ching*) can combine with the vital energy (*ch'i*). There are divergent views as to where in the body this fusion of *ching* and *ch'i* occurs. Some maintain it takes place in the respiratory tract, to which the essence ascends; others say it occurs in the lower cinnabar field, to which the breath descends. Once combined, the semen and the vital energy circulate through the body until they once again rise from the lower to the upper cinnabar field—more precisely, that part of it known as → *ni-huan,* whereby the brain is repaired. Some Taoists practice *huang-ching pu-nao* as a preliminary to meditative breathing exercises of the Inner Alchemy School (→ *nei-tan*).

Taoists are convinced that this method of preventing ejaculation was already known at the time of the legendary Yellow Emperor (→ Huang-ti), who is said to have had successive sexual intercourse with twelve hundred concubines, suffering no damage to his health. In any case, it is certain that the practice was widespread by the time of the Han Dynasty.

Most Taoist works stress that the essential generating factor of this technique is the primordial essence of the semen rather than the semen itself. The process of the *huan-ching pu-nao* practice begins at the moment an erection becomes manifest and sexual energy is aroused. In the Taoist view an erection need, however, not always be dependent on sexual arousal; rather it is taken to indicate that energy is present in sufficient quantity to circulate freely through the body. Furthermore, an erection may occur during meditation if the practitioner reaches a state free of thought and desire. *Huan-ching pu nao* can thus also be practiced by Taoists who reject sexual techniques involving a partner of the opposite sex.

Huang-chin Chin., lit. "yellow cloth," "Yellow Turbans"; a term descriptive of the followers of the Way of Supreme Peace (→ *t'ai-p'ing tao*) founded by → Chang Chüeh. They wore around their heads a yellow cloth in honor of the Yellow Emperor (→ Huang-ti) who, together with → Lao-chün, was considered the original founder of the *t'ai-p'ing tao* movement as a whole.

A rebellion organized in 184 C.E. by the followers of the Way of Supreme Peace has gone down in history as the Rising of the Yellow Turbans (*huang-chin ch'i-i*).

Huang-ch'üan Chin., lit. "yellow springs"; the Underworld, to which yin souls (→ yin-yang, → *p'o*) return after death. The *huang-ch'üan* is traditionally believed to be a watery place, situated in the North. That is why in ancient times the dead were buried in the northern part of the town and with their heads pointing north.

Huang-lao Chin., lit. "Yellow-old"; Taoist deity. The *Huang* component refers to → Huang-ti, the Yellow Emperor, and the *lao* component to → Lao-tzu. Religious Taoism (→ *tao-chiao*) considers both as its founders, and they have been jointly venerated as Huang-lao since ca. 200 B.C.E. Later, Huang-lao developed into one of the most important deities of early Taoism, → Huang-lao-chün, the main deity of the Way of Supreme Peace (→ *t'ai-p'ing tao*).

Huang-lao-chün Chin., lit. "Ancient Yellow Lord"; important deity of early Taoism and main god of the Way of Supreme Peace (→ *t'ai-p'ing tao,* → Huang-lao). The common people considered Huang-lao-chün to be the ruler of the world, who descends to Earth to guide and assist mankind. From the beginning of the world he is said to have appeared, again and again, in the shape of Taoist masters to spread the teachings about the Tao. One of his incarnations was → Lao-tzu.

Huang-ti Chin., lit. "Yellow Emperor"; one of the legendary emperors, whose life span is variously given as 2697–2597 B.C.E. or 2674–2575 B.C.E. He is venerated as one of the founders of religious Taoism (→ *tao-chiao*) and furthermore credited with the creation of mankind, the invention of writing, the compass, the pottery wheel, and the breeding of silkworms. In addition, the Yellow Emperor is considered to have been a determining influence in establishing the Chinese social order, in that he allocated a name to each family. Lastly he is the alleged author of the → *Huang-ti nei-ching*, the first medical treatise in the history of China.

According to one tradition Huang-ti spontaneously came into being as a result of the fusion of energies that marked the beginning of the world. He created man by placing earthen statues at the cardinal points of the world, leaving them exposed to the breath of the world's beginning for a period of three hundred years. When they were totally pervaded by the energy of that breath, the statues were able to speak and move. In this way the various races of mankind came into being. Since the Warring States Period, Taoists have associated Huang-ti with the cult of the immortals. On his travels to the Sacred Mountains, Huang-ti met Master Kuan Cheng, who initiated him in the practices for the realization of the Tao. This encounter is described by → Chuang-tzu (Book 11, Chapter 3) as follows (Kuan Cheng speaking): "See nothing; hear nothing; let your soul be wrapped in quiet, and your body will begin to take proper form. Let there be absolute repose and absolute purity; do not weary your body nor disturb your vitality–and you will live forever. For if the eye sees nothing and the ear hears nothing, and the mind thinks nothing the soul will preserve the body and the body will live forever. Cherish that which is within you and shut off that which is without; for much knowledge is a curse. Then I will place you upon that abode of Great Light, which is the source of the positive Power (*yang*) and escort you through the gate of Profound Mystery, which is the source of the negative Power (*yin*)" (Giles 1961). At the age of 100 Huang-ti was possessed with magical powers and produced the golden elixir (→ *chin-tan*). He attained immortality on Ching Mountain, whereupon he ascended to Heaven riding a dragon (→ *fei-sheng*) and became one of the five mythological emperors, who rule over the five cardinal points (the fifth being the center, ruled by Huang-ti).

Huang-ti nei-ching Chin., lit. *"Inner Classic of the Yellow Emperor"*; first medical treatise in the history of China. Although the *Huang-ti nei-ching* is ascribed to the Yellow Emperor (Huang-ti), in all probability it dates from the 3d or 2d Century B.C.E. The basic theories of Chinese medicine contained in the *Huang-ti nei-ching* have retained their validity to the present day. The title of the work is generally translated as *The Yellow Emperor's Classic of Internal Medicine*.

Huang-t'ing ching   Chin., lit. "*Classic Treatise on the Yellow Hall* [or *Castle*]"; 3d century Taoist treatise describing the most important deities of the body (→ *shen*) and their functions. In addition, the *Huang-t'ing ching* contains instructions for breathing exercises, above all on letting the breath circulate through the body. (→ *hsing-ch'i*), sexual practices (→ *fang-chung shu*), and other techniques aimed at attaining immortality. The earliest known mention of the term *yellow castle* occurs in an inscription dating from the year 165 C.E. in honor of → Lao-tzu: "Enter into and depart from the cinnabar hut, ascend from and descend to the yellow castle" (Homann 1971, p. 57).

The somewhat ambiguous term *yellow castle* refers primarily to the notion of a center and to the connections that can be established—by following the instruction of the *Huang-t'ing ching*—between the centers of Heaven, of man, and of the Earth. In the case of man, the term *yellow castle* (as employed in the *Huang-t'ing ching*) refers to the heart as the central organ and ruler over thoughts and emotions. Other texts, however, associate the term with the pancreas.

The repeated recitation of the *Huang-t'ing ching* is said to ward off evil, allow the adept to regain his former youthful appearance, and to bestow physical invulnerability. Such recitation, moreover, causes the various deities of the body to appear before the inner eye of the practitioner and helps him to contact these deities so as to obtain instructions on how to attain immortality. In the Taoist view, the effectiveness of the *Huang-t'ing ching* is due to the fact that it reveals the actual names of the deities; by reciting their names the deities can be invoked.

Huan-tan   Chin., lit. "recycled cinnabar"; a term used by Taoist alchemists to describe a life-prolonging elixir obtained by a method of cyclic transformation: cinnabar powder is heated and thereby turned into mercury. As a result of the consequent oxidation of the mercury, the alchemist obtains a vermilion-colored oxide, which explains the origin of the term *cinnabar.* As a rule, this process was repeated nine times, thereby producing *chiu-huan-tan,* the "nine times recycled Elixir."

For the followers of the Inner Elixir School (→ *nei-tan*) the term *huan-tan* designates the → *ch'i* produced and accumulated in the body. This *ch'i* is capable of transforming aged body tissue to resemble that of a new-born child. In this way, the adherents of this school believe it to be possible to attain physical immortality.

Hua T'o   Taoist physician of 2d/3d century C.E. He was a renowned surgeon, the first anaesthetist in Chinese medicine, and made an important contribution to the development of Taoist gymnastic exercises (→ *tao-yin*).

According to Hua T'o physical exercise effects a removal of negative energies resulting from eating grain (→ *pi-ku*), and ensures the unimpeded circulation of blood. *Tao-yin* exercises are capable of restoring a youthful appearance to the aging body. Hua T'o is furthermore credited with the invention of the *ch'i-kung* exercise known as "movements of the five animals" (*wu-ch'in-hsi*), which consists of imitating the movements of a tiger, a stag, a bear, a monkey, and a bird, thereby stimulating and balancing the flow of → *ch'i* within the body and enhancing the practitioner's health. (For a detailed description of this exercise, see Zoller 1984, p. 256 ff.)

Hui Shih   ca. 370–310 B.C.E.; a philosopher of the Warring States Period, who represented the School of Names, which concerned itself with the problem of the relationship between names and reality. Hui Shih was a friend of Chuang-tzu, in whose writings his thoughts have come down to us. Within the philosophical School of Names Hui Shih represented a faction supporting the unification of opposites. His central idea is that of the unity of the universe, forming a single whole. This thought finds expression in the equation of varying concepts of size: "There is nothing beyond the infinitely great, which I call the Great One [→ T'ai-i]; there is nothing within the infinitely small, which I call the Small One [Hsiao-i]" (trans. from Kaltenmark, *Laotzu und der Taoismus;* see Kaltenmark 1969).

Hui Shih sees all differences and opposites in relative terms: thus Heaven and Earth are not to be considered as different from each other. This proposition finds its direct and most positive expression in a nondifferentiating love for all things. Hui Shih's celebrated paradoxes aim at questioning deeply rooted notions concerning the qualities of things and the nature of beings.

The writings of Hui Shih have not been preserved in their entirety; fragments of his teaching are found in the → *Chuang-tzu,* → *Lieh-tzu,* and → *Lü-shih ch'un-ch'iu.*

Book 33 of the *Chuang-tzu* contains some of Hui Shih's most famous paradoxes:

"That which is without dimension cannot be piled up, yet it measures a thousand li."

"Heaven and Earth are equally low. Mountain and marsh are equally level."

"The sun at noon is the sun setting; when an animal is born, it dies."

"The Center of the World is north of Yen and south of Yueh (Yen was the northernmost and Yueh the southernmost region of ancient China)." A commentator has interpreted this last paradox as expressing the idea that the world is infinite and its center everywhere. (Quotes from Giles 1961.)

Hui-tsung 1082–1135 C.E.; Sung Dynasty emperor and one of the staunchest supporters and promoters of Taoism. During his reign numerous Taoist temples and monasteries (→ *kuan*) were built. He referred to himself as "nobleman of the Tao" and bestowed upon the Jade Emperor (→ Yü-huang)—an important Taoist deity—the title *Shang-ti* (god). In addition he greatly encouraged the compilation of the Taoist canon (→ *Tao-tsang*).

Hun Chin., "breath soul," spirit soul; one of two souls said to reside in each human being, the other being the so-called body soul (→ *p'o*). The life and health of a person depend on the harmonious interplay of these two souls, or energies. When *hun* and *p'o* separate, death ensues.

Each human being has, in fact, three *hun*, which are considered to be higher souls that form at birth, after the seven *p'o* souls. The *hun* represent the *yang* energy (→ yin-yang), the active force, and regulate the higher physical functions. At death, they leave the body and return to Heaven. They are also capable of manifesting in another form or shape, because they may leave the body of a person, without that person dying, e.g., when someone loses consciousness or faints. This view is also reflected by the old custom of "recalling the *hun*" (*chao-hun*), in which the souls of people who have drowned, lost consciousness, or been hanged are beckoned to return and thereby revive their former bodies.

Hung-fan   Chin., lit. great plan, great norm; a chapter of the *Book of Writings* (*Shu-ching*), a classic Confucian treatise, which contains the first exposition of the teaching of the five elements (→ *wu-hsing*).

The *Hung-fan* considers the five elements (water, fire, wood, metal, and earth) to be concrete substances instead of—a later view—abstract energies, and teaches that the world of nature is dependant on the world of man: the inadequate conduct of a ruler will cause abnormal phenomena in nature. Later, this view was more fully developed by the Yin-Yang School (→ *yin-yang chia*).

✣   ✣   ✣

I   Chin., roughly honesty, uprightness, duty; a concept in

I   Chin., lit. "change, transformation" → *I-ching* Confucianist philosophy. To act in accordance with *i* means to respond to the demands of a situation from a sense of moral obligation and without any thought of gain (*li*). *I* and *li* are total opposites. Uprightness is one of the five cardinal virtues of Confucianism (→ *wu-ch'ang*, → K'ung-tzu).

The *Analects* (*Lun-yü*) of Confucius state (4.16), "A noble man understands what is moral; a small man understands what is profitable."

I-ching   Chin., lit. "*Book of Change(s)*"; a Chinese book of wisdom and oracles, dating from the transition period between the Yin and Chou dynasties. The essential philosophy of the *I-ching* is based on Confucianism, but there are also Taoist ideas present. The *Book of Change(s)* is based on the idea of two polar energies, by whose activities all things are brought about and come into being. Initially, these two energies were simply called the light and the dark, but later were referred to as yin and yang (→ yin-yang). The interaction of yin and yang produces change (*i*), which is to be understood as the movement of the → Tao.

The basic structure of the *Book of Change(s)* is formed by the eight trigrams (→ *pa-kua*), which consist of three broken and/or unbroken horizontal lines. The various combinations of these trigrams in pairs produce the sixty-four hexagrams. The root text of the *Book of Change(s)* describes the individual hexagrams and their lines, representing states or tendencies of transformation, and explains the social and political aspects of whatever sign is under discussion. The various commentaries (→ *Shih-i*) on this root text were added later and are Confucianist interpretations.

In all probability the *I-ching* was originally used as a manual of prophecy. When oracles were first cast in China, the answer to a question would be simply *Yes* or *No,* indicated by either an unbroken (—) or a broken (– –) line. In the face of the complexity of reality, this method of prediction soon proved inadequate, and this led to the introduction of trigrams and hexagrams composed of broken and/or unbroken lines.

These trigrams and hexagrams reflect events in Heaven and on Earth, and the prediction is based on the transformation of one state into another. The relevant processes are described in concise sayings that refer to basic cosmic or social situations. Change is inherent in the hexagrams themselves, because they are said to be in a continuous state of motion, so that one or several lines may change into their opposite and thus into another of the sixty-four hexagrams. This makes it possible to embrace the whole of reality in the prediction.

Traditionally, oracles were cast by throwing fifty yarrow stalks or—in a simplified procedure—three coins. The best-known translations of the original Chinese text of the *I-ching,* containing also a description of the method of obtaining a prediction, are Wilhelm 1967 (an English translation of Wilhelm's German translation) and Blofeld 1965.

The hexagrams of the *I-ching* were adopted by the followers of the Inner Alchemy (→ *nei-tan*), to symbolize various internal processes (→ *ch'ien* and *k'un,* → *k'an* and *li*).

In the traditional view the *Book of Change(s)* goes back to → Fu Hsi, who is said to have invented the eight trigrams and some of the sixty-four hexagrams. The remaining hexagrams allegedly originated with King Wen, one of the founders of the Chou Dynasty. Some scholars say both the trigrams and the hexagrams should be attributed to King Wen, while others hold that King Wen created the trigrams, and the Duke of Chou the hexagrams. The main commentary (also called the *Ten Wings*) on the root text is attributed to Confucius (→ K'ung-tzu) but in actual fact stems from a later period, in all probability the early Han Dynasty.

The *I-ching* is the only philosophical work to survive the burning of the books ordered in 213 C.E. by Ch'in Shih-huang-ti, the first historical emperor of China, who himself consulted the *I-ching* as a book of prophecy. The *I-ching* was commonly used for purposes of divination at the time, both by the → *fang-shih* and the followers of the → *yin-yang chia.* Subsequently it came to be considered primarily a book of wisdom and of the official state doctrine.

The *I-ching* has been used for casting oracles since the time of the Chou Dynasty. During the Han Dynasty methods of prediction by the use of emblems and numbers began to spread and reached their highest popularity in Confucianist circles during the Sung Dynasty. The most common—and at the same time, most reliable—method of putting a question to the oracle was by throwing fifty yarrow stalks. This method symbolizes the harmony between the macrocosmic order of nature and the microcosmic order at the precise moment of consultation.

I-chuan   Chin., lit. *"Commentary on the Changes"*; another name for the *Ten Commentaries* on the *Book of Change(s)* (→ *I-ching*). For further details → *Shih-i*.

Inner Deity Hygiene School   a movement within religious Taoism (→ *tao-chiao*) which allocated deities (→ *shen*) to the various parts and organs of the human body. By means of right nourishment, appropriate invocations, and meditation practices these deities were induced to protect the body and grant the practitioner immortality. The inner deities are identical with the deities inhabiting the Taoist heavens. The basic philosophical tract of this movement, which flourished between the 2d and 6th century C.E., is the → *Huang-t'ing ching*.

The inner pantheon—like the outer—consists of 36,000 deities. The most important of these reside in the three vital centers of the body, i.e., the three cinnabar fields (→ *tan-t'ien*). They are the three ones (→ *san-i*) who are ruled by the Supreme One (→ Tai-i). A further important inner deity is → Ssu-ming, the Ruler of Fate.

The allocation of deities to the various organs of the body is not uniform and varies from one text to the next; in the course of time more and more deities were admitted to the pantheon. Each practitioner has a special relationship with one of these deities and is capable of establishing direct contact with it; the higher this deity is placed in the overall hierarchy of the *shen* the greater the benefit the practitioner can derive from his association with it.

The followers of the Inner Deity Hygiene School consider the presence of these 36,000 deities within the body of a prerequisite for life: if the deities leave the body, the person in question dies. Taoist adepts employ various methods to prevent the deities from leaving the body.

A practitioner may try to visualize the deities (→ *nei-kuan*) and keep a specific diet: he will neither eat meat nor drink wine, because the deities are said to dislike the smell of both. In addition, he may abstain from eating grain (→ *pi-ku*), which is said to serve as nourishment for the three worms, the enemies of the deities (→ *san-ch'ung*).

However, all these practices are of no avail if the practitioner leads an immoral life, in which case the deities will withhold their support. In this way good deeds and charitable works, such as the construction of roads and bridges, the establishment of orphanages, and similar projects became a very important aspect of religious practice.

During the 6th century C.E. the Inner Deity Hygiene School was displaced by the School of the Magic Jewel (→ *ling-pao p'ai*, → *Ling-pao ching*) and the consequent externalization of the inner deities.

Inner Elixir   → *nei-tan*

✻   ✻   ✻

Jen   Chin., roughly humanity, love of fellow man; central virtue of → Confucianism and the most important characteristic of the ideal man (*chün-tzu*, lit. "duke's son") in the teachings of Confucius (→ K'ung-tzu). *Jen* is the manifestation of pure untarnished human nature in accordance with the requirements of morality (→ *li*). Its basis is a natural sympathy for one's fellow beings, its expression the maintenance of mutuality (*shu*) and loyalty (*chung*).

In the *Analects* (*Lun-yü*) Confucius states (6.28), "To apply one's own wishes and desires as a yardstick by which to judge one's behavior toward others is the true way of *jen*." Asked about the essence of *jen*, the master replied, "To love your fellow men."

The roots of *jen* are piety (*hsiao*), i.e., the veneration shown by children for their parents in life and after their death, and fraternal obedience (*ti*), i.e., the subordination of the younger brother to the older: "A noble person will cultivate the root; if the root is rooted firmly, the path will grow. Piety and obedience: these are the roots of *jen*." An analysis of the pictogram for *jen* allows us to arrive at a deeper understanding of the term: the pictogram consists of the sign for "human being" and the sign for "two." *Jen* thus embraces all the moral qualities governing—and expressed by—the ideal behavior of one human being toward another.

Juan Chi   → *chu-lin ch'i-hsien*

Juan Hsien   → *chu-lin ch'i-hsien*

Ju ching   Chin., lit. "to enter into the silence"; the cultivation of quietude prior to Taoist meditation. To cultivate this stillness the adept withdraws to a quiet place, closes his eyes, eliminates all distracting thoughts, and empties his mind. Only then is he ready to begin his actual meditation.

Ju-i Chin. (Jap., nyoi), lit. "as one wishes"; name for the "wish-fulfilling scepter," a frequent attribute of Taoist or Buddhist saints or masters.

The *ju-i* is carved from bamboo, jade, bone, or other materials. The upper end usually has the form of the immortality mushroom (→ *ling-chih*). It is easily wielded.

☆   ☆   ☆

K'an and Li Chin.; the twenty-ninth and thirtieth hexagrams of the → *I-ching*; two of the eight trigrams (→ *pakua*). The trigram *k'an* consists of a broken, an unbroken, and another broken line: ☵ . The hexagram *k'an* is a duplication of that trigram: ䷜ . The trigram *li* consists of an unbroken, a broken, and another unbroken line: ☲ . The hexagram *li* is a duplication of that trigram: ䷝ .

K'an and *li* represent a combination of yin and yang (→ yin-yang), which are symbolized by the trigrams and hexagrams *ch'ien* ☰ ䷀ and *k'un* ☷ ䷁ . They furthermore represent the function of the → Tao, which pervades Heaven (*ch'ien*) and Earth (*k'un*), i.e., the macrocosm and the microcosm. As stated in the *Book of Change(s)*, yin and yang cannot be fixed or brought to rest, but circulate in the spaces between the lines of a hexagram and thus give rise to the remaining hexagrams. Together with *ch'ien* and *k'un* they are said to be the parents of the remaining hexagrams.

In the writings of Taoist alchemists (→ *nei-tan*, → *wai-tan*) *k'an* and *li* designate the ingredients of the elixir (of life).

In the texts of the Inner Alchemy (→ *nei-tan*) there is frequent mention of the fusion of *k'an* and *li;* this fusion produces the sacred embryo (→ *sheng-t'ai*) in the body of the Inner Alchemy practitioner: the broken yin line of *li* descends and unites with the ascending yang line of *k'an*. The upward movement of the yang line symbolizes the purification of the essence (→ *ching*) and the energy (→ *ch'i*); the downward movement of the yin line symbolizes the crystallization of the spirit (→ *shen*).

Common alchemical symbols for *k'an* are: the white tiger (*pai-hu*), the crescent moon, and the hare; in addition, *k'an* is associated with winter, the North, water, the color black, the kidneys, and lead.

Li is symbolized by the green dragon (*ch'ng-lung*), the sun, or a crow and is further associated with summer, the South, the color red, the heart, fire, and mercury.

One of the most important texts of the Inner Alchemy School—the *Chou-i ts'an-t'ung-ch'i* of → Wei P'o-yang states:

"The transformation rests on *k'an*—the nature of which is symbolized by water, the abysmal, the heart, the soul, light, and reason [*logos*]—and *li*—the nature of which is symbolized by fire, that which clings, brightness, and nature in its glorified state; and these two, *k'an* and *li,* are functions, respectively, of the creative and the receptive.

"These two functions have no fixed position; they weave and knit to and fro between the six empty positions. Coming and going are not bound by energy; above and below float freely, they sink into the hidden, they disappear into the twilight.

"The transformation and exchange (of *k'an* and *li*) occur in the six empty spaces between the lines of the hexagram. They embrace myriads of manifestations and thus become the great principle of the Tao" (trans. from Miyuki 1984).

Kan Chi   → Yü Chi

Ko Hung   284–364 C.E.; influential Taoist alchemist and theoretician, author of the *Pao-p'u-tzu,* an encyclopedia of methods and practices for attaining immortality. The esoteric chapters of the *Pao-p'u-tzu* describe procedures for changing one's outer appearance, making talismans, producing spells and magical formulae, etc. Ko Hung, in compiling the *Pao-p'u-tzu,* made use of all Taoist texts known to him. This explains a number of contradictions between entries. The exoteric part is not confined to Taoist texts but also contains Confucianist ideas.

Ko Hung's major contribution consisted in systematically arranging all known teachings on how to attain immortality and in combining these with the central teachings of → Confucianism (→ K'ung-tzu). He emphasizes that immortality cannot be attained by physical, sexual, or meditative practices alone; the practitioner must also train himself in the Confucianist virtues (→ *wu-ch'ang*). Ko Hung therefore had a decisive influence on the moral orientation of Taoism. He opposed the neo-Taoist → *ch'ing-t'an* movement (→ *hsüan-hsüeh*), which he considered to be totally devoid of any religious value.

In addition, Ko Hung was a prominent physician. One of his treatises contains the first known descriptions of smallpox and psittacosis.

In the *Pao-p'u-tzu* Ko Hung argues that immortality can only be attained through the workings of the secret elixir of Life (→ *nei-tan,* → *wai-tan*); physical exercises and sexual practices are merely methods for prolonging life. Alchemy furthermore made it possible to acquire certain supernatural abilities, such as walking on water, calling back the dead, securing whatever official post one desired, etc. In addition, Ko Hung describes the preliminary spiritual exercises for attaining immortality. The most important of these is the veneration of the Supreme One (→ T'ai-i), of the Spirit of the Hearth (→ Tsao-chün), and of → Lao-tzu.

Ko Hung classifies immortals hierarchically according to their practices. He allocates the highest rank to those who have ingested elixirs of gold or jade and performed twelve hundred meritorious deeds. They rise to Heaven in broad daylight (→ *fei-sheng*) but may remain in this world if that is their wish: in that case they make it their task to explain the teachings of Confucius to the common people and to initiate advanced adepts into the secrets of alchemy. Other immortals do not have such a choice, although they liberate both themselves as well as others. They withdraw from the world to devote themselves exclusively to hygiene exercises.

Ko Hung was renowned for his profound knowledge of the classics. He held several high military and public posts, which gained him the respect of Confucianists. He also played an important part in the successful suppression of a peasant uprising. After that he turned his back on public life and withdrew to the mountains near Canton to devote himself to alchemical practices.

K'ou Ch'ien-chih 365–448 C.E.; Taoist master, initially a follower of the Five-Pecks-of-Rice School (→ *wu-tou-mi tao*). After → Lao-tzu had appeared to him in several visions, K'ou Ch'ien-chih brought about various reforms within the Five-Pecks-of-Rice School with the aim of eliminating its sexual practices. In 415 C.E. he assumed the title Celestial Master (→ *t'ien-shih*). As a result of his endeavors Taoism was accorded the status of an official state religion. In addition, K'ou Ch'ien-chih initiated the persecution of Buddhists in Northern China during the seven years from 438 to 445 C.E.

In K'ou Ch'ien-chih's visions Lao-tzu predicted that K'ou would cleanse Taoism of the false teachings of → Chang Chüeh and abolish the practice of "combining the breaths" (→ *ho-ch'i*) as well as the payment of five pecks of rice to priests as a fee for performing certain ceremonies. Lao-tzu furthermore taught him how to perform certain → *tao-yin* and breathing exercises. K'ou stressed the importance of good deeds in the life of a Taoist. The newly reformed Taoism became known as the New Way of the Celestial Master or the Northern Way of the Celestial Master.

K'ou feared the competition of Buddhist teachings and rituals and, together with the reactionary Confucianist Ts'ui Hao, convinced the emperor of the Northern Way Dynasty that Buddhism constituted a danger to the state. In consequence Taoism was proclaimed a state religion. In 438 C.E. the emperor, influenced by K'ou, passed a law forbidding any man aged over fifty to become ordained as a Buddhist monk. In 441 C.E. the majority of Buddhist monasteries and temples were closed down. In 444 C.E. Buddhist monks were forbidden to lead a nomadic life; in 445 C.E. all the monks in the capital were killed, and soon after, the remaining monks in Northern China. It must be said that K'ou objected to such radical measures, but his Confucianist ally was determined to "kill the evil ones in order to help the good." Taoist temples were constructed in the capital, and the emperor assumed the title of True Prince of Supreme Peace.

K'ou-ch'ih Chin., lit. "chattering of teeth"; Taoist health exercise consisting of clapping one's teeth together thirty-six times. It is performed as a preliminary to most breathing exercises and other hygiene practices and is said to stimulate the production of saliva (→ *yü-chiang*)

77

and, according to the Inner Deity Hygiene School, attract the attention of the body deities (→ *shen*).

Kuan Chin., lit. seeing, beholding; designation for a Taoist monastery or nunnery. *Kuan* were constructed on the pattern of Buddhist monasteries. In the early days of Taoism they were the abode of either celibate monks (→ *tao-shih*) or lay priests and their families. Under → Sung Wen-ming (6th century C.E.) these *kuan* were turned into strict monasteries or nunneries, so that married Taoist teachers (*shih-kung*) and their families had to live outside the monastery walls.

Tradition explains the use of a term meaning "seeing" or "beholding" to designate a monastery or nunnery as follows: In ancient times (i.e., some centuries before the Christian era) when → Yüan-shih t'ien-tsun walked upon the Earth in the shape of → Lao-tzu to teach people the Way [→ Tao] there lived in Western China a fervent believer in the Tao. His name was → Yin Hsi, the Guardian of the [Mountain] Pass. He built himself a hut from brushwood to practice "seeing." According to one tradition Yin Hsi was informed by a supernatural manifestation of light in the eastern sky that Lao-tzu was approaching his mountain pass. Another tradition says that Yin Hsi was an astrologer who gazed at the stars, which told him that Lao-tzu would be passing his way. He set out to meet Lao-tzu, became his pupil, and received from him the → *Tao-te ching*. Yin Hsi's hut was thus a precursor of Taoist monasteries.

Kuan-ti Chin., lit. "Emperor Kuan"; Taoist war god, who opposed all disturbers of the peace. He had the task of protecting the realm against all external enemies and internal rebels and began to be venerated sometime in the 7th century C.E. He was also worshipped as a protector of

it by the cor-
ames (cheng-
at all things
ond with the
ribed to them
ames (appella-
other words, a
to behave like a

as had a strong
s heavenly voca-
luntarily submit-
celestial mandate
ing), the will of
His teachings are
in the *Analects* (*Lun-yü*).

Portrait of K'ung-tzu.

tzu was born into a noble family in Lu (now Shan-
vince and grew up in humble circumstances. At the
teen he decided to pursue a career as state official;
was twenty years old he held an official post as
per and later became a supervisor of the royal
Under various teachers he studied the thoughts and
of the ancients and soon gathered a group of pupils
him. At the age of fifty he held the post of justice
r, but political intrigues forced him to abandon it
into exile. He spent several years traveling through
provinces in the hope that his views on political and
reform would find favor, because he was convinced
ey were capable of renewing the world. At the age of
even he was allowed to return home, where he died in
.E.

state officials, who accorded him special veneration. In
popular religious belief he was known primarily for casting out demons and was called Fu-mo ta-ti, the Great
Ruler Who Banishes Demons. He is portrayed as a nine-
foot tall giant with a two-foot-long beard. His face is scarlet, his eyes like those of a phoenix, and his eyebrows like
silkworms. Frequently he is shown standing beside his
horse, in full armor and carrying a halberd. Sometimes,
however, he is portrayed as a military mandarin, in a sitting position, unarmed, stroking his beard with one hand
and in the other holding one of the classic Confucianist
works, the *Spring and Autumn Annals* (*Ch'un-ch'iu*).

The deity Kuan-ti is a historical personality, namely the 3d-
century general Kuan Yü, who served under the founder of
one of the three realms and, in 220 C.E., was executed on the
orders of a hostile ruler. His life story forms the theme of one
of the most popular Chinese novels and of many plays.

The cult around Kuan-ti as a deity is of a relatively recent
origin and was strongly influenced by Buddhist ideas. Kuan-ti
has even been described as a Bodhisattva. During the 7th century C.E. he was one of the protectors of Buddhist temples and
monasteries. In the 16th century he was accorded the title
Great Just Emperor Who Assists Heaven and Protects the State
and admitted to the Taoist pantheon. In the 19th century the
then emperor bestowed upon him the title Military Emperor
and elevated him to the level of Confucius (→ K'ung-tzu).

Temples were erected in his honor throughout the realm,
and imperial officials made offerings to him on the thirteenth
day of the first and fifth month of each year. This practice
continued until the end of the Chinese empire (1911 C.E.).
Furthermore, Kuan-ti was called upon during spiritualist
seances to guide the brush of the medium and provide, inter

alia, information about people who had died, prophecies concerning the future, and knowledge about divine recompense or retaliation for good or evil deeds.

Kuei Chin., lit. ghost, spirit, demon; spirit of the dead formed of the negative yin components (→ yin-yang) of a person's soul—i.e., the *p'o* souls—after death.

The term *kuei* applies to all dead souls except those of members of one's own family. *Kuei* are feared, because they are believed to be capable of avenging injustices or insults suffered by them when they were alive. This particularly applies to the *kuei* of people who die by drowning or hanging or die a long way from home but also to the souls of those for whom no ancestral tree (→ *tzu*) has been erected. They are the so-called hungry ghosts.

Offerings of paper money are made to placate the *kuei* and accumulate merit in their world: at these sacrificial ceremonies bundles of bank notes, issued by the "bank of the Lower World," are burned, sometimes also houses constructed of paper. In the seventh month of each year a feast of the hungry ghosts is celebrated, at which the community endeavors to appease theses lost souls by ceremonial sacrifices.

According to popular belief the clothes worn by *kuei* have no hems. Their body casts no shadow so that people can perceive them only as a breath of air. The *kuei,* on their part, perceive living humans as a dim red light. Their voices do not sound like those of the living. In the teachings of the inner elixir (→ *neitan*) it is said that the sacred embryo (→ *sheng-t'ai*) must consist of pure yang, because even the presence of a minute trace of yin in the embryo renders it susceptible to falling victim to the *kuei.*

K'ung-fu-tzu → K

Kung Sun-lung (States Period. He be studied the relation was a contemporary (main pursuit consiste the restoration of a pr and realities. (Also → K

A well-known parad(white horse is not a hors sential difference betweei because the former was g that reason he considered separate concepts.

By his analysis of the det the differences between them tion to the development of lo

K'ung-tzu 551–479 B.C.E. *fu-tzu;* Confucius, founder school, whose teachings wer(public life in China, Japan, the 20th century. Confucius vaging the ideals of the ancien He reformulated and systemati and ideas contained in the classi tion later accredited to him. Th philosophy were → *jen* (humanei and → *li* (morality, uprightness, these to be the indispensable virt (*chün-tzu*), the Confucianist ide were essentially based on the idea

brought abo rection of *ming*) so t will corresp qualities as by their n tions). In prince has prince.

Confuci sense of hi tion and v ted to the (→ *t'ien-n* Heaven. preserved

K'ung-tung) pr age of fi when he storeke lands. custom around minist and g variou social that t sixty-479 B

According to tradition, K'ung-tzu, toward the end of his life, wrote a number of works which have come to be considered the classic teachings of → Confucianism. He is credited with the authorship of the *Shi-ching* (*Book of Songs*), the *Shu-ching* (*Book of Writings*), and the *Ch'un-ch'iu* (*Spring and Autumn Annals*), the first Chinese historical work. In addition, parts of the → *I-ching* and the *Chia-yü* (*Instructive Discourses*) are attributed to him. The *Yüeh-ching* (*Book of Music*) and the *Li-ch'i* (*Book of Rites*) are said to have been edited by him. His pupils—of whom there were approximately three thousand—compiled his sayings in the *Analects* (*Lun-yü*). (All the above works have been translated into the major European languages.)

The central concept of his teachings was that of *jen* (humaneness, loving-kindness toward one's fellow men): "Do not unto others what you would not have them do unto you" (*Analects* 15.23). The practice of *jen* is governed by *li* (morality): "To conquer oneself and turn to *li;* that is humaneness" (*Analects* 12.1). This concept of humaneness and benevolence furthermore embraces the virtues of conscientiousness (*chung*) and reciprocity (*shu*). Social intercourse is governed by the five relationships (→ *wu-lun*), which regulate moral behavior and allocate a proper place to each member of society. The five relationships are those between father and son, husband and wife, older and younger brother, ruler and subject, and friend and friend. To bring order into the world it is necessary to first create order within the family, and then within the territorial provinces. Once that is done, the realm will naturally fall into order. Order within the family depends on the respect and piety shown by children toward their parents.

Confucius adopted a somewhat reserved attitude toward the religious ideas of his time. His philosophy contains no religious speculations, although he felt that he had a heavenly

($\rightarrow$ *t'ien*) vocation. It was not his intention to abolish ancestor worship—the basis of the official religion of the time—and he went so far as to include it, together with the rites of mourning, in the duties of piety toward ancestors. He refused to pronounce on the fate of the dead: "We do not even know what life is; how then can we know anything about death?" Confucianist philosophy has little room for superstition. The respect Confucius held for the official cult of ancestor worship was based on ethical rather than religious considerations. He was of the opinion that it made no sense to ask the deities for their help. In his view the will of Heaven could not be changed by our prayers.

His ideas about government are simple: if the ruler is righteous and honest, so will his subjects be. Reforms must begin at the top. When asked what would be the first measure he would take if he were appointed to govern, Confucius replied, "Correct the names; because if the names are incorrect, the words will not be correct either; and if the words are incorrect, actions will not be properly carried out; and if the actions are not properly completed, rites [*li*] and music cannot flourish; if rites and music do not flourish, punishments will not fit the crime; if punishments do not fit the crime, the common people will not know where to put hand and foot. Therefore a noble person takes care to ensure that names are properly used in speech and that what he says will in all circumstances be practicable. A noble person will not tolerate disorder in his words. That is what matters" (*Analects* 13.3).

And elsewhere, "Let the prince be prince, the minister minister, the father father, and the son son" (*Analects* 12.11).

The first step toward the correction of names thus consists in the prince behaving like a prince, whereby all remaining names are also put in order and society, too, can be restored to order. Every name contains qualities that correspond to the essence of the thing referred to by that name. If a ruler follows the → Tao of a ruler he will rule in accordance with the essence and qualities of a ruler and not merely in name. There is then a harmonious correspondence between name and external reality. Confucius therefore states that everyone—father, son, wife, etc.—must act in accordance with the duties arising from his or her appellation. He further considered it to be his task to give rulers a true idea of their calling so that they might live up to and act in accordance with the requirements of rulership.

Although the Confucian model of society had no immediate effect on the society of his time, it became—for over two thousand years—a model and example for the people of China, Japan, and Korea, in that their whole life was oriented toward Confucianist ideas. (Also → Confucianism.) (Quotes from Opitz 1968.)

K'un-lun mountain range in Western China, glorified as a Taoist paradise. It is the abode of the Royal Mother of the West (→ Hsi wang-mu) and of the immortals (→ *hsien*). The K'un-lun—one of the ten continents and three islands in Taoist cosmology—is said to be three (or nine, according to some texts) stories high. Whoever is capable of ascending to its top gains access to the heavens. The K'un-lun furthermore extends three (or nine) stories below the Earth, thereby connecting the subterranean watery realm—the dwelling place of the dead—with the realm of the gods. In the K'un-lun the Royal Mother of the West grows the peaches of immortality, which Taoists have again and again set out to discover in countless expeditions.

The → Inner Deity Hygiene School equates K'un-lun with the human head.

According to tradition the first to visit this paradise was King Mu of Chou, who there discovered a palace of the Yellow Emperor (→ Huang-ti) and erected a stone memorial. He was then received by the Royal Mother of the West.

The K'un-lun has been a popular subject of Chinese literature since the early days of the Han Dynasty. According to the → *Huai-nan-tzu* "the mountains' Hanging Garden, Cool Breeze and Fenced Paulonia Gardens form the municipal parks of K'un-lun City, and the lakes to be found in these parks are plenished by yellow water, which, after flowing through the park, returns to its source. This water is known as cinnabar water, and whoever drinks it becomes immortal. . . . One may also attain immortality by climbing the first and lowest of the three mountains of K'un-lun—the mountain called Cool Breeze. Whoever reaches the top of the second mountain, called Hanging Garden and twice as high as the first, will become a spirit capable of magic and of commanding wind and rain. Those who climb the third and highest mountain . . . can step from its peak directly into Heaven and become a spirit of the gods (→ *shen*), because they have reached the palace of the Supreme Celestial Emperor (Ta-ti)" (Bauer 1974).

Kuo Hsiang   → *hsüan-hsüh*

Ku-shen   Chin., lit. "Spirit of the Valley"; a deity mentioned in the → *Tao-te ching* and said to be identical with the mysterious Primordial Mother (Hsüan-p'in), who herself is a symbol of the → Tao. According to Chapter 6 of the *Tao-te ching,* "The Valley Spirit never dies; it is the woman, primal mother. Her gateway is the root of heaven and earth. It is like a veil barely seen. Use it; it will never fail" (Feng & English 1972).

This passage has been cited by later followers of religious Taoism (→ *tao-chiao*) to justify various sexual practices, the alleged purpose of which was to attain immortality.

In the *Tao-te-ching* the valley is a symbol of the Tao or the → *te*. It signifies emptiness or the void (→ *wu*) and also points towards the place to which all waters flow. It can thus be understood as a general symbol for the true Taoist's philosophy of life.

In a narrow sense *ku* designates a mountain spring. This allows the possible conclusion that the Spirit of the Valley may originally have been a spirit of springs.

☆   ☆   ☆

Lan Ts'ai-ho   → *pa-hsien*

Lao-chün   Chin., lit. "Master Lao"; also called T'ai-shang lao-chün ("Supreme Master Lao"); name of → Lao-tzu in his deified form. Together with → Yüan-shih t'ien-tsun and → T'ai-shang tao-chün, Lao-chün is one of the highest deities of religious Taoism (→ *tao-chiao*).

The deification of Lao-tzu began in the 2d century B.C.E. He already was a legendary figure at the time and was reported to have lived to an unusually ripe old age. During the Eastern or Late Han Dynasty he became one of the most important deities of Taoism. Some followers of the Tao considered him to be an emanation of the primordial chaos. It is said that he reincarnated many times as a human being in order to teach mankind. He is reputed to have been initiated into the secret practices of longevity characteristic of most later Taoist sects.

Although Lao-chün is generally acknowledged to have been a revealer of sacred writings and a teacher of mankind, not all Taoists look upon him as their highest deity. Often he is placed below Yüan-shih t'ien-tsun and some Taoists have gone so far as to question his divinity altogether, e.g., → Ko Hung, who believed him to be an extraordinary human being but not a god.

Lao Tan   early Taoist designation for → Lao-tzu. *Tan* means "long ears," a symbol of longevity (→ Li Erh).

Lao-tzu   Chin., lit. "Old Master," also known as → Lao Tan or → Li Erh; traditionally considered to be the author of the → *Tao-te ching* and a contemporary of Confucius (6th century B.C.E. → K'ung-tzu). The biography of Lao-tzu in the *Historical Records* (*Shih-chi*), dating from the 2d/1st century B.C.E., mentions that he was born in Hu-hsien in the state of Ch'u (now Honan Province). His family name was Li, his first name Erh, and his majority name Tan. Most philosophical texts refer to him as either Lao-tzu or Lao Tan.

According to the *Shih-chi* Lao-tzu was keeper of archives at the court of the king of Chou when he first met Confucius. This encounter has frequently been described but cannot be considered historical. Disputes at the royal court prompted Lao-tzu to resign from his post. He traveled west and at the mountain pass of Hsien-ku met → Yin Hsi, the Guardian of the Pass, at whose request he wrote the *Tao-te ching,* consisting of five thousand pictograms. After that his traces vanish.

Although tradition considered Lao-tzu to be the author of the *Tao-te ching,* scholars have established that this work cannot have been written before the 4th or 3d century B.C.E. and thus did not originate with Lao-tzu.

state officials, who accorded him special veneration. In popular religious belief he was known primarily for casting out demons and was called Fu-mo ta-ti, the Great Ruler Who Banishes Demons. He is portrayed as a nine-foot tall giant with a two-foot-long beard. His face is scarlet, his eyes like those of a phoenix, and his eyebrows like silkworms. Frequently he is shown standing beside his horse, in full armor and carrying a halberd. Sometimes, however, he is portrayed as a military mandarin, in a sitting position, unarmed, stroking his beard with one hand and in the other holding one of the classic Confucianist works, the *Spring and Autumn Annals* (*Ch'un-ch'iu*).

The deity Kuan-ti is a historical personality, namely the 3d-century general Kuan Yü, who served under the founder of one of the three realms and, in 220 C.E., was executed on the orders of a hostile ruler. His life story forms the theme of one of the most popular Chinese novels and of many plays.

The cult around Kuan-ti as a deity is of a relatively recent origin and was strongly influenced by Buddhist ideas. Kuan-ti has even been described as a Bodhisattva. During the 7th century C.E. he was one of the protectors of Buddhist temples and monasteries. In the 16th century he was accorded the title Great Just Emperor Who Assists Heaven and Protects the State and admitted to the Taoist pantheon. In the 19th century the then emperor bestowed upon him the title Military Emperor and elevated him to the level of Confucius (→ K'ung-tzu).

Temples were erected in his honor throughout the realm, and imperial officials made offerings to him on the thirteenth day of the first and fifth month of each year. This practice continued until the end of the Chinese empire (1911 C.E.). Furthermore, Kuan-ti was called upon during spiritualist seances to guide the brush of the medium and provide, inter alia, information about people who had died, prophecies concerning the future, and knowledge about divine recompense or retaliation for good or evil deeds.

Kuei   Chin., lit. ghost, spirit, demon; spirit of the dead formed of the negative yin components (→ yin-yang) of a person's soul—i.e., the *p'o* souls—after death.

The term *kuei* applies to all dead souls except those of members of one's own family. *Kuei* are feared, because they are believed to be capable of avenging injustices or insults suffered by them when they were alive. This particularly applies to the *kuei* of people who die by drowning or hanging or die a long way from home but also to the souls of those for whom no ancestral tree (→ *tzu*) has been erected. They are the so-called hungry ghosts.

Offerings of paper money are made to placate the *kuei* and accumulate merit in their world: at these sacrificial ceremonies bundles of bank notes, issued by the "bank of the Lower World," are burned, sometimes also houses constructed of paper. In the seventh month of each year a feast of the hungry ghosts is celebrated, at which the community endeavors to appease theses lost souls by ceremonial sacrifices.

According to popular belief the clothes worn by *kuei* have no hems. Their body casts no shadow so that people can perceive them only as a breath of air. The *kuei*, on their part, perceive living humans as a dim red light. Their voices do not sound like those of the living. In the teachings of the inner elixir (→ *neitan*) it is said that the sacred embryo (→ *sheng-t'ai*) must consist of pure yang, because even the presence of a minute trace of yin in the embryo renders it susceptible to falling victim to the *kuei*.

K'ung-fu-tzu → K'ung-tzu

Kung Sun-lung Chinese philosopher of the Warring States Period. He belonged to the School of Names, which studied the relationship between name and reality, and was a contemporary of → Chuang-tzu and → Hui Shih. His main pursuit consisted in the "correction of names," i.e., the restoration of a proper correspondence between names and realities. (Also → K'ung-tzu.)

A well-known paradox of Kung Sun-lung states that "a white horse is not a horse": he argued that there was an essential difference between the terms *horse* and *white horse*, because the former was general and the latter specific. For that reason he considered them to be different names, i.e., separate concepts.

By his analysis of the determinateness of all concepts and the differences between them he made an important contribution to the development of logic in Chinese philosophy.

K'ung-tzu 551–479 B.C.E., also transcribed as *K'ung-fu-tzu;* Confucius, founder of the first Chinese wisdom school, whose teachings were a determining influence on public life in China, Japan, and Korea until the time of the 20th century. Confucius set himself the task of salvaging the ideals of the ancients from the general decline. He reformulated and systematically ordered the thoughts and ideas contained in the classical writings, which tradition later accredited to him. The central concepts of his philosophy were → *jen* (humaneness, love of fellow men) and → *li* (morality, uprightness, custom). He considered these to be the indispensable virtues of a princely person (*chün-tzu*), the Confucianist ideal. His political views were essentially based on the idea that order can only be brought about by the correction of names (cheng-ming) so that all things will correspond with the qualities ascribed to them by their names (appellations). In other words, a prince has to behave like a prince.

Confucius had a strong sense of his heavenly vocation and voluntarily submitted to the celestial mandate (→ t'ien-ming), the will of Heaven. His teachings are preserved in the Analects (Lun-yü).

Portrait of K'ung-tzu.

K'ung-tzu was born into a noble family in Lu (now Shan-tung) province and grew up in humble circumstances. At the age of fifteen he decided to pursue a career as state official; when he was twenty years old he held an official post as storekeeper and later became a supervisor of the royal lands. Under various teachers he studied the thoughts and customs of the ancients and soon gathered a group of pupils around him. At the age of fifty he held the post of justice minister, but political intrigues forced him to abandon it and go into exile. He spent several years traveling through various provinces in the hope that his views on political and social reform would find favor, because he was convinced that they were capable of renewing the world. At the age of sixty-seven he was allowed to return home, where he died in 479 B.C.E.

According to tradition, K'ung-tzu, toward the end of his life, wrote a number of works which have come to be considered the classic teachings of → Confucianism. He is credited with the authorship of the *Shi-ching* (*Book of Songs*), the *Shu-ching* (*Book of Writings*), and the *Ch'un-ch'iu* (*Spring and Autumn Annals*), the first Chinese historical work. In addition, parts of the → *I-ching* and the *Chia-yü* (*Instructive Discourses*) are attributed to him. The *Yüeh-ching* (*Book of Music*) and the *Li-ch'i* (*Book of Rites*) are said to have been edited by him. His pupils—of whom there were approximately three thousand—compiled his sayings in the *Analects* (*Lun-yü*). (All the above works have been translated into the major European languages.)

The central concept of his teachings was that of *jen* (humaneness, loving-kindness toward one's fellow men): "Do not unto others what you would not have them do unto you" (*Analects* 15.23). The practice of *jen* is governed by *li* (morality): "To conquer oneself and turn to *li;* that is humaneness" (*Analects* 12.1). This concept of humaneness and benevolence furthermore embraces the virtues of conscientiousness (*chung*) and reciprocity (*shu*). Social intercourse is governed by the five relationships (→ *wu-lun*), which regulate moral behavior and allocate a proper place to each member of society. The five relationships are those between father and son, husband and wife, older and younger brother, ruler and subject, and friend and friend. To bring order into the world it is necessary to first create order within the family, and then within the territorial provinces. Once that is done, the realm will naturally fall into order. Order within the family depends on the respect and piety shown by children toward their parents.

Confucius adopted a somewhat reserved attitude toward the religious ideas of his time. His philosophy contains no religious speculations, although he felt that he had a heavenly

($\rightarrow$ *t'ien*) vocation. It was not his intention to abolish ancestor worship—the basis of the official religion of the time—
and he went so far as to include it, together with the rites of
mourning, in the duties of piety toward ancestors. He refused
to pronounce on the fate of the dead: "We do not even know
what life is; how then can we know anything about death?"
Confucianist philosophy has little room for superstition. The
respect Confucius held for the official cult of ancestor worship was based on ethical rather than religious considerations. He was of the opinion that it made no sense to ask the
deities for their help. In his view the will of Heaven could not
be changed by our prayers.

His ideas about government are simple: if the ruler is righteous and honest, so will his subjects be. Reforms must begin at the top. When asked what would be the first measure
he would take if he were appointed to govern, Confucius
replied, "Correct the names; because if the names are incorrect, the words will not be correct either; and if the words
are incorrect, actions will not be properly carried out; and if
the actions are not properly completed, rites [*li*] and music
cannot flourish; if rites and music do not flourish, punishments will not fit the crime; if punishments do not fit the
crime, the common people will not know where to put hand
and foot. Therefore a noble person takes care to ensure that
names are properly used in speech and that what he says will
in all circumstances be practicable. A noble person will not
tolerate disorder in his words. That is what matters"
(*Analects* 13.3).

And elsewhere, "Let the prince be prince, the minister minister, the father father, and the son son" (*Analects* 12.11).

The first step toward the correction of names thus consists
in the prince behaving like a prince, whereby all remaining
names are also put in order and society, too, can be restored

to order. Every name contains qualities that correspond to the essence of the thing referred to by that name. If a ruler follows the → Tao of a ruler he will rule in accordance with the essence and qualities of a ruler and not merely in name. There is then a harmonious correspondence between name and external reality. Confucius therefore states that everyone—father, son, wife, etc.—must act in accordance with the duties arising from his or her appellation. He further considered it to be his task to give rulers a true idea of their calling so that they might live up to and act in accordance with the requirements of rulership.

Although the Confucian model of society had no immediate effect on the society of his time, it became—for over two thousand years—a model and example for the people of China, Japan, and Korea, in that their whole life was oriented toward Confucianist ideas. (Also → Confucianism.) (Quotes from Opitz 1968.)

K'un-lun   mountain range in Western China, glorified as a Taoist paradise. It is the abode of the Royal Mother of the West (→ Hsi wang-mu) and of the immortals (→ *hsien*). The K'un-lun—one of the ten continents and three islands in Taoist cosmology—is said to be three (or nine, according to some texts) stories high. Whoever is capable of ascending to its top gains access to the heavens. The K'un-lun furthermore extends three (or nine) stories below the Earth, thereby connecting the subterranean watery realm—the dwelling place of the dead—with the realm of the gods. In the K'un-lun the Royal Mother of the West grows the peaches of immortality, which Taoists have again and again set out to discover in countless expeditions.

The → Inner Deity Hygiene School equates K'un-lun with the human head.

According to tradition the first to visit this paradise was King Mu of Chou, who there discovered a palace of the Yellow Emperor (→ Huang-ti) and erected a stone memorial. He was then received by the Royal Mother of the West.

The K'un-lun has been a popular subject of Chinese literature since the early days of the Han Dynasty. According to the → *Huai-nan-tzu* "the mountains' Hanging Garden, Cool Breeze and Fenced Paulonia Gardens form the municipal parks of K'un-lun City, and the lakes to be found in these parks are plenished by yellow water, which, after flowing through the park, returns to its source. This water is known as cinnabar water, and whoever drinks it becomes immortal. . . . One may also attain immortality by climbing the first and lowest of the three mountains of K'un-lun—the mountain called Cool Breeze. Whoever reaches the top of the second mountain, called Hanging Garden and twice as high as the first, will become a spirit capable of magic and of commanding wind and rain. Those who climb the third and highest mountain . . . can step from its peak directly into Heaven and become a spirit of the gods (→ *shen*), because they have reached the palace of the Supreme Celestial Emperor (Ta-ti)" (Bauer 1974).

Kuo Hsiang   → *hsüan-hsüh*

Ku-shen   Chin., lit. "Spirit of the Valley"; a deity mentioned in the → *Tao-te ching* and said to be identical with the mysterious Primordial Mother (Hsüan-p'in), who herself is a symbol of the → Tao. According to Chapter 6 of the *Tao-te ching*, "The Valley Spirit never dies; it is the woman, primal mother. Her gateway is the root of heaven and earth. It is like a veil barely seen. Use it; it will never fail" (Feng & English 1972).

This passage has been cited by later followers of religious Taoism (→ *tao-chiao*) to justify various sexual practices, the alleged purpose of which was to attain immortality.

In the *Tao-te-ching* the valley is a symbol of the Tao or the → *te*. It signifies emptiness or the void (→ *wu*) and also points towards the place to which all waters flow. It can thus be understood as a general symbol for the true Taoist's philosophy of life.

In a narrow sense *ku* designates a mountain spring. This allows the possible conclusion that the Spirit of the Valley may originally have been a spirit of springs.

✻   ✻   ✻

Lan Ts'ai-ho   → *pa-hsien*

Lao-chün   Chin., lit. "Master Lao"; also called T'ai-shang lao-chün ("Supreme Master Lao"); name of → Lao-tzu in his deified form. Together with → Yüan-shih t'ien-tsun and → T'ai-shang tao-chün, Lao-chün is one of the highest deities of religious Taoism (→ *tao-chiao*).

The deification of Lao-tzu began in the 2d century B.C.E. He already was a legendary figure at the time and was reported to have lived to an unusually ripe old age. During the Eastern or Late Han Dynasty he became one of the most important deities of Taoism. Some followers of the Tao considered him to be an emanation of the primordial chaos. It is said that he reincarnated many times as a human being in order to teach mankind. He is reputed to have been initiated into the secret practices of longevity characteristic of most later Taoist sects.

Although Lao-chün is generally acknowledged to have been a revealer of sacred writings and a teacher of mankind, not all Taoists look upon him as their highest deity. Often he is placed below Yüan-shih t'ien-tsun and some Taoists have gone so far as to question his divinity altogether, e.g., → Ko Hung, who believed him to be an extraordinary human being but not a god.

Lao Tan early Taoist designation for → Lao-tzu. *Tan* means "long ears," a symbol of longevity (→ Li Erh).

Lao-tzu Chin., lit. "Old Master," also known as → Lao Tan or → Li Erh; traditionally considered to be the author of the → *Tao-te ching* and a contemporary of Confucius (6th century B.C.E. → K'ung-tzu). The biography of Lao-tzu in the *Historical Records* (*Shih-chi*), dating from the 2d/1st century B.C.E., mentions that he was born in Hu-hsien in the state of Ch'u (now Honan Province). His family name was Li, his first name Erh, and his majority name Tan. Most philosophical texts refer to him as either Lao-tzu or Lao Tan.

According to the *Shih-chi* Lao-tzu was keeper of archives at the court of the king of Chou when he first met Confucius. This encounter has frequently been described but cannot be considered historical. Disputes at the royal court prompted Lao-tzu to resign from his post. He traveled west and at the mountain pass of Hsien-ku met → Yin Hsi, the Guardian of the Pass, at whose request he wrote the *Tao-te ching*, consisting of five thousand pictograms. After that his traces vanish.

Although tradition considered Lao-tzu to be the author of the *Tao-te ching*, scholars have established that this work cannot have been written before the 4th or 3d century B.C.E. and thus did not originate with Lao-tzu.

The author of the *Shih-chi* tells us that "Lao-tzu lived in accordance with the Tao and the *te*. He taught that one should live anonymously and in obscurity" (trans. from Kaltenmark, *Lao-tzu und der Taoismus;* see Kaltenmark 1969). His simple view of life also is reflected in a dialogue between him and Confucius: "When Confucius went to the land of

Lao-tzu riding a water buffalo. (19th-century wood carving)

Chou, he questioned Lao-tzu about the observance of the rites (→ *li*). Lao-tzu replied, 'The bones of those of whom you speak have long since turned to dust; only their words have been preserved for us. In any case, if time and fortune favor a person, he will travel to court in a carriage. If they do not favor him, he will roam about in unpretentious attire. I have heard it said that a good merchant will conceal his wealth and act as if he were poor. A noble person with sufficient inner virtue may give the appearance of a fool. Therefore, give up your high-handed manner, your desires, your vanity, and your zeal—for they are of no use to you.' Confucius then withdrew and said to his pupils, 'I know that birds can fly, that fish can swim, and that quadrupeds can roam about on the earth. Roaming animals may be caught in a pit or cage, fish with a net or rod, and birds can be shot down with an arrow. The dragon however cannot be caught by such cleverness. It wings towards

Heaven on wind and clouds. Today I have seen Lao-tzu. He is like a dragon!' (trans. from Kaltenmark, *Lao-tzu und der Taoismus;* see Kaltenmark 1969).

Religious Taoism (→ *tao-chiao*) has admitted Lao-tzu to the Taoist pantheon. He is venerated as either → T'ai-shang lao-chün, Tao-te t'ien-tsun (Celestial Noble of the Tao and Te), or Lao-chün and is considered to be the founder of religious Taoism. He is, moreover, the subject of numerous legends. His disappearance after traveling west is explained by his having allegedly traveled to India, where he met the Buddha, who became his pupil—a claim Taoists are wont to make in their disputes with Buddhists (→ *Hua-hu ching*).

Lei-kung   Chin., lit. "Thunder Duke"; god of thunder. In the Taoist pantheon Lei-kung is an official in the Ministry of Thunder, which forms part of the celestial administration.

Lei-kung is portrayed with the beak, wings, and claws of an eagle owl. His body has the shape of a human and is blue. He wears a loin cloth and carries a drum, which he beats with a hammer to produce thunder. His image can be found in many Taoist temples.

Li   Chin., roughly rites, customs, morality; central concept of Confucianism (also → K'ung-tzu); the rules governing interhuman relations as well as ceremonies and how to act in a given situation. *Li* also serves as a means of expressing man's inherent benevolence (→ *jen*). It is the right expression of the right view. The concept of *li* is extensively discussed in a Confucianist classic known as *Li-chi* (see Chai & Chai 1965; Legge 1964).

In the *Analects* (*Lun-yü*) of Confucius we read (8.2), "Deference that lacks form [*li*] becomes servility, caution without form becomes timidity, courage without form becomes rebelliousness, honesty without form becomes rudeness."

To apply these rules correctly and distinguish between that which is proper and that which is not requires wisdom (*chih*), i.e., the ability to discriminate without confusion. → Mengtzu (also transcribed as *Mencius*), a famous Confucianist of the 4th century B.C.E., writes concerning this wisdom, "When it is a question of whether or not to accept a gift or favor, it is less selfish not to accept. If there is doubt as to whether or not one should make a present, it is more considerate not to make one. If it is a question of whether or not to die, it is more courageous not to die" (trans. from Wilhelm 1982).

In pre-Confucianist China *li* mainly governed the performance of religious rituals or ceremonies connected with the veneration of ancestors. Because of the tremendous importance of these rituals in the political life of the country, *li* gradually came to be applied to the notion of correct behavior in general, instead of remaining confined to the proper performance of such rituals.

Liang-i   Chin., two forms or basic energies, a concept in the *Book of Change(s)* (→ *I-ching*). The two basic energies referred to are the yin and yang (→ yin-yang). According to one commentary—*Hsi-tz'u* (11.5)—there is in the *Changes* the supreme ultimate (→ *t'ai-chi*), which produces the two basic energies. The basic energies in turn give rise to the four images (→ *ssu-hsiang*) and these in turn to the eight trigrams (→ *pa-kua*).

The same idea is expressed in Chapter 42 of the → *Tao-te ching*: "The Tao begot one. One begot two. Two begot three. And three begot the ten thousand things" (Feng & English 1972).

Li-chiao shih-wu-lun   Chin., → *ch'üan-chen tao*

Lieh-tzu Taoist philosopher of the Warring States Period and the alleged author of a work named after him but also known as the *Ch'ung-hsü chen-ching* (roughly, "True Book of the Expanding Emptiness"). Scholars have however established that this is a much later work, dating from the Chin Dynasty. Lieh-tzu was fond of transmitting his ideas and thoughts by reinterpreting ancient folk tales and myths. A characteristic feature of his view of life was that nature and life were mechanical processes, not admitting of free will. To further illustrate his ideas he made reference to the basic themes of Confucius (→ K'ung-tzu) as well as the → *Tao-te ching* and the → *I-ching*. Chapter 7 of the *Lieh-tzu* is devoted to the teachings of → Yang Chu. (An English version of Lieh-tzu's work has been published in Giles 1912. See also Wilhelm 1981b.)

The *Lieh-tzu* contains the earliest known reference to the isles of the immortals (→ P'eng-lai, → Fang-chang, →Ying-chou), the abode of the → *hsien*. During the later period of religious Taoism (→ *tao-chiao*), these descriptions led to numerous expeditions being dispatched, although there can be little doubt that Lieh-tzu meant them to be understood allegorically, i.e., referring to soul journeys.

Little is known about Lieh-tzu's life. He lived for forty years in one place and remained relatively unknown. He questioned Kuan-yin-tzu (→ Yin Hsi) concerning the Tao and had several other teachers. After nine years of Taoist practices he was able to rise on the wind. In Chapter 2 of the work accredited to him Lieh-tzu describes his state of mind after becoming one with the Tao: "After nine years of study I can set my mind completely free, let my words come forth completely unbound as I speak. I do not know whether right or wrong, gain and loss, are mine or others. I am not aware that the old

Master Shang-tzu is my teacher and that Pai-kao is my friend. My self, both within and without, has been transformed. Everything about me is identified. My eye becomes my ear, my ear becomes my nose, my nose my mouth. My mind is highly integrated and my body dissolves. My bone and my flesh melt away. I cannot tell by what my body is supported or what my feet walk upon. I am blowing away, east and west, as a dry leaf torn from a tree. I cannot even make out whether the wind is riding on me or I am riding on the wind" (Chang Chung-yuan 1963, p. 87).

Lien-ch'i Chin., lit. "melting the breath"; Taoist breathing exercise, in which the breath is allowed to flow unimpeded through the whole of the body instead of being directed along certain channels (→ *hsing-ch'i*). The practice of *lien-ch'i* is thought to be helpful in curing illnesses, acquiring supernatural abilities, and attaining immortality.

To practice *lien-ch'i* the adept withdraws to a quiet room, discards all restrictive clothing and lies down on a firm support, legs and arms extended. He harmonizes the breath (→ *t'iao-ch'i*) and swallows it (→ *yen-ch'i*), endeavoring to hold it for as long as possible (→ *pi-ch'i*). At the same time he strives to eliminate all thoughts and to calm the mind. The breath is then allowed to roam freely throughout the body without any intervention on the part of the practitioner. When he can no longer hold his breath, he opens his mouth and permits the breath to escape slowly.

The exercise is best performed after practicing → *fu-ch'i* and should be repeated ten times; a well-trained practitioner is capable of repeating it fifty times or more. If *lien-ch'i* is properly performed the breath is felt throughout the body; blockages are loosened and dissolved and the pores opened. The best indication for the effectiveness of the practice is perspiration. Because of its strong effect, *lien-ch'i* should be practiced at intervals of five to ten days.

Lien-tan   Chin., lit. "melting the cinnabar"; a method of Taoist alchemy for attaining immortality (→ *ch'ang-sheng pu-ssu*).

Originally *lien-tan* referred to a procedure in which various substances such as gold, cinnabar, mercury, and lead were melted over a trivet with the aim of producing the golden elixir (→ *chin-tan*). It was believed that whoever ingested this elixir would become immortal. Later this form of *lien-tan* came to be considered an outer elixir (→ *wai-tan*) practice and was gradually replaced by an inner elixir (→ *nei-tan*) practice, in which the adept fuses the life energy (→ *ch'i*), the semen (→ *ching*), and the mind (→ *shen*) within his body, thereby producing the sacred embryo (→ *sheng-t'ai*), the symbol of spiritual immortality.

Li Erh   according to Chinese historical sources the true name of → Lao-tzu, ascribed to him by the historian Ssu-ma Ch'ien (2d–1st century B.C.E.) on the basis of the ancestral tree of a family from Shantung by the name of Li, which was attached to an early biography of Lao-tzu.

Although this assertion cannot be proven historically, the family name Li, in Chinese tradition, became so closely linked with Lao-tzu that the later emperors of the T'ang Dynasty bearing that name looked upon Lao-tzu as their original ancestor.

Li Hsüan   → *pa-hsien*

Ling-chih   Chin., lit. "magic herb"; Taoist plant of immortality. The *ling-chih* is portrayed variously as grass, or as a trufflelike mushroom. It grows on the isles of the immortals (→ P'eng-lai, → Ying-chou, → Fang-chang). Like many others, Ch'in Shih-huang-ti, the first historical emperor of China, dispatched expeditions to gain possession of this magic herb, the ingestion of which is said to confer immortality for at least five hundred years.

In Taoist art the *ling-chih* symbolizes the female yin energy (→ yin-yang). Often, in popular illustrations, a stag or crane is shown holding the *ling-chih* in his mouth or beak—a twofold symbol of immortality.

Ling-pao ching   Chin., lit. *"Scriptures of the Magic Jewel"*; a body of writings forming the doctrinal basis of the School of the Magic Jewel (→ *ling-pao p'ai*), an independent stream of religious Taoism (→ *tao-chiao*). The *Ling-pao ching* describes the hierarchy of the Taoist pantheon, the rites by which believers may summon the various deities, and also contains instructions on how to conduct funeral ceremonies, etc. The oldest sections of the *Ling-pao ching* date from the 3d century; those explaining the Taoist doctrine, from the 4th and 5th centuries. Because of a commentary by the Taoist scholar → Sung Wenming (ca. 550 C.E.) the *Ling-pao ching* became an authoritative text of religious Taoism.

According to Taoist tradition these writings came into being spontaneously at the beginning of the world and were in the form of golden signs written on small tiles of jade. Their meaning is communicated to the deities at the beginning of each aeon by the Celestial Venerable of the Primordial Beginning (→ Yüan-shih t'ien-tsun), who alone is capable of reading them. Some of these deities have passed the teachings on to certain human beings, which is how they are said to have come into the possession of → Chang Tao-ling.

Ling-pao p'ai   Chin., lit. "School of the Magic Jewel"; a branch of religious Taoism (→ *tao-chiao*) that developed in the 4th/5th century C.E. and was based on the scriptures of the Magic Jewel (→ *Ling-pao ching*).

The School of the Magic Jewel reformed rites and practices to bring them into line with its own teaching, which was strongly influenced by Buddhism. It teaches that a person's salvation (or liberation) largely depends on the help that person is able to obtain from the venerable celestial deities (→ *t'ien-tsun*). This constitutes a simplification of the original Taoist doctrine. The deities are projected out from within the body (→ Inner Deity Hygiene School) and rule the whole universe. The Magic Jewel School owed its rapid spread to this simplification. The most important practices of the school were so-called fasting ceremonies (→ *chai*).

Li Shao-chün   ?–133 B.C.E.; Taoist sorcerer (→ *fang-shih*) who declared the aim of the Taoist path to be the attainment of immortality by alchemical methods. He himself claimed to be immortal and to have visited the isles of the immortals (→ P'eng-lai, → Ying-chou, → Fang-chang). He also knew prescriptions for prolonging life, performed hygiene exercises, and abstained from eating grain (→ *pi-ku*). In addition, he introduced the veneration of the deity of the hearth (→ Tsao-chün). He died of an illness. Taoist literature records his death as the first example of a separation from the corpse (→ *shih-chieh*).

In 133 B.C.E. Li Shao-chün persuaded the emperor Han Wu-ti to permit experiments, the aim of which consisted in transforming cinnabar into gold. These were the first recorded alchemical experiments in the history of mankind.

The transformed cinnabar, however, was not ingested, as was the case later. Instead it was fashioned into crockery. Anyone eating from such crockery would enjoy a long life (but not immortality) and behold the immortals of the isles of P'eng-lai. Li promised the emperor immortality, if, upon beholding the → *hsien*, he were to perform certain sacrifices.

According to Li Shao-chün cinnabar could not be transformed into gold without the help of Tsao-chün, the hearth deity. These alchemical practices thus marked the beginning of the cult of the hearth deity, which continues to this day.

Li T'ieh-kuai → *pa-hsien*

Liu-fu Chin., lit. "six containers"; six bodily organs—stomach, gallbladder, small intestine, large intestine, bladder, and the alimentary and respiratory tracts (these two being classed as one)—of particular importance in Taoist breathing and hygiene exercises.

Liu Ling → *chu-lin ch'i-hsien*

Liu Te-jen → *chen-ta-tao chiao*

Lung Chin., lit. "dragon." In Taoism, the dragon represents the yang principle (→ yin-yang) and is often portrayed surrounded by clouds or water (both symbols of yin).

Chinese mythology knows five types of dragon: celestial dragons, who guard the abodes of heavenly deities; dragon spirits, who rule over wind and rain but can also cause flooding; earth dragons, who cleanse the rivers and deepen the oceans; treasure-guarding dragons; and finally imperial dragons, who have five claws instead of the usual four.

Lung-hu Chin., lit. "dragon [and] tiger"; symbols, respectively, for yang and yin (→ yin-yang) in Taoist alchemy (→ *nei-tan*, → *wai-tan*).

In the teachings of the Inner Alchemy it is said that the dragon arises from *li* (→ *k'an* and *li*), i.e., "out of the fire"; the tiger (yin) is associated with *k'an,* which is associated with water. For that reason the tiger is said to arise from the water. The fusion of *k'an* and *li* leads to the realization of → Tao.

The dragon's color is green; it is further associated with the East, the liver, wood, and spring. The tiger's colour is white, and it is associated with the West, the lungs, metal, and autumn.

Lung-hu-shan   Chin., lit. "Dragon [and] Tiger Mountain"; famous Taoist mountain (situated in Chiang-shi Province), which from the 3d century C.E. until 1949 was the abode of the celestial masters (→ *t'ien-shih*), the descendants of → Chang Tao-ling and the subsequent patriarchs of Five-Pecks-of-Rice Taoism (→ *wu-tou-mi tao,* → *tao-chiao*).

Lung-men School   → *ch'uan-chen tao*

Lung-wang   Chin., lit. "dragon king[s]"; mythological figures who, in the Taoist view, are ruled by the Celestial Venerable of the Primordial Beginning (→ Yüan-shih t'ientsun), to whom they ascend once a year in order to submit their reports. The *lung-wang* have jurisdiction over rain and funerals; during a drought they are supplicated to produce rain. If mistakes or omissions occur at a funeral ceremony, which might result in misfortunes or disaster for descendants of the person that has died, the dragon kings are similarly implored to help. Taoism distinguishes between various types of *lung-wang:* the celestial dragon kings, the dragon kings of the four oceans, who live in splendid palaces at the bottom of the sea, and the *lung-wang* of the five cardinal points.

Lü Pu-wei → *Lü-shih ch'un-ch'iu*

Lü-shih ch'un-ch'iu Chin., lit. *"Spring and Autumn of Master Lü"*; Philosophical work dating from the 3d century B.C.E. and compiled by Lü Pu-wei (?–235 B.C.E.), a rich merchant of the Warring States Period, who is said to have assembled as many as 10,000 scholars of the various philosophical schools at his court and recorded their teachings in his annals. The *Lü-shih ch'un-ch'iu* contains Taoist, Confucianist, Legalist, and Mohist ideas. (See Wilhelm 1979.)

Lü Tung-pin → *pa-hsien*

✻   ✻   ✻

Magic Jewel School → *ling-pao p'ai*

Mao-shan p'ai Chin., lit. "School of Mount Mao"; one of the talisman schools (→ *fu-lu p'ai*) of religious Taoism (→ *tao-chiao*). The Mount Mao movement was founded in the 6th century by → T'ao Hung-ching and is based on the teachings of the brothers Mao (2d century), whom T'ao venerated.

Its doctrinal basis is the *Scriptures of the Magic Jewel*. Its followers endeavored to summon the deities and banish evil spirits by the use of spells and talismans. They abstained from eating grain (→ *pi-ku*), practiced → *tao-yin,* and carried out alchemical experiments. The Mao-shan movement flourished during the Sui and T'ang dynasties and in the 13th century was absorbed by the Way of Right Unity (→ *cheng-i tao*).

Meditation   general term for a multitude of religious practices, often quite different in method, but all having the same goal: to bring the consciousness of the practitioner to a state in which he can come to an experience of "awakening," "liberation," "enlightenment."   Esoteric schools of various religions, i.e., schools practically concerned with individuals' *own* religious experience, have developed different "ways" or "paths" leading to this experience, corresponding to different historical and geographical circumstances as well as to the psychological dispositions and personality types of different individuals or groups. If an individual religion comes to a conclusion concerning a specific unwholesome state of mind of people in a culture which it is its goal to cure, then the "medicine" to accomplish the cure will be the path of meditative training developed within that religion. Such training, while not a goal in itself, should also not be regarded as a mere means to an end; for, as many religious traditions stress, "the path *is* the goal." At the same time, however, it is said that it is futile to hang on to a method when the goal has already been reached, as though one were to carry a boat about after one had already crossed the river.

A common mark of all forms of meditation is that practice of the meditation concentrates the mind of the practitioner, calms and clarifies it like the surface of a turbulent body of water, the bottom of which one can see only when the surface is still and the water is clear. This is accomplished through different techniques, depending on the method of training—for example, by physical or breathing exercises as in hatha-yoga, by concentration on symbolic forms (for example, mandalas, *thangkas*, yantras) or sounds (mantra) as in Indian Tantra or Tantric Buddhism, on feelings such as love or compassion, on pictorial representations (visualization), on a kōan in Zen, or by resting in collected, contentless wakefulness in the practice of *mahāmudrā*, *dzogchen*, or Zen (*shikantaza*).

Diligent practice of meditation leads to a nondualistic state of mind in which, the distinction between subject and object having disappeared and the practitioner having become one with "god" or "the absolute," conventions like time and space are transcended in an "eternal here and now," and the identity of life and death, phenomenal and essential, samsāra and nirvāna, is experienced. If this experience, in the process of endlessly ongoing spiritual training, can be integrated into daily life, then finally that stage is reached which religions refer to as salvation, liberation, or complete enlightenment.

Meng-tzu also known as Meng K'o and latinized as *Mencius;* Confucianist philosopher, 372–289 B.C.E., Meng-tzu is representative of the idealistic branch of Confucianism. His basic thesis postulates that man is inherently good. (See Legge 1861–1872, 1964; Wilhelm 1982.)

Meng-tzu argued that human beings are inherently capable of experiencing pity, shame, and modesty and have an inborn sense of right and wrong. These inherent qualities generate benevolence ($\rightarrow$ *jen*), uprightness ($\rightarrow$ *i*), morality ($\rightarrow$ *li*), and wisdom. They are what distinguishes man from the animals and have to be further developed and cultivated. In this context Meng-tzu stressed the importance of education and the environment. The above seed qualities find their perfect expression in the Confucianist saint. Meng-tzu further emphasized that all rulers must possess proper ethical qualifications;

only a wise man can be a true ruler. If a king lacks these qualifications, the people—by virtue of being the most important element in the state—have a right to rebel. This view influenced Chinese politics up to the 20th century.

Men-shen Chin., lit. "gods of the doorway"; deities in syncretistic Chinese folk religion who, as guardians of the gate, protect the double doorway of a domestic dwelling or public building. *Men-shen* are commonly believed to have been Ch'in Shu-pao and Hu Ching-te, two generals of the T'angDynasty emperor T'ang T'ai-tsung—who have been venerated as guardians of the doorway since the 13th/14th century. According to legend they also defended the 6th emperor against attacks by demons while he was asleep, and popular belief continues to consider it their task to keep away or ward off ghosts and evil spirits. They figure as protectors in many folk tales.

The doorways of private and public buildings are ornmented with color prints of the two *men-shen*. They are usually shown in military uniform and/or armor, with tiny banners affixed to their shoulders to signify their rank. They are armed with a rapier or halberd. Their facial expression is appropriately terrifying. The veneration of *men-shen* is not part of a specific cult; people simply fix their picture to the front entrances to their houses at the beginning of the new year. The back door is guarded by the less popular deity Wei Ch'eng, a former minister of the emperor T'ang T'ai-tsung.

Ming Chin., lit. "luminosity"; Taoist enlightenment. According to Lao-tzu this enlightenment consists in the realization of the law of return to the source (→ *fu*). This law, to which all beings are subject, is characterized by the eternal and enduring (→ *ch'ang*). To know and understand it is a characteristic of the saint, who lives in accordance with it, by returning to the → Tao and realizing its simplicity, unity, and emptiness.

Chapter 16 of the → *Tao-te ching* (Feng & English 1972) explains as follows:

Empty yourself of everything

Let the mind rest at peace.

The ten thousand things rise and fall while the Self watches their return.

They grow and flourish and then return to the source.

Returning to the source is stillness, which is the way of nature.

The way of nature is unchanging (*Ch'ang*).

Knowing constancy is insight (*Ming*).

Not knowing constancy leads to disaster.

Knowing constancy, the mind is open.

With an open mind, you will be openhearted.

Being openhearted, you will act royally.

Being royal, you will attain the divine.

Being divine, you will be at one with the Tao.

Being at one with the Tao is eternal.

And though the body dies, the Tao will never pass away.

Ming　Chin., roughly, fate, destiny, celestial mandate; a concept of → Confucianism, in which *ming* originally denoted the celestial mandate, i.e., the will of Heaven (→ *t'ien*) and later referred to the totality of all energies and conditions of the universe that are beyond the influence of the human will. The successful outcome of an action therefore essentially depends on *ming*.

To understand *ming* means to act in accordance with the requirements and obligations of a given situation, without being concerned about the success or failure of such action.

To know *ming* means to accept the inevitability of the world as it is. This acceptance is considered one of the outstanding characteristics of the ideal man of Confucius.

Ming-men   Chin., lit. "door of destiny"; a location situated between the kidneys of the human body and considered to be the source of the vital energy (→ *ch'i*).

Miu Chi   → T'ai-i

Mo-chia   Chin. → Mo Ti

Mohism   → Mo Ti

Mo Ti   also known as Mo-tzu (Master Mo), about 468–376 B.C.E.; opponent of Confucius (→ K'ung-tzu) and founder of Mohism (Chin., *mo-chia*). His doctrines are contained in a work known as *Mo-tzu*, which in all probability was compiled by his pupils around 400 B.C.E. (see Graham 1978; Mei 1929; Watson 1967).

Mo Ti initially studied the teachings of Confucius (→ K'ung-tzu), but was unable to agree with his definition of morality (→ *li*). He thus developed his own philosophy, the central idea of which was an all-embracing love, not confined to the family or clan (as in the case of Confucius) and subject to the will of Heaven (→ *t'ien*). In his philosophy Mo Ti personifies Heaven and sees it as a supreme being, which will intervene unfavorably in the lives of men who do not love each other. Mo Ti furthermore bases his doctrine on the existence of spirits and demons, who also punish those who do not live in accordance with the principle of all-embracing love and reward those who do.

Mo Ti rejects offensive warfare, criticizes the elaborateness of Confucianist rites, and considers the cultivation of music— an important feature of Confucianist doctrine—as a mere waste of time. For about two centuries, Mohism held its own against the teachings of Confucius but later was gradually displaced by it. The followers of Mo Ti were tightly organized in groups, some of which continued to study problems of logic and dialectics and even matters of technology, which led to an elaboration of certain materialist aspects of Mohism.

Mo-tzu   Chin. → Mo Ti

    *   *   *

Nan-hua chen-ching   Chin. → Chuang-tzu

Nan-hua chen-jen   → *chen-jen*

Nei-ch'i   Chin., lit. "inner breath"; vital energy stored within the body, as opposed to → *wai-ch'i*, the outer breath, which designates the air we inhale. In the Taoist view, a person's *nei-ch'i* corresponds to the primordial breath (→ *yüan-ch'i*) of the cosmos, the primal energy from which Heaven (→ *t'ien*) and Earth arose at the beginning of the world. The primordial *ch'i* enters the human body at birth and in fact forms the mind (→ *shen*), the body itself, the saliva (→ *yü-chiang*) and spermatozoa (→ *ching*). A Taoist practitioner strives to conserve and strengthen his *nei-ch'i* and restore it to the pure state in which it was at the time of birth. If the inner breath is allowed to escape during exhalation this results in a shortening of that person's life span.

Since the time of the T'ang Dynasty Taoist authors have consistently emphasized that the instructions on how to perform breathing exercises such as embryonic breathing (→ *t'ai-hsi*) refer to the inner rather than the outer breath (→ *fu-ch'i*, → *hsing-ch'i*, → *yen-ch'i*). The *nei-ch'i* is stored in the ocean of energy (→ *ch'i-hai*) and circulates in harmony with the outer breath but separate from it. As the outer *ch'i* ascends during exhalation, the inner breath follows it; but they must not mix. In an untrained person the inner breath will leave the body together with the outer. Once the inner *ch'i* is exhausted, death ensues. The Taoist adept, however, swallows the inner *ch'i* before it can leave his body (→ *yen-ch'i*) and during inhalation channels it back to the *ch'i-hai*.

Nei-kuan also known as *nei-shih*, Chin., lit. "inner viewing"; a Taoist practice in which the practitioner visualizes the inside of his body until the smallest details appear with great clarity before his inner eye. The practice of *nei-kuan* facilitates the circulating of the breath (→ *hsing-ch'i*). In the → Inner Deity Hygiene School it is used for visualizing and contacting the various body deities. The successful practice of *nei-kuan* depends on the elimination of all external disturbances and the effective calming of all thought processes.

Nei-shih Chin. → *nei-kuan*

Nei-tan Chin., lit. "inner cinnabar"; the inner elixir, the inner alchemy. In the language of the Taoist School of the Inner Elixir *nei-tan* refers to the development of an immortal soul from the three life-preserving energies: the essence (→ *ching*), the vital energy (→ *ch'i*) and the spirit (→ *shen*). This process often is described in the language of the Outer Alchemy (→ *wai-tan*), which endeavors to produce an elixir of immortality (→ *ch'ang-sheng pu-ssu*) by combining various chemical substances. The Inner Alchemy compares the melting pot of the Outer Alchemy to the human body in which the essence and the life force—

corresponding to the chemical substances employed by the Outer Alchemy—are fashioned into a sacred embryo (→ *sheng-t'ai*) with the help of the mind.

In the practice of *nei-tan* the inner amalgamation and sublimation are brought about by taming and sublimating the thought processes of the mind. All processes that normally result in the death of a person can be reversed by concentrating and purifying

An adept of the Inner Alchemy (nei-tan).

the life energies within the body, thus making them independent of the world of the senses. By various meditative breathing techniques the practitioner causes a new being—the so-called sacred embryo—to develop within him. This sacred embryo is synonymous with our idea of an immortal soul and—like the soul—leaves the dying body at the moment of death to ascend to Heaven. Taoists frequently refer to the sacred embryo as the golden flower, which opens when the adept has attained enlightenment. In a philosophical sense the enlightenment of the followers of the inner elixir consists in a return to nothingness. The goal of the Inner Alchemy therefore is the same as that of the philosophical Taoism (→ *tao-chia*) of Lao-tzu or Chuang-tzu: to become one with the Tao by balancing yin and yang (→ yin-yang).

The practice of *nei-tan* began to replace those of the outer elixir during the Sung Dynasty. It was particularly widespread in the School of the Realization of Truth (→ *ch'üan-chen tao*) and its various branches and strongly influenced by Buddhism, especially Zen.

The most famous representatives of the School of the Inner Elixir were → Wei P'o-yang, → Chen T'uan, and → Chang Po-tuan. One of the most important Inner Alchemy texts is the → *T'ai-i chin-hua tsung-chih*, known as *The Secret of the Golden Flower*.

The main teaching of the School of the Inner Elixir states that the three vital energies of man—*ching, ch'i,* and *shen*—have both a material, visible aspect, which is active within the body, and an immaterial, invisible aspect, which is active in the universe. Practitioners of the Inner Alchemy perform meditative breathing exercises with the aim of purifying the essence and transforming it into *ch'i* and thereafter purifying *ch'i* and transforming that into *shen* (*lien-ching hua-ch'i, lien-ch'i hua-shen*). The final stage of the *nei-tan* path consists in purifying the mind and returning to nothingness (*lien-shen fu-hsü*), i.e., integrating the self with the universe.

The strengthening of one's own essence is a prerequisite for the successful practice of *nei-tan*. Frequently, various sexual techniques (→ *fang-chung shu*) are employed to that effect. However, many Taoist scholars categorically reject such practices, the most important of which consists in "returning the essence [semen] to strengthen the brain" (→ *huan-ching pu-nao*).

The actual work of the inner alchemist begins with the creation of channels within himself along which the energy can circulate. The first of these is the so-called lesser celestial circulation (*hsiao-chou-t'ien*), which begins at the heart and from there descends via the middle of the abdomen to the kidneys. In Taoist texts this path of the inner circulation is often related to the five elements (→ *wu-hsing*), the annual seasons, the cardinal points, physical organs, animals, etc.

The lesser circulation forms the basis for the greater, which engages the whole of the body, in that the energy rises from the lower end of the spine along the vertebral column to the top of the head and from there, via the face, chest, and abdominal surface, back down to the end of the spine. The ascending current of energy is referred to as *tu-mai,* or the controlled path. Its most important centers are situated (1) at the lowest point of the spine, (2) at the level of the kidneys, (3) at the halfway point of the vertebral column, and (4) at the connecting point between the spine and the head. The topmost of these centers is the so-called upper cinnabar field (→ *tan-t'ien*), or, more specifically, the → *ni-huan.*

The descending channel is called *jen-mai,* or involuntary path. Its most important centers are the middle and lower cinnabar fields, the yellow castle (*huang-t'ing*) in the middle of the abdomen, and the hall of light (*ming-t'ang*) between the eyes.

Alchemical texts sub-divide the whole circulatory path into twelve sections that are symbolized by hexagrams from the → *I-ching* or by signs corresponding to the twelve months of the year or twelve two-hour periods of the day.

In addition, the texts often describe the ascent and descent of the energy as a fusion of → *k'an* and *li* or of dragon (yang) and tiger (yin), whereby the actual aim of *nei-tan* is realized.

Detailed description of the practice of Inner Alchemy may be found in Chang Chung-yuan 1963; Wilhelm 1938; Miyuki 1984.

Neo-Confucianism   → Confucianism, → Chu Hsi

Neo-Taoism   → *hsüan-hsüeh*

Ni-huan   Chin., lit. "ball of clay"; name given by the → Inner Deity Hygiene School of religious Taoism (→ *tao-chiao*) to the most important area of the upper cinnabar field (→ *tan-t'ien*), in which the Great One (→ T'ai-i), the highest body deity, resides. The term *ni-huan* may, however, also refer to the brain in general or to a deity associated with the brain.

Nü-kua   female figure in Chinese mythology. Nü-kua is considered to have created mankind. A text dating from the Han Dynasty states that after Heaven and Earth had separated, Nü-kua began to form human figures out of yellow earth. But this method proved too tedious and time-consuming, so she dipped a rope into mud and then swung it about her so that lumps of mud fell to the ground. The original handmade humans became the wealthy and noble, and those that arose from the splashes of mud the poor and common. In addition, Nü-kua is said to have restored the universal order after a devastating attack by the mythical monster Kung Kung. In this role she is usually represented in the company of → Fu Hsi, her alleged husband. They are shown as a couple in human form but with intertwining dragon tails. Fu Hsi holds a set square, and Nü-kua a compass, symbols of Heaven and Earth.

Nü-kua is also credited with having instituted marriage. In addition, she tamed wild animals and—together with other mythological figures—instructed mankind in the art of building dikes and dams as well as channels for regulating flood water and for purposes of irrigation.

Another myth states that beyond the northwestern ocean there live ten ghosts who were fashioned from the bowels of Nü-kua.

→ Lieh-tzu gives the following description of Nü-kua's activities: "At one time it was found that the cardinal points were no longer in the proper place. The nine provinces lay exposed. Heaven no longer fully covered Earth, and the Earth in turn supported Heaven only in places. Fire burned continuously. Water flowed incessantly. Wild animals devoured peaceable human beings. Predatory birds carried off old men and children. Then Nü-kua melted colored stones to mend the azure skies. She cut off the legs of a turtle to support the cardinal points. She slayed the black dragon to save the land of Ch'i. On the river bank she piled up the ashes of reeds to dam the overflowing water. And all was calm again and everyone lived in peace" (Christie 1968, p. 84).

* * *

Outer elixir → *wai-tan*

* * *

Pa-hsien Chin., lit. "eight immortals"; a group of eight immortals (→ *hsien*), who are among the best known figures of Taoist mythology. The earliest descriptions of them date from the T'ang Dynasty, but their present grouping was not established until the Ming Dynasty. The eight immortals are Li T'ieh-kuai (also called Li Hsüan), Chang Kuo-lao, Ts'ao Kuo-chiu, Han Hsiang-tzu, Lü Tung-pin, Ho Hsien-ku, Lan Ts'ai-ho and Chung Li-ch'üan (also called Han Chung-li). Chang Kuo-lao, Lü Tung-pin, Ts'ao Kuo-chiu and Chung Li-ch'üan are historical figures.

Throughout China the eight immortals are a symbol for good fortune. In addition, they represent eight different

111

conditions of life: youth, old age, poverty, wealth, nobility, the populace, the feminine, and the masculine.

The *pa-hsien* are a favorite theme in artistic representations. They can be found on fans, porcelain, picture scrolls, etc. and also figure prominently in many literary works.

1. *Li T'ieh-kuai* (lit. "Li with the Iron Crutch") is usually portrayed with an iron crutch and a pumpkin containing magic potions. According to tradition, the Royal Mother of the West (→ Hsi Wang-mu) healed an abscess on Li's leg and taught him how to become immortal. She also gave him the iron crutch.

Another legend explains how Li came to have a crippled leg: Lao-tzu had descended from Heaven to initiate Li in the Taoist teachings. Soon after that Li attained immortality and left his body to travel to sacred Mount Hua-hsan. He told one of his pupils to guard his body during his absence but to burn it if he did not return within seven days. After Li had gone six days, this pupil received a message to say that his mother was dying. To enable him to fulfill his duty as a son, he burned the body of his master and went to his dying mother. When Li returned all he found was a heap of ashes and thus was forced to enter the body of a dead beggar, who had a black face, a pointed head, matted hair, a crippled leg, and big protruding eyes. Li did not want to live in such a body but Lao-tzu begged him to accept his fate and presented him with a band of gold to keep his tousled hair in place and with an iron crutch to help him walk.

2. *Chang Kuo-lao* was a Taoist who lived during the T'ang Dynasty. Legend tells us that he owned a white donkey capable of traveling a thousand miles a day. This magic donkey could be folded like a handkerchief and carried in one's pocket. To revive it, Chang had only to sprinkle a handful of water over the handkerchief. Chang's

symbol is the so-called fish drum, an instrument for raising a loud noise.

Chang held a high official post and attracted the curiosity of the emperor who had questioned a famous Taoist master about him. This Taoist master told the emperor that he knew the true identity of Chang but was afraid to reveal it, because he had been told that he would fall dead to the ground if he were to do so. However, if the emperor in person were to go barefoot and bareheaded to ask Chang to forgive such a betrayal, Chang could bring him back to life. The emperor promised to do so whereupon the master told him that Chang was an incarnation of the primordial chaos. The master immediately fell dead to the ground. After the emperor had begged forgiveness of Chang he brought the Taoist master back to life by sprinkling water over his body. Soon after, Chang became ill and withdrew to the mountains where he died between 742 and 746 C.E. When his pupils opened his grave they found it to be empty (→ *shih-chieh*).

3. *Ts'ao Kuo-chiu* (d. 1097 C.E.) was the brother-in-law of a Sung Dynasty emperor. His younger brother became a murderer. In shame, Ts'ao withdrew to the mountains and decided to spend his life as a hermit. He is usually portrayed holding a pair of castanets.

According to legend Ts'ao one day encountered Chung Li-ch'üan and Lü Tung-pin, who asked him what he was doing in the mountains. Ts'ao answered that he was following the Way (→ Tao) whereupon they wanted to know where the Way was. Ts'ao pointed at Heaven. Lü and Chung then wanted to know where Heaven was. Ts'ao pointed at his heart. At this Chung Li-ch'üan smiled and said, "The heart is Heaven and Heaven is the Way. I see that you know the original face of things." They then taught Ts'ao how to attain perfection and within a few days he became an immortal.

Another legend says that the emperor gave Ts'ao a golden medal which would allow him to overcome all obstacles. One day, when Ts'ao had to cross the Yellow River, he showed that medal to the ferryman. Thereupon a poorly dressed Taoist priest asked Ts'ao why he—a follower of the Way—stooped to employ such methods. At this Ts'ao begged the priest to cast the medal into the river. The priest took him aside and said, "Have you heard of Lü Tung-pin? I am he and have come to help you attain immortality."

4. *Han Hsiang-tzu* is generally believed to be the nephew of Han Yü, a famous literary figure and statesman of the T'ang Dynasty, who had been entrusted with Hsiang-tzu's education. Han Hsiang-tzu had a stormy temper and possessed various supernatural abilities. He is usually portrayed holding a flute, a bouquet of flowers, or a peach.

Once Han caused peonies of many colors to blossom forth in the middle of winter. On the petals of these peonies appeared the following poem: "Clouds veil the peaks of Ch'in-ling mountain. Where is your home? Deep lies the snow on Lan Pass and the horses will go no further." Han Hsiang-tzu saw a hidden meaning in these lines, but his uncle dismissed them as nonsense. Soon after, Han Yü fell in disgrace with the emperor and was banished. When he reached Lan Pass the snow was so deep that he could make no further progress. Then Han Hsiang-tzu appeared and cleared away the snow. He told his uncle that he would regain his official post and return to the bosom of his family, which prophecy soon came true.

5. *Lü Tung-pin* was born in 798 C.E. in Northern China. His family were civil servants. As a young man he traveled to Mount Lü in the south of the country where he met a fire dragon who presented him with a magic sword that enabled him to conceal himself in Heaven.

On a journey to the capital he came upon the immortal Chung Li-ch'üan, who was warming up some wine. Lü fell asleep and dreamt that he had been promoted to a high official post and possessed enormous wealth. In his dream he lived the life of a rich man for the next fifty years until a crime caused his family to be banished and exterminated. When he awoke from his dream he found that only a few moments had passed. The dream, which has become proverbial in China, brought him to his senses and he decided to forgo an official career and follow Chung Li-ch'üan into the mountains. Chung initiated him into the secrets of alchemy and taught him the art of swordsmanship. At the age of 100 Lü still retained his youthful appearance and was capable of traveling 100 miles in a matter of seconds.

Lü Tung-pin considered compassion to be the essential means of attaining perfection. He transformed the methods of the Outer Alchemy (→ *wai-tan*) into those of the Inner (→ *nei-tan*). To him his sword—his symbol—was not a tool for killing enemies but for conquering passion, aggression, and ignorance. Through his example Lü had a decisive influence on the development of Taoism, and the school of → *ch'üan-chen tao* venerated him as the teacher of its founder.

6. *Ho Hsien-ku* is the only female among the *pa-hsien*. She lived during the T'ang Dynasty and spent her life as a hermit in the mountains. When she was fourteen, a spirit appeared to her in a dream and told her to grind a stone known as "mother of clouds" into powder and eat that powder. She would then become as light as a feather and attain immortality. She followed these instructions and furthermore vowed never to get married. Thereafter she was able to fly from one mountain peak to the next; as she did so she gathered fruit and berries for her mother. She

herself no longer had any need of nourishment. One day the emperor summoned her to the court but on her way there she disappeared and became an immortal. Legend further reports that she was sighted several times after her earthly demise.

According to another legend young Ho Hsien-ku lost her way in the mountains while gathering tea and met a → *tao-shih*, who gave her a peach to eat. After that she never again felt hungry. This *tao-shih* is said to have been none other than Lü Tung-pin, the fifth of the eight immortals.

7. *Lan Ts'ai-ho* is sometimes portrayed with female features. He is dressed in rags, wears a belt made of black wood, and wears a boot on one of his feet, the other being bare. In his hand he carries a basket of flowers.

In summer he would wear a thick overcoat but dress lightly in winter. His breath was like hot steam. According to legend he roamed the streets as a beggar, accompanying his songs with castanets. Most of the time he was drunk. When people gave him money he used to string the coins on a cord, which he dragged behind him. One day he stopped at an inn, took off his boot, belt, and cloak, and disappeared into the clouds, riding on a crane.

8. *Chung Li-ch'üan* allegedly lived during the Han Dynasty. His symbol was a fan made of feathers or palm leaves. He is usually portrayed as a corpulent man, bald, but with a beard that reaches down to his navel. In representations of the eight immortals he can also be recognized by the wisps of hair that grace his temples. Reports about his life vary greatly: according to some he was a field marshal, who withdrew to the mountains in his old age; others claim that he was a vice-marshal who, after losing a battle against the Tibetans, fled into the mountains, where five Taoist saints

initiated him into the teachings of immortality. Several hundred years later he is said to have taught Lü Tung-pin.

Various legends give conflicting versions as to how he became an immortal: according to one he met an old Taoist master in a forest, who at his request gave him prescriptions on how to attain immortality. As Chung was leaving this venerable master, he turned to cast a last glance at his hut but found that it had vanished.

Another version claims that during a famine Chung produced silver coins by miraculous means and distributed them among the poor, thereby saving numerous lives. One day, a wall of his hermitage collapsed as he was meditating and behind it appeared a jade vessel which contained prescriptions for attaining immortality. He followed these and—to the accompaniment of heavenly sounds—was borne away to the abode of the immortals on a shimmering cloud.

Pai-yün kuan Chin., lit. "Monastery of the White Clouds"; a Taoist monastery (→ *kuan*) in Peking; the main monastery of the School of the Realization of Truth (→ *ch'üan-chen tao*). *Pai-yün kuan* was constructed in 739 C.E. and restored in 1167.

During the 13th century this monastery was the residence of Ch'ui Ch'u-chih, the founder of the northern (or dragon gate) faction of the *ch'üan-chen tao*, who is also buried there. The present layout of the monastery dates from the Ch'ing Dynasty. It is now the headquarters of the Taoist Society of China.

Pa-kua Chin., eight trigrams; eight signs that form the basis of the *Book of Change(s)* (→ *I-ching*) and from which the sixty-four hexagrams are derived. Each trigram consists of three lines, each of which may be either yin (– –)

117

or yang (—) (→ yin-yang).
There are eight possible
combinations:

The most important tri-
grams are → *ch'ien* and
k'un because they symbolize the primordial energy
from which all phenomena
arise. *Ch'ien* is pure yang,

Ch'ien *Tui* *Li* *Chen*

Sun *K'an* *Ken* *K'un*

pure male energy; whereas *k'un* represents yin or female
energy. Their material manifestations are, respectively,
Heaven and Earth. The intermingling of *ch'ien* and *k'un*
gives rise to the remaining six trigrams.

Two further important trigrams are → *k'an* and *li*, because their configuration remains unchanged when they
are turned upside down. Each, when doubled, gives rise to
a hexagram bearing the same name.

The *pa-kua* are considered to be images of concrete
reality:

Ch'ien, the creative, is strong, Heaven, the father.

K'un, the receptive, is yielding, Earth, the mother.

Chen, the arousing, is movement, thunder, the first son.

K'an, the abysmal, is danger, water or clouds, the second
son.

Ken, keeping still, is rest, mountain, the youngest son.

Sun, the gentle, is penetrating, wind or wood, the oldest
daughter.

Li, the clinging, is luminous, the sun or lightning, the second daughter.

Tui, the joyous, is joyful, the lake, the youngest daughter.

According to tradition, the eight trigrams originated with
the legendary emperor → Fu Hsi: A dragon-horse emerged

from the Yellow River, carrying on its back the so-called river diagram (→ *Ho-t'u* and *Lo-shu*); and a turtle, emerging from the River Lo, carried on its back the Lo River diagram. From these two magic number diagrams (similar to magic squares) Fu Hsi derived the *pa-kua*. The ancient historian Ssu-ma Ch'ien, on the other hand, states that the trigrams as well as the hexagrams go back to King Wen, one of the founders of the Chou Dynasty. Fu Hsi established correspondences between

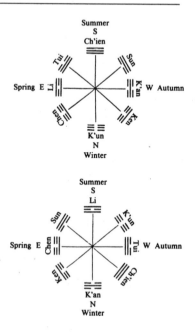

these trigrams, the cardinal points, and the seasons. His arrangement of the trigrams is known as the precelestial ordering (above). The postcelestial ordering was established by King Wen (bottom diagram).

In addition, the trigrams are of considerable importance in the alchemical teachings of the inner and outer elixir (→ *nei-tan*, → *wai-tan*). → Wei P'o-yang's *Ts'an-t'ung-ch'i* states, "Ch'ien and *k'un* are the gate and entrance to change [i.e., the beginning of all transformation] and the father and mother of the remaining signs." *K'an* and *li* are symbolic of the function of *ch'ien* and *k'un*, i.e., the influences of Heaven and Earth. In the language of the alchemists *ch'ien* and *k'un* stand for, respectively, the furnace and the melting pot; and

119

k'un and *li* for the various ingredients from which the elixir is produced.

P'an-ku   creator of the world; first human being. According to a myth dating from the 3d century B.C.E., P'an-ku arose out of chaos, which had the form of a chicken's egg. Then the constituent parts of the egg separated into those which were heavy and pervaded by yin (→ yin-yang), which led to the formation of the Earth, and those that were light and pervaded by yang, which caused Heaven to come into being.

Over a period of 13,000 years the distance between Heaven and Earth increased at the rate of ten feet per day. P'an-ku grew at the same rate so that he always filled the space between the two. After his death the different parts of his body were transformed into the various regions of the world. Different sources describe this transformation in various ways.

According to a 6th-century text P'an-ku's head turned into the four sacred mountains. His eyes became sun and moon, his fatty tissues the rivers and oceans, his hair and beard the grasses and trees.

Other traditional texts state that his ears were transformed into rivers, his breath into wind, his voice into thunder, and the pupils of his eyes into lightning.

P'an-ku holding the World Egg.

Pao-p'u-tzu Chin., lit. *"He Who Embraces the Unhewn Block* [→ *p'u*]"; the most important work of → Ko Hung, in which all the methods for attaining immortality known in his time are systematically set out. The expression *unhewn block* stands for artless simplicity, the natural primordial state of man. For that reason *Pao-p'u-tzu* is sometimes translated as *The Master Who Prefers His Simplicity.*

Pa-tuan-chin Chin., roughly "eight elegant exercises"; a series of Taoist physical exercises (→ *ch'i-kung*) allegedly dating from the 12th century and originally consisting of eight movements, to which others were added in the course of time.

There are two forms of *pa-tuan-chin:* the northern (difficult) and the southern (easier). The latter are attributed to Liang Shih-ch'ang, the former to Yo Fei, but it is more likely that both have an as yet undiscovered common source.

The eight elegant exercises may be performed in a sitting position or standing up.

The oldest texts list the following eight standing exercises:

1. Grasping Heaven with both hands extended, thereby regulating the "triple heater" (*san-chiao,* an acupuncture meridian).
2. Adopting the position of an archer aiming at an eagle (toward either the left or the right).
3. To regulate and harmonize the pancreas and stomach one should extend one arm upwards;
4. To perceive the difficulties and sorrows of one's past existence one should look behind oneself;
5. Simultaneously rocking the head and the posterior from side to side will expel the fire of the heart;

6. The seven sorrows and one hundred illnesses disappear behind the back.
7. Clenching the fists and making the eyes fierce intensifies the energy.
8. Grasping the tips of the toes with both hands makes kidneys and hips firm. (cf. Pálos 1980).

P'eng-lai Chin., lit. "Rampant Weeds"; an island in the East China Sea, which Taoists believe to be inhabited by immortals (→ *hsien*). In Chinese mythology *p'eng-lai* epitomizes bliss, because this is where the legendary mushroom of immortality grows, in search of which numerous expeditions were dispatched as long ago as the 4th century B.C.E. All these expeditions failed, because any ship approaching the legendary island either capsized or was driven off course, or the island itself sank into the sea before the very eyes of the ship's crew. The earliest mention of P'eng-lai in Taoist literature is in the work of → Lieh-tzu (Book 5, Chapter 2). The motive of the search for the mushroom of immortality was an important element in the development of religious Taoism (→ *tao-chiao*).

Lieh-tzu describes the Isle of P'eng-lai as follows: "Up there everything consisted of gold and precious stones; birds and animals shone a glittering white, trees of pearl and coral grew in dense forests, all the flowers were exquisitely fragrant and the fruit deliciously sweet. Anyone eating that fruit felt himself to be liberated from old age and death. Those living there were either fairies or immortals; day and night they would fly in great numbers to visit each other" (Bauer 1974, p. 145).

Ch'in Shih Huang-ti, the first historical emperor of China, dispatched several expeditions to gain possession of the mushroom of immortality. The most famous of these was led by Hsü Fu, who recruited an expeditionary force of three thousand young men. They took with them different kinds of grain as well as plant seeds. However, Hsü Fu never returned: he and his men settled in a fertile region, where he appointed himself king.

P'eng-tzu   figure in Chinese mythology, representing longevity. Religious Taoism (→ *tao-chiao*) maintains that the Taoist sexual practices for prolonging life (→ *fang-chung shu*) were introduced by P'eng-tzu.

According to legend he was born during the Hsia Dynasty and by the end of the Yin Dynasty had reached the age of 777 years (over 800 years according to some sources). King Yin appointed him his physician. His outer appearance was that of a youth. To keep young he swallowed mica dust and the ground antlers of a species of elk. He considered it wrong to withdraw from the world and claimed that the enjoyment of its delights would not impede progress along the Way.

His biography is contained in the writings of → Ko Hung, from which we quote the following passage: "Whoever would follow the Way should eat sweet delicious food; dress in light, becoming gowns; and give his sexual desires their due. He may also accept official and honorary posts. His bones will be hard and firm, his face contented and healthy. He will age without becoming decrepit and, always being in the present, prolongs his life span and thus enjoys a long and happy life in human company. Neither cold nor heat, wind, or fog can harm him; while ghosts and other specters will not dare approach him. . . . Neither displeasure nor joy, pain, or fame will move him. Well might such a man be considered an estimable person. An ordinary man should, by virtue of his life energy, reach an age of 120 years, even without resorting to magical potions, providing he looks after himself. Those that die sooner have willfully abused their life energy. Anyone with no more than a slight knowledge of the Way can reach an age of 240 years and—if he knows a little more than that—480 years. If he makes full use of the power of his spirit he need not die at all. . . . The Way of longevity simply consists in never offending against life. In winter one should keep warm, and cool in summer, and never fail to adjust to the inherent harmony of the four seasons: in this way a man attunes his body to the natural flow. In darkened rooms he may enjoy the company of women, thereby banishing lascivious fantasies: in this way his life force is allowed to flow freely. As for owning carriages and official gowns, as well as possessing power and influence, a man should know what is sufficient and have no desires beyond that: in this way he will harness his will. The eight tones and five colors are welcome to delight our eyes and ears: thus are our hearts guided" (Bauer 1974, p. 157).

Pi-ch'i Chin., lit. "holding the breath"; Taoist breathing technique, in which the breath is first harmonized (→ *t'iao-ch'i*), then swallowed (→ *yen-ch'i*), and finally retained for as long as possible.

A beginner may retain his breath for the duration of three to nine heartbeats; this is known as the small round. Advanced practitioners practice the great round lasting 120 heartbeats. At this level it is possible to heal sicknesses in one's body. However, only those who are able to stop their breath for a duration of 1,000 heartbeats are approaching immortality.

When practicing *pi-ch'i* with the aim of curing himself of illness, the adept should begin by concentrating his mind on the sick area of his body and then direct and collect his breath at that point. In this way blockages—the most frequent cause of illness—can be dissolved with the breath. The practitioner then exhales. This process is repeated between twenty and fifty times, i.e., until perspiration appears at the affected area. The practice is continued until all signs of the illness have disappeared.

Pi-hsia yüan-chün Chin., lit. "Princess of the Azure Clouds"; Taoist deity, daughter of the god of Mount T'ai (→ T'ai-shan, → T'ai-yüeh ta-ti). Pi-hsia yüan-chün is also known as the Lady of T'ai-shan (T'ai-shan niang-niang) or the Holy Mother (Sheng-mu). She is the protectress of women and children and in this role is often compared to the Buddhist Kuan-yün. Her temple on top of Mount T'ai continues to be visited by many pilgrims who beseech the Princess of the Azure Clouds to bless them with children.

The veneration of Pi-hsia yüan-chün can be traced back to the time of the Han Dynasty. She is the subject of many legends. Generally she is shown in the company of two female assistants: the Lady of Good Sight, who protects children from eye infections, and the Lady Who Bestows Children (Sung-tzu niang-niang). Often there are six further deities by her side, who have the task of protecting children of different ages. Pi-hsia yüan-chün, her two assistants, and the six subordinate deities form a group known as the "nine ladies" (*chiu niang-niang*) to whom temples (*nai-nai miao*) were dedicated throughout China.

Pi-ku Chin., lit. "abstaining from eating grain"; Taoist practice indispensable for the attainment of immortality. The practice is based on the notion that the five types of grain forming the staple diet of the Chinese—i.e., rice, barley, wheat, millet, and beans—also are the nourishment of the three worms (→ *san-ch'ung*), who are the cause of illnesses and thus shorten a person's life span. Another reason why they are considered to be harmful is that they are the essence of Earth. In the Taoist view the physical damage and diseases caused by eating these grains can be passed on from one generation to the next.

Abstinence from eating grain, in order to be successful, must be accompanied by other methods, i.e., the practitioner is not allowed to drink alcohol or eat meat and should avoid all fatty food.

P'o Chin.; body soul, one of two types of soul that, according to Chinese belief, inhabit every human being. The other is the so-called breath, or spirit, soul (→ *hun*).

Every human being has seven *p'o* souls, which owe their existence to the passive yin energy (→ yin-yang) and regulate the lower body functions. They cling to the human body; if they depart from it, death ensues. In that case the *p'o* souls rejoin the Earth, which is pure yin.

P'u Chin., lit. "rough timber, an unhewn block"; simplicity, plainness, innocence. A symbol used by Lao-tzu in the → *Tao-te ching* to describe the original, simple, and unpretentious nature of man. This original human nature is also compared to that of a new-born child (*ying-erh*) or to raw silk (*su*). It is the goal we must regain, because *p'u* is the ultimate destination of the return to our source (→ *fu*). Its predominant characteristic is spontaneous action (→ *wu-wei*) and freedom from desire. The return to this primordial state is only possible by shedding our desires and attachments. Chapter 19 of the *Tao-te ching* (Wei 1982, p. 152) states,

Display plainness (*su*), embrace simplicity (*p'u*),
Reduce selfishness and decrease desires.
Forswear learning

and vexation will vanish.

Lao-tzu considers the desire for wealth, fame, and sensuous pleasures the main hindrance to our development, because they give rise to envy and hatred. A person who attains true inner simplicity thereby gains power over the whole world (Chap. 32, Feng & English 1972):

The Tao is forever undefined.
Small though it is in the unformed state,
   it cannot be grasped.
If kings and lords could harness it,
the ten thousand things would naturally obey.
. . .
Men would need no more instruction
   and all things would take their course.

Pu-nao   Chin. → *huan-ching*

    ✻   ✻   ✻

Ru-chia   Chin. → Confucianism

    ✻   ✻   ✻

San-ch'ing   Chin., lit. "the three pure ones"; the three Taoist heavens (→ *t'ien*) and the three deities inhabiting them.

The first of these is *yü-ch'ing,* the Heaven of Jade Purity, inhabited by → Yüan-shih t'ien-tsun, the Celestial Venerable of the Primordial Beginning. He is also known as T'ien-pao-chün or Lord of the Heavenly Jewel. According to some sources this first and highest heaven also is ruled by → Yü-huang, the Jade Emperor. In popular belief Yü-huang is considered the ruler of Heaven and Earth and thus ranks higher than Yüan-shih t'ien-tsun.

The second heaven—*shang-ch'ing*—is the Heaven of Great Purity and is reserved for Ling-pao t'ien-tsun, the Heavenly Venerable of the Magic Jewel. He is sometimes called Tao-chün, Lord of the Tao, and considered to be the guardian of magical writings (→ *Ling-pao ching*). He has existed since the beginning of the world and it is his task to calculate time, allocate it to the various epochs, and to regulate yin and yang (→ yin-yang).

The third heaven—*t'ai-ch'ing*—is the Heaven of Highest Purity, ruled by Tao-te t'ien-tsun, the Heavenly Venerable of the → Tao and the → *te*. He is identical with T'ai-shang lao-chün, Supreme Master Lao, i.e., Lao-tzu (also → Lao-chün). This heavenly venerable reveals the Taoist teachings contained in the writings guarded by the Heavenly Venerable of the Magic Jewel. He will assume a great variety of forms—e.g., that of Lao-tzu—to bring the people of the "world of dust" closer to the teachings of the Tao.

San-ch'ung   Chin., lit. "three worms"; three transcendental beings whom Taoists believe to inhabit the three cinnabar fields (→ *tan-t'ien*). Having no permanent form, they may take on the appearance of demons or of human beings.

The three worms endeavor to shorten the life of those whose bodies they inhabit and thus prevent them from attaining immortality. They are the cause of a great variety of diseases and also inform Heaven of people's transgressions so that the deities might shorten their lives (→ Ssu-ming). A Taoist adept striving for immortality therefore tries to rid himself of the three worms by abstaining from eating grain (→ *pi-ku*) because grain is their nourishment. As an additional measure, he may meditate and fast on the days when the three worms ascend to Heaven to inform → Yü-huang, the Jade Emperor, of man's good and evil deeds. The meditation and fasting prevent the worms from ascending to Heaven.

The first worm lives in the palace (→ *ni-huan*) of the upper cinnabar field situated in the head. It causes blindness and deafness, loss of teeth and hair, as well as foul-smelling breath and congestion of the nose. The second worm resides in the middle cinnabar field situated near the heart. It causes heart disease, asthma, and melancholy. The third worm inhabits the lower cinnabar field in the region of the navel and causes intestinal malfunctions, skin diseases, rheumatism, and lack of will power.

San-hsing Chin., lit. "three stars"; three stellar deities or gods of good fortune, which are a favorite motif in Chinese folk art: Fu-hsing (Lucky Star) is most frequently portrayed in the company of a child or in his symbolic form of a bat—a sign of good luck. Lü-hsing (Star of Honor or Status) often appears in his symbolical form of a stag. Shou-hsing (Star of Longevity) has an enormously high bald head. He supports himself on a knotty staff, a symbol of

The three gods of good fortune: left, Shou-hsing; center, Lu-hsing; right, Fu-hsing.

129

the immortals (→ *hsien*). In his other hand he holds the peach of immortality. Symbolically he is represented by a mushroom or a turtle (→ Shou-lao). The *san-hsing* are historical personalities who were deified in recognition of the special merits they accumulated.

Fu-hsing, according to tradition, was a 6th-century government official by the name of Yang Ch'eng. He came from the village of Tao-chou, all the inhabitants of which were of extremely short stature. Every year, the emperor would summon a large number of people from this village to his court, because he loved to surround himself with dwarfs. In consequence, the population of Tao-chou was greatly reduced as the years went on. Yang Ch'eng addressed a petition to the emperor asking him to show consideration for the people of his home town. The emperor was so touched by Yang Ch'eng's petition that he never again summoned them to his court.

There are, however, other historical personalities to whom the function of Fu-hsing is ascribed. The most prominent of these is the 8th-century general Kuo Tzu-i, who saved the T'ang Dynasty from destruction after an uprising. It is said that the Heavenly Weaver—a female mythological figure—appeared to him. When he asked her to grant him fame and fortune, she replied that he himself was the god of wealth. This encounter is the subject of many artistic representations. In popular belief, Fu-hsing is frequently confused with the Ruler of Heaven (→ *san-kuan*).

Lü-hsing, who is also known as Kuan-hsing (Star of State Officials), is supposed to have been Shih Fei, a vassal of the founder of the Han Dynasty. Another tradition identifies Lü-hsing with the god of literature (→ *Wen-ch'ang*).

Shou-hsing came to be known as Shou-lao in later popular belief and is also called the Old Man of the South Pole. A legend tells of one Chao Yen who, as a child, was told by a physiognomer that he had only nineteen more years to live. He therefore advised the child to go on a certain day to a certain field and take with him a jar of wine and dried meat. In that field he would find two men playing draughts under a mulberry tree. Chao Yen should offer them wine and meat but on no account answer any of their questions. Chao Yen followed the physiognomer's advice.

After they had partaken of the wine and meat offered to them by Chao Yen, the two players discussed how they might best thank the boy for his hospitality. In the end they decided to reverse the digits of the number of years the boy could be expected to live, thus changing the *19* into a *91*. Later the physiognomer told Chao Yen that one of the two players had been the God of the North Pole, who determines the day on which people are born, and the other the God of the South Pole, who fixes the dates of death.

San-hsüan Chin., lit. "three unfathomables"; neo-Taoist (→ *hsüan-hsüeh*) collective term for the → *Tao-te ching* of Lao-tzu, the → *Chuang-tzu*, and the → *I-ching*.

San-huang Chin., lit. "three nobles"; three legendary emperors of China, namely → Fu Hsi, → Shen-nung, and Yen-ti. The period during which they are believed to have ruled is variously given as 2852–2697 B.C.E. or 2952–2490 B.C.E. They were succeeded by the five legendary emperors (→ *wu-ti*).

San-i Chin.,, lit. "the three ones"; three deities who, according to the Inner Deity Hygiene School of religious Taoism (→ *tao-chiao*), guard the three cinnabar fields (→ *tan-t'ien*) situated respectively in the head, near the heart, and in the abdominal region. The *san-i* are in turn ruled by the Supreme One (→ T'ai-i), who dwells in a particular compartment of the upper cinnabar field. The task of the three ones consists in guarding the three cinnabar fields— the focal points of man's life energy—against ghosts and evil breath. They are the enemies of the three worms (→ *san-ch'ung*).

The term *san-i* may also designate the trinity of mind (→ *shen*), life force (→ *ch'i*), and essence (→ *ching*). In Taoist texts from the Han Dynasty the three ones refer to the Celestial One (T'ien-i), the Earthly One (Ti-i), and the Supreme One (→ T'ai-i).

The idea of the three ones originated with a passage of the *Tao-te ching* (chap. 42, Feng & English 1972):

The Tao begot one
one begot two
two begot three
and three begot the ten thousand things.

Due to the tendency of Taoism to personalize abstract concepts, this "one" that arises from the Tao quickly became transformed into a deity, the Supreme One (T'ai-i), who for a long time was the most important deity in religious Taoism. The splitting up of the One into three ones proved necessary as a result of the fusion of two practices, which until then had been independent of each other: (1) meditation aimed at becoming one with the Tao, based on the teachings of → Lao-tzu and → Chuang-tzu, who considered the preservation of → *shou-i* to be indispensable, and (2) the practice of "allowing the breath to circulate" through the cinnabar fields of the body (→ *hsing-ch'i*). Since there are three fields and the ultimate principle of the One resides in each of them it became necessary to assume the existence of three ones, which dwell in three different places but nevertheless form a unity.

San-kuan Chin., roughly "three rulers"; three Taoist deities, namely T'ien-kuan (Ruler of Heaven); Ti-kuan (Ruler of the Earth), and Shui-kuan (Ruler of Water). These three play an important part in the religious life of the Chinese. According to popular belief the Ruler of Heaven bestows wealth and good luck, the Ruler of the Earth forgives sins and transgressions, and the Ruler of Water helps the believer to overcome obstacles. In addition, all three keep a register of the good and evil deeds of people.

The veneration of the *san-kuan* goes back to the beginning of religious Taoism (→ *tao-chiao*) because both → Chang Chüeh and → Chang Tao-ling, the respective leaders of the Way of Supreme Peace (→ *t'ai-p'ing tao*) and Five-Pecks-of-Rice Taoism (→ *wu-tou-mi tao*), enlisted their help during healing ceremonies.

At these healing sessions the sick would list their sins—which were considered to be the cause of their illness—on three strips of paper, one for each of the three rulers. The paper strip intended for T'ien-kuan was either burned or deposited on the peak of a mountain; that addressed to the Ruler of the Earth was buried in the ground; and that intended for the Ruler of Water thrown into a river.

Under → K'ou Ch'ien-chih, the *san-kuan* cult was reformed and the three rulers became functionaries of the gods, responsible for supervising rites and rewarding believers. In ancient times, each city had a hall or temple dedicated to the three rulers.

In representations they are not often seen together. When they are, they sit next to each other and are dressed as mandarins. In their hands they hold the register of the good and evil deeds. However, representations showing the Ruler of

Heaven on his own are quite common: he is usually shown standing and holding a scroll with the inscription, "The Ruler of Heaven bestows good fortune." For that reason he is also venerated as a god of good fortune (→ *san-hsing*).

San-pao Chin., lit. "three treasures"; the term *san-pao* occurs in the → *Tao-te ching* and refers to love, moderation, and the renunciation of fame and honor.

Chapter 67 of the *Tao-te ching* (Lin 1949) states:
I have Three Treasures;
Guard them and keep them safe:
The first is Love.
The second is, Never too much.
The third is, Never be the first in the world.
Through Love, one has no fear;
Through not doing too much, one has amplitude
   [of reserve power];
Through not presuming to be the first in the world,
One can develop one's talent and let it mature.
If one forsakes love and fearlessness,
Forsakes restraint and reserve power,
Forsakes following behind and rushes in front,
He is dead!
For love is victorious in attack,
And invulnerable in defence.
Heaven arms with love
Those it would see destroyed.

In religious Taoism (→ *tao-chiao*) the term *san-pao* has varied meanings: (1) similar to the three treasures of Buddhism, it refers to the Way (→ Tao), the Taoist scriptures (→ *Tao-tsang*), and the masters of the Way (→ *tao-shih*). Taoists venerate these three treasures in numerous ceremonies; (2) the three cinnabar fields (→ *tan-t'ien*); (3) the so-called inner treasures: primordial essence (→ *ching*), primordial energy (→ *yüan-ch'i,* → *ch'i*), and the primordial spirit (→ *shen,* → *san-yüan*).

The three outer treasures—as opposed to the inner ones—are the ears, eyes, and mouth.

San-ts'ai　Chin., lit. "three powers"; a term found in the → *I-ching,* referring to Heaven (→ *t'ien*), Earth, and man. Elsewhere the term *san-ts'ai* also may designate the trinity of Heaven and Earth (taken as one constituent), man, and the ten thousand things (→ *wan-wu*).

In the *Shuo-kua* ("Explanation of the Trigrams") of the *I-ching* (see also → *Shih-i* and → *pa-kua*) it is stated: "Therefore they determined the Tao of Heaven and called it the dark and the light. They determined the Tao of the Earth and called it the yielding and the firm. They determined the Tao of Man and called it love (→ *jen*) and rectitude (→ *i*). They combined these three fundamental powers and doubled them; therefore in the Book of Changes is always formed by six lines" (Wilhelm 1967).

San-yüan　Chin., lit. "three origins, three foundations"; in Taoist literature the term *san-yüan* refers to various groupings of three: (1) Heaven, Earth, and Water (→ *san-kuan*); (2) the three cinnabar fields (→ *tan-t'ien*); (3) primordial essence (→ *ching*), primordial energy (→ *yüan-ch'i*), and primordial spirit (→ *shen*); i.e., essence, energy, and spirit in the unborn state to which, according to the Taoist teachings, we must return to attain perfection.

School of the Magic Jewel　→ *ling-pao p'ai*

Shang-ch'ing　Chin. → *san-ch'ing*

Shan Tao　→ *chu-lin ch'i-hsien*

Shen Chin., deity, spirit; in Taoism *shen* refers both to the deities that inhabit the universe (and, in the view of some schools, the human body) and to the personal spirit (or mind)—one of the three life energies of man.

The macrocosm, i.e., the universe, is inhabited by 36,000 deities, who, according to the → Inner Deity Hygiene School, exist also within the body of each human being. To attain immortality, the Taoist adept must prevent these deities from leaving his body by the performance of various meditative, breathing, and hygiene exercises. Each of the *shen* has its own name and area of responsibility. The highest *shen* are the three pure ones (→ *san-ch'ing*).

In addition, *shen* designates the personal spirit of a human being, which arises from the union of → *ching*, the essence, with the primordial energy (→ *yüan-ch'i*) of the universe and enters the body with the first breath of a newborn child. This *shen* leaves the body at the moment of death. While in the body, it determines our thoughts and feelings. Its seat is in the upper cinnabar field (→ *tan-t'ien*).

In the Confucianist view *shen* constitutes the spiritual element inherent in the ancestral family tree that is venerated by the relatives of the dead.

In the sense of "mind," *shen*—according to the meditative schools of Taoism—refers to ordinary consciousness (*shih-shen*) and spiritual consciousness (*yüan-shen*). The former consists of the senses, feelings, thoughts, perceptions, etc. accumulated by a person in the course of life. The spiritual consciouness, on the other hand, exists already before birth and is part of the energy that pervades the whole of the universe.

After birth, it becomes invisible, because it is covered over by our ordinary consciousness. By meditating (→ *nei-tan*) the Taoist adept is able to reestablish contact with his spiritual consciousness and at the same time eliminate the influence of his ordinary consciousness.

Frequently *shen* is considered to be the opposite of → *kuei,* in that it refers to the heavenly yang spirits as opposed to the yin demons (*kuei*) (→ yin-yang).

Sheng-jen   Chin., lit. "sage, saint"; one of the names by which → Chuang-tzu describes the ideal man, who has attained perfection (→ *chih-jen,* → *chen-jen,* → *shen-jen*). The *Chuang-tzu* (Book 2, Chapter 1) describes the qualities of a *sheng-jen* as follows:

"For the true sage, beyond the limits of an external world, the so-called 'Eight Predicables' (right and left, relationship and obligation, division and discrimination, emulation and contention) exist, but are not recognised. By the true sage, within the limits of an external world, they are recognised, but are not assigned. And so, with regard to the wisdom of the ancients, as embodied in the canon of *Spring* and *Autumn,* the true sage assigns, but does not justify by argument. And thus, classifying, he does not classify, arguing, he does not argue. The true sage keeps his knowledge within him, while men in general set forth theirs in argument, in order to convince each other. And therefore it is said that in argument he does not manifest himself. Perfect Tao does not declare itself. Nor does perfect argument express itself in words. Nor does perfect charity show itself in act. Nor is perfect honesty absolutely incorruptible. Nor is perfect courage absolutely unyielding. For the Tao which shines forth is not the Tao. Speech which argues falls short of its aim. Charity which has fixed points loses its scope. Honesty which is absolute is

137

wanting in credit. Courage which is absolute misses its object. These five are, as it were, round, with a strong bias towards squareness. Therefore knowledge that stops at what it does not know is the highest knowledge. Who knows the argument which can be argued without words? (Who knows) the Tao which does not declare itself as Tao? He who knows this, may be said to be of god. To be able to pour in without making full and pour out without making empty in ignorance of the power by which such results are accomplished,—this is accounted Light" (Giles 1961).

Sheng-mu → Pi-hsia yüan-chün

Sheng-t'ai Chin., lit. "sacred embryo"; an embryo or fetus that, according to Taoist beliefs, comes into being by the fusion of the inner *ch'i* (→ *nei-ch'i*, → *ch'i*) and the essence (→ *ching*) in the lower cinnabar field (*tan-t'ien*), where it is nourished by the breath and slowly develops into a new purified body within the physical body. This embryo is the immortal soul of Taoists. When the physical body dies, this pure body departs from its mortal sheath and the practitioner becomes an immortal (→ *hsien*).

In the teachings of the Inner Alchemy (→ *nei-tan*) the development of the sacred embryo is described in great detail—albeit in the language of the Outer Alchemy (→ *wai-tan*)—and is said to have nine stages, which are analogous to the effect of the ninefold-purified cinnabar of the alchemists: (1) the living *ch'i* circulates freely and unimpeded throughout the body; (2) the essence, the semen (*ching*), collects in the lower cinnabar field; (3) the sacred embryo begins to assume the form of a human embryo; (4) the two souls (→ *hun* and → *p'o*) of the sacred embryo come into being; (5) the embryo is fully formed and has various supernatural powers; (6) inner and outer yin and yang (→ yin-yang) reach their highest intensity and the embryo merges with the body of the adept; (7) the five internal organs (→ *wu-tsang*) are transformed by the power of *ch'i* into those of an immortal; (8) an umbilical cord develops, through which the breath is channeled during a practice known as embryonic breathing (→ *t'ai-hsi*); (9) form and → Tao combine and clouds form below the feet of the practitioner, on which he ascends toward Heaven (→ *fei-sheng*), thereby completing the metamorphosis.

Texts that are not as strongly influenced by the Outer Alchemy describe the sacred embryo—at the beginning of its development—as a pearl or a rust-colored drop; → Wei P'o-yang for instance refers to it as a child of a pearl. Other texts speak of a mysterious pearl (*hsüan-chu*). Sometimes the embryo is also compared to a grain of corn or a drop of water. Syncretist movements combining Taoism, Buddhism, and Confucianism compare the Taoist *sheng-t'ai* to the Buddhist *tathagatagarbha* or the *dharmakaya*.

The term *sheng-t'ai* furthermore occurs in the writings of Tsung-mi, a patriarch of the Hua-yen School of Chinese Buddhism. In a passage on the origin of Zen, Tsung-mi speaks of nourishing the spirit (→ *shen*) and allowing the sacred embryo to grow. Ma-tzu Tao-i, one of the most famous Zen masters of the 8th century, also used the term.

Shen-jen Chin., lit. "spiritual man"; a term used by → Chuang-tzu to describe his ideal man, i.e., one who has realized the Tao (→ *chen-jen*, → *chih-jen*, → *sheng-jen*). According to the *Chuang-tzu*, "the highest man [*chih-jen*] is free of "I'; the spiritual man (*shen-jen*) is free of action; the realized saint (*sheng-jen*) is free of name" (Wilhelm 1969).

Shen-nung   Chin., lit. "Divine Countryman"; figure in Chinese mythology, one of the three noble ones (→ *san-huang*). He is said to have invented the plow and taught man the art of agriculture as well as the cultivation of forests. Furthermore, he is credited with having introduced the use of medicaments. Lastly, he is considered to be the god of wind, and, as such, was the ideal of various movements in Chinese history that were hostile to civilization and romantically enthused by nature.

Shih-chieh   Chin., lit. "separation from the corpse"; a theory in Taoist tradition to explain the physical death of an immortal (→ *hsien*) by postulating that an immortal only appears to change into a corpse before he ascends to Heaven in broad daylight (→ *fei-sheng*).

In such cases, the coffin—when opened sometime after "death"—is found to be empty, or else just contains the staff, sword, sandals, or some other item of clothing of the adept, who has become an immortal.

One Taoist text describes the process of *shih-chieh* as follows: "'Separation from a corpse' means to present one's body as apparently dead, without in fact being dead. . . . Whenever a dead person's body looks as if it were still alive, i.e., when the skin does not wrinkle, the blood does not drain from the feet, the light of the eyes is not extinguished, . . . whenever such a 'dead' person returns to life after death or causes his corpse to disappear before he is buried, so that nothing but his clothes are left behind in the coffin, while his physical body dissolves of its own account or floats away—in all such cases we may speak of a 'separation from the corpse'" (Bauer 1974, p. 160).

The followers of Taoism could not ignore the fact that even immortals are subject to physical death. Only very few *hsien* are said to have withdrawn to the mountains and lived as hermits for hundreds of years, occasionally revealing their true identity to ordinary mortals. In this way, religious Taoism considered death itself a means of overcoming death: dying became an indispensable prerequisite for a transformation, without which immortality was unattainable.

Shih-i Chin., lit. *"Ten Wings";* the commentaries (*i-chuan*) on the → *I-ching,* which explain the main part of the *Book of Change(s)* from a Confucianist point of view.

The *Ten Wings* are: *Tuan-chuan* (*Commentary on the Decisions of Judgments* [2 parts]); *Hsiang-chuan* (*Commentary on the Images* [2 parts]); *Hsi-tz'u*—also called *Ta-chuan*—(*Great Commentary on the Appended Judgments* [2 parts]); *Wen-yen* (*Commentary on the Words of the Text*); *Sho-kua* (*Discussion of the Trigrams* [→ *pa-kua*]); *Hsü-kua* (*Sequence of the Hexagrams*); and *Tsa-kua* (*Miscellaneous Notes*).

The *Tuan-chuan* gives exact interpretations of decisions (judgments) on the basis of the structure and other elements of the hexagrams.

The *Hsiang-chuan* consists of two commentaries: one on the great images and one on the small images. The term *great images* refers to images associated with the two trigrams of each hexagram; *small images* refers to the individual lines of a hexagram. The commentary as a whole is based on the idea that each trigram of a hexagram represents certain images, which reflect the objective conditions prevailing in the world as well as the relevant laws of change. Therefore, a knowledge of the meaning of the trigrams and of their individual lines is indispensable for a genuine understanding of the meaning of the various hexagrams.

The *Hsi-tz'u* is the most important commentary of the *I-ching*. It explains the underlying concepts of the main text and their application in nature and society. The *Hsi-tz'u* is based on the premise that the → Tao arises from the interaction of yin and yang (→ yin-yang) and that the succession of yin and yang—rest and motion, soft and hard, and other opposites—is a basic law of nature.

The *Wen-yen* deals with the hexagrams → *ch'ien* and *k'un*, which are the most important, because they can be considered the basis of all other hexagrams.

The *Sho-kua* explains the eight trigrams (*pa-kua*) with reference to the things and concepts they represent.

The *Hsü-kua* explains the present sequence of the sixty-four hexagrams of the *Book of Change(s)*.

The *Tsa-kua* deals with the relationships between pairs of individual hexagrams, although the order followed in this commentary essentially differs from the present arrangement of the hexagrams.

According to tradition, the *Ten Wings* are said to have originated with Confucius (→ K'ung-tzu), but scholars have established that they date from the Warring States Period, i.e., the Ch'in or Han dynasty.

Shou Chin., lit. "long life"; preliminary stage of immortality (→ *ch'ang-sheng pu-ssu*). An almost magical power attaches to the pictogram for *shou,* which, for that reason, is represented in every conceivable shape.

Three ornamental representations of shou.

Taoists believe that a person's life span may be extended by the performance of certain exercises. In this context breathing and physical exercises, meditation, the avoidance of certain food substances, and sexual techniques are of particular significance.

Shou-hsing   → *san-hsing*

Shou-i   Chin., lit. "preserving the One"; Taoist meditation practice, in which deities believed to dwell within the body of the practitioner (→ *shen,* → Inner Deity Hygiene School) are visualized with a view to preventing them from leaving the body. The most frequently visualized deity is the Supreme One (→ T'ai-i), with whom the practitioner tries to unite.

The oldest form of this meditation is described in the → *T'ai-p'ing ching* as a "method for preserving the light of the One": "The method for preserving the light of the One forms the basis of the art of ensuring a long life (→ *ch'ang-sheng pu-ssu*). It enables the practitioner to seek out the deities and cause radiant light to appear from their abode. In order to preserve the light of the One the practitioner should, as soon as he perceives the first flicker of the flame, hold on to that image. At first the flame is red, then it becomes white and—after some considerable time—green. It is a radiant luminosity, which seems to spread ever wider. The practitioner should, however, try to gather and collect it. In this way he will create light throughout his body and drive out all illness. Anyone capable of maintaining this inner luminosity without interruption could be said to have mastered the art of living for 10,000 years" (trans. from Kaltenmark, *Lao-tzu und der Taoismus;* see Kaltenmark 1969).

This form of meditation on light was already known in the early stages of Taoism; e.g., → Lao-tzu often speaks of an inner light. In the → *Huai-nan-tzu* the appearance of light in the antechamber of the heart symbolizes the presence of the Tao.

The inner deities did not become objects of meditation until after the personification of the T'ai-i and its subsequent division into the three ones (→ *san-i*). Later, Taoists came to believe that by means of *shou-i* the essence (→ *ching*) could be spread throughout the body, that the three ones could then be made to become visible, and that the sacred embryo (→ *sheng-t'ai*) comes into being through a transformation of the breath (→ *ch'i*). An adept who succeeds in effecting such a transformation has attained immortality and ascends to Heaven in broad daylight (→ *fei-sheng*).

Shou-lao   Chin.; Taoist god of long life (→ *ch'ang-sheng pu-ssu*). Shou-lao is the popular name of Shou-hsing (→ *san-hsing*), the stellar deity of longevity. In representations he is usually shown with an enormously enlarged head. He carries a long staff and a pumpkin gourd, which contains the water of life. In his other hand he holds the peach of immortality, on which another symbol of immortality—a crane—is often depicted.

Shui-kuan   → *san-kuan*

Shun   2255–2205 B.C.E. or 2233–2184 B.C.E.; one of the legendary five emperors (→ *wu-ti*) and the successor of → Yao, who, on the suggestion of Four Mountains, the ruler of the four points of the compass, chose Shun to succeed him instead of his son. According to classical texts, Shun was an eastern barbarian, a potter, who cultivated his own fields. He is said to have traveled throughout the four directions and banished the ominous beings guarding their entrances. His successor was Yü the Great (→ Ta-yü).

In the *Analects* (*Lun-yü*) of Confucius (→ K'ung-tzu) and other Confucianist texts, Shun and his predecessor Yao are described as ideal rulers of the golden age and held up as a model for all future kings and emperors.

Ssu-hsiang Chin., lit. "four images"; a concept found in the → *I-ching*. Each of the four images—the building blocks of the sixty-four hexagrams—consists of two lines, each of which can be either yin or yang, the former being indicated by a broken line (– –), the latter by a continuous line (——). Yin symbolizes Earth, yang Heaven. The four images, with the permutations of yin and yang lines, represent the four possible combinations of Heaven and Earth, which give rise to the four seasons of the year.

The first image consists of two yang lines ═══ and is known as *t'ai-yang* (ripe yang); it signifies summer.

The second image consists of a yang line below a yin line ══; it is known as *shao-yin* (young yin) and signifies spring.

The third image consists of a yin line below a yang line ══, is known as *shao-yang* (young yang), and signifies autumn.

The fourth image consists of two yin lines ═ ═, is called *t'ai-yin* (ripe yin), and signifies winter.

By adding a third line (either yin or yang), which is meant to represent man as a link between Heaven and Earth, one arrives at the eight trigrams (→ *pa-kua*), the basic signs of the *Book of Change(s)*.

In another context, however, *ssu-hsiang* may also refer to the four seasons of the year, the four elements (water, fire, wood, and metal), or the four cardinal points.

The *Hsi-tz'u* (→ *Shih-i*) of the *I-ching* states,

"In change there is the supreme ultimate [→ *t'ai-chi*]. It created the two forms [→ *liang-i*]. From them arose the four images, and from these, in turn, the eight trigrams."

Ssu-ming Chin., lit. "Lord of Fate," better known as →
Tsao-chün, the hearth deity; one of the most important
deities of religious Taoism (→ *tao-chiao*). Ssu-ming determines the life span of each individual. He keeps a register
of our transgressions and omissions, of which he informs
the Supreme One (→ T'ai-i), at the same time asking him
to lengthen or shorten the life span of the individual in
question accordingly. Ssu-ming's *Book of Death* contains
the names of all who must die; his *Book of Life,* those of
the immortals (→ *hsien*).

According to the teaching of the Inner Deity Hygiene
School, Ssu-ming—like the Supreme One—lives in one
of the compartments of the inner cinnabar fields (→ *tan-t'ien*).

Ssu-ming goes back to the 8th century B.C.E. He is one of
the deities with whom shamans—the precursors of the later
Taoist → *fang-shih*—made contact. Even then, it was their
task to determine the life span of human beings. In the course
of time (→ Li Shao-chün), Ssu-ming became identified with
the hearth god Tsao-chün, who continues to be the most important deity in Chinese folk religion.

Sung Wen-ming Taoist writer and reformer, who lived
during the 6th century and—basing himself on the Buddhist model—popularized the idea of celibacy for Taoist
monks. He wrote commentaries on the works of → Chang
Tao-ling and played a decisive role in the spread of the
School of the Magic Jewel (→ *ling-pao p'ai*).

Sun Ssu-miao 581–682 C.E.; famous Taoist physician
and scholar of the T'ang Dynasty, on whom the Emper-
or Sung Hui-tsung—in recognition of his medical knowledge—bestowed the title *true human being* (→*chen-jen*).

Sun Ssu-miao systematized the clinical and diagnostic knowledge of his time, collected prescriptions, and was interested in acupuncture. A well-known collection of breathing exercises, known as *Thousand Ducet Recipes* (*Ch'ien-chin fang*) is attributed to him. In addition, he was the author of treatises on the prolongation of life, a method of meditation known as → *ts'un-ssu,* and a longevity breathing exercise known as "melting the breath" (→ *lien-ch'i*).

☆   ☆   ☆

Ta-i   Chin. → T'ai-i

T'ai-chi   Chin., lit. "ridge beam"; a term denoting the supreme ultimate. The concept occurs in the → *I-ching,* where it refers to ultimate reality, the primordial ground of being from which everything arises. The notion of *t'ai-chi* is of particular importance in neo-Confucianist philosophy (→ Chu Hsi). Essentially *t'ai-chi* is synonymous with → T'ai-i, the Supreme One.

The *I-ching* states, "Thus there is in the changes the great primordial beginning [*t'ai-chi*], which produces the two original energies [→ yin-yang]. These in turn produce the four images [→ *ssu-hsiang*], from which arise the eight trigrams [→ *pa-kua*]."

In neo-Confucianism *t'ai-chi* denotes the fusion of the two basic principles of the universe, namely → *li,* the normative, structural principle, and → *ch'i,* the formative primordial substance, matter. *T'ai-chi* itself is unlimited; since it contains *li* it is capable of giving rise to all things. This creative process is marked by alternating phases of rest and activity—rest being characteristic of yin, activity of yang. *T'ai-chi* combines these two. The alternation of the two energies produces the five elements (→ *wu-hsing*), which form the basis of all material existence.

T'ai chi ch'uan   Chin., lit. the "fist (-fighting method) of the supreme ultimate (→ *t'ai-chi*)"; a form of meditation based on physical movements and a method of self-defense.

The origins of T'ai chi ch'uan are said to go back to the 14th century. It is practiced by performing a sequence of soft, flowing, and slowly executed movements, which co-ordinate mind and body—i.e., consciousness, breath, and the body as such—and thereby produce a harmonization of the energies of yin and yang (→ yin-yang). T'ai chi ch'uan enhances the general state of health of the practitioner, dissolves tensions in the body, and removes blockages in the energy meridians. There are at present five main styles, the best known being the Yang style, named after its originators Yang Lu-ch'an and Yang Ch'eng-fu.

T'ai chi ch'uan is normally practiced alone, but there is a method known as *t'ui-shou* (roughly "pushing hands"), which involves a partner. T'ai chi ch'uan can also be performed with a lance, knife, or sword.

T'ai-ch'ing   Chin. → *san-ch'ing*

T'ai-chi-t'u   Chin., lit. "diagram of the supreme ultimate (→ *t'ai-chi*)"; a cosmological diagram created by the neo-Confucianist philosopher Chou Tun-i (1017–73 C.E.) to describe the process of how the ten thousand things (→ *wan-wu*) arise from the supreme ultimate (*t'ai-chi*), which he considered to be identical with → *wu-chi,* the unconditioned. From it arise the two energies of the → yin-yang, which in turn give rise to the four seasons, the five elements (→ *wu-hsing*), and the ten thousand things.

In his diagram Chou Tun-i connects Confucianist ideas with those of religious Taoism.

Chou Tun-i's commentary on the *t'ai-chi-t'u* states, "The unconditioned also is the supreme ultimate. The supreme ultimate moves and thereby creates yang. After this movement has reached its extreme, it returns to rest. Through this rest yin is created. When this rest has reached its extreme, it once again transforms into movement; thus movement and rest alternate and give rise to each other. When yin and yang act separately, the two energies [→ *liang-i*] can be clearly perceived. By the fusion of yin and yang the two energies become transformed into the five elements—fire, water, wood, metal, and earth [→ *wu-hsing*]. These five 'breaths' [→ *ch'i*], i.e. the elements, spread out in harmonious order and the four seasons come into being. The five elements are the same as yin and yang; yin and yang are the same as the supreme ultimate. The supreme ultimate originally is the unconditioned. When the five elements are brought into existence, each of them has its characteristic nature. The reality of the unconditioned, and the essences of the two energies and of the five elements, in miraculous fashion are one. The *ch'ien* principle becomes the masculine, and the *k'un* principle the feminine [→ *ch'ien* and *k'un*]. By their combination, the two energies yin and yang create the ten thousand things. By their unceasing production and reproduction, the ten thousand things transform themselves and are never exhausted."

T'ai-hsi   Chin., lit. "embryonic breathing"; a Taoist mediation practice for prolonging life. *T'ai-hsi* consists in learning to breathe like an embryo in the mother's body. Essentially it is a combination of holding the breath (→ *pi-ch'i*) and then allowing it to circulate (→ *hsing-ch'i*), thereby creating an immortality body, which is nourished by the breath (→ *shen-t'ai*). When the adept dies, this embryo separates from the corpse (→ *shih-chieh*) and the practitioner becomes an immortal (→ *hsien*).

At first the adept must learn to hold his breath. By daily practice he will manage to do so for ever longer periods—three, five, seven, nine (etc.) heartbeats until he can do so for approximately one thousand heartbeats. At this

Kuan-yin surrounded by magic formulae for producing embryonic breathing.

point, the practitioner can cure himself of any illnesses by means of the breath and is said to be approaching immortality. As the breath is held, it is directed through the body of the practitioner. This is done by a technique known as inner vision (→ *nei-kuan*). Normally, the air we inhale only reaches as far as the heart, entrails, liver, and kidneys; the Taoist practitioner, however, endeavors to direct it to the lower cinnabar field (→ *tan-t'ien*) situated in the region of the navel, and from there right down to the soles of his feet. The breath should then be made to rise along the spine to the brain, i.e., the upper cinnabar field, from there to the chest (middle cinnabar field), and from there, via the lungs, back to the throat. When it reaches the throat the breath is gradually swallowed. In this way the practitioner nourishes himself by the breath.

While the practitioner directs the breath through his body he endeavors to produce as much saliva (→ *yü-chiang*) as possible, by pressing his tongue against the palate. This accumulated saliva is swallowed, together with the breath. Breath and saliva are considered to be the best nourishment for those who strive for immortality: it is said that their body becomes light and transparent, so that they are able to ride on the clouds.

To realize the importance of embryonic breathing as a Taoist practice, it is necessary to remember that in the Taoist view man consists of breath, i.e., energy (→ *ch'i*). The body of a human being is formed by coarse Earth energies, while the life energy of a person circulates between Heaven and Earth. To attain immortality it is necessary to transform the coarse energies into pure energy. For that reason, practitioners of *t'ai-hsi* must also refrain from eating grain (→ *pi-ku*) because it is believed to consist of coarse energy.

Over the centuries, the Taoist understanding of embryonic breathing has radically changed. At first it was believed that the "breath" that is allowed to circulate through the body was the actual air the practitioner inhales. Since the time of the T'ang Dynasty, however, relevant texts state that what circulates through the body is the inner breath (→ *nei-ch'i*), which is synonymous with the primordial breath (→ *yüan-ch'i*) and corresponds to the energies that give rise to Heaven and Earth. This primordial breath the adept must preserve within his body. Normally it escapes through the mouth. The practitioner of *t'ai-hsi* therefore tries to store it in the lower cinnabar field and prevent it from mingling with the ordinary outer breath, i.e., the air he inhales. Both these breaths move synchronously within the body: as the outer breath rises during exhalation, the inner breath ascends from the lower cinnabar field; and as the outer breath sinks during inhalation, the inner breath descends to the lower cinnabar field.

The practice of allowing the inner breath to circulate begins by swallowing it (→ *yen-ch'i*), thereby preventing it from leaving the body together with the outer breath. After that the inner breath is collected and channeled toward the lower cinnabar field (also called → *ch'i-hai*, "ocean of the breath") via the alimentary tract, and from there through the whole of the body. The practitioner may also allow the inner breath to circulate freely without directing it in any way. This method is known as "melting the breath" (→ *lien-ch'i*).

T'ai-i   Chin., lit. "the Supreme One," also called Ta-i, "the Great One"; a Taoist concept that has undergone many changes of meaning in the course of its development. In philosophical Taoism (→ *tao-chia*) T'ai-i denotes the original cause of all appearances and thus is synonymous with → Tao.

The → Inner Deity Hygiene School considered the Supreme One to be the most important deity within the human body. As abstract concepts became personified, T'ai-i became → *san-i*, the highest deity of religious Taoism (→ *tao-chiao*).

Frequently, T'ai-i is synonymous with → *t'ai-chi*.

The origin of the notion of a Supreme One goes back to a time when shamanism was practiced in China. In the *Nine Songs* (*Chiu-ko*), which contain shamanistic ideas of the 4th and 3d century B.C.E., sacrifices to the Supreme One are already mentioned. In philosophical Taoism the idea of the "one" or "unique" can be traced back to the → *Tao-te ching*, Chapter 42 of which states, "Out of Tao, One is born; Out of One, Two; Out of Two, Three; Out of Three, the created universe (the Ten Thousand Things)" (Lin 1949).

The → *Chuang-tzu,* too, mentions the concept of T'ai-i or Ta-i. The following quote is from the *Spring and Autumn Annals* (→ *Lü-shih ch'un-ch'iu*): "T'ai-i produces the two forms; the two forms cause yin and yang (→ yin-yang) to arise." In a philosophical sense, the concept of T'ai-i constitutes an attempt at postulating a unity that forms a common ground of the multiplicity of appearances. At first the Supreme One was understood to be that which existed before the ten thousand things (→ *wan-wu*) came into being; later it was taken to be that in which the opposite qualities of yin and yang are united.

During the Han Dynasty the Supreme One was venerated as part of the triad of the three ones (→ *san-i*) and became a personalized deity. In the 2d century B.C.E. the Taoist magician Miu Chi introduced the T'ai-i cult to the ruler's court. Sacrifices were made to the Supreme One in the Palace of Long Life. The followers of this cult believed that the Supreme One was assisted by → Ssu-ming (Lord [or Ruler] of Fate). T'ai-i became the highest deity, and was said to dwell in the polar star, while the five legendary emperors—as rulers of the five cardinal points—became subjects of T'ai-i. The followers of the later Inner Deity Hygiene School believed that the Supreme One resides in the brain—specifically, in one of the nine compartments of the upper cinnabar field (→ *tan-t'ien*)—and from there rules the triad of the three ones. An adept of this school would endeavor to visualize T'ai-i as the supreme deity within his body and make contact with it so as to prevent it from leaving the body, thereby removing the inevitability of death.

Other schools venerate T'ai-i together with the god of the sun.

T'ai-i chin-hua tsung-chih Chin., lit. *"Teaching of the Golden Flower of the Supreme One"* (→ T'ai-i); 17th-century Taoist text in the tradition of one of the great movements of religious Taoism—the School of the Realization of Truth (→ *ch'üan-chen tao*). The *Teaching of the Golden Flower* is a synthesis of the meditative breathing exercises of the Inner Elixir School (→ *nei-tan*) and Chinese Zen (Ch'an) Buddhism.

The *T'ai-i chin-hua tsung-chih* became relatively well known in the West, owing to an (incomplete) translation (with a commentary by C. G. Jung) by the German sinologist Richard Wilhelm under the title *Das Geheimnis der goldenen Blüte* (English: *The Secret of the Golden Flower*; see Wilhelm 1938). In the original illustrations to this text, C. G. Jung saw parallels to symbols of psychic processes described by him. A complete translation of the text into German has been made by the Japanese Taoist scholar Mokusen Miyuki (1984).

The central feature of the *T'ai-i chin-hua tsung-chih* is the circulation of light (*fan-chao*). The (inner) light corresponds to pure yang (→ yin-yang), i.e., the true precelestial (→ *hsien-t'ien*) breath. The practitioner causes this light to circulate (→ *hsing-ch'i*) within his body and ultimately to crystallize, forming the "golden flower." By this method the mortal body can give birth to a new immortal being, the sacred embryo (→ *sheng-t'ai*).

The correct circulation of the light brings about a "return to the source" (→ *fu*), "where form and spirit have not yet separated within consciousness into knowing and understanding. This process is quite simply a search for a wholeness that existed within our body before Heaven and Earth came into existence" (trans. from the German version based on Mokusen Miyuki).

Some of the practical instructions for this form of meditation are similar to those for Buddhist shamatha/vipashyana (peaceful abiding/insight) meditation.

T'ai-i tao Chin., lit. "Way of the Supreme One"; a school of religious Taoism (→ *tao-chiao*). The *t'ai-i tao* was founded in the 12th century C.E. by Hsiao Pao-chen and is related to an earlier movement, the → *cheng-i tao* (Way of Right Unity), whose priests conducted ceremonies to cure diseases by the use of talismans (→*fu-lu*), magic formulae, and exorcism. The *t'ai-i tao* also contained Confucianist elements. Its followers were committed to strict obedience of monastic rules. It became extinct during the middle period of the Yüan Dynasty.

T'ai-p'ing ching Chin., lit. *"Book of Supreme Peace"*; a Taoist text existing in a number of differing versions, one of which has been ascribed to → Yü Chi. Only fragments of this text have been preserved. It formed the doctrinal basis of a school known as the Way of Supreme Peace (→ *t'ai-ping tao*) and dealt with all aspects of ancient Taoist teachings on such subjects as → yin-yang and the five elements (→ *wu-hsing*). In addition, it contained descriptions of deities and one of the earliest forms of Taoist meditation (→ *shou-i*) known to us.

T'ai-p'ing tao Chin., lit. "Way of Supreme Peace"; early Taoist school founded between 172 and 178 C.E. by → Chang Chüeh. It derived its name from its basic doctrinal text, the → *T'ai-ping ching*.

As a result of his spectacular methods of healing, Chang Chüeh attracted a vast following. In this he was helped by the extremely poor living conditions of the peasants, who not only had suffered epidemics and natural disasters but were also cruelly oppressed by the rulers of the Han Dynasty. Chang Chüeh's healing methods were based on magic. To be healed a believer had to confess his or her sins—which Chang Chüeh considered to be the root of their afflictions—at public mass ceremonies. A further important ritual of the *t'ai-p'ing tao* was fasting ceremonies (→ *chai*). In addition, the priests or officials of this school made use of talismans (→ *fu-lu*), holy water (*fu-shui*), magic formulae, etc. The *t'ai-p'ing tao* tried to explain some of its practices by a willfully convenient interpretation of the *Tao-te ching*. In actual fact, its teachings are very similar to those of Five-Pecks-of-Rice Taoism (→ *wu-tou-mi tao*). As a mass movement the *t'ai-p'ing tao* was furthermore of political importance. Its followers were organized on a strictly hierarchical basis which, moreover, fulfilled certain military functions. Its influence extended over eight provinces, subdivided into thirty-six districts, with between seven thousand and ten thousand followers in each. Every one of these districts was under the charge of a "general," while Chang Chüeh and his brothers were the leaders of the *t'ai-p'ing tao* as a whole. Chang named himself *celestial duke-general*. His two brothers bore the titles *terrestrial duke-general* and *people's duke-general,* respectively.

In 184 C.E. 36,000 followers of the Way of Supreme Peace rose against the central government. The rebels wore yellow head bands, which is why this rebellion is recorded in Chinese history as the Rising of the Yellow Turbans (*Huang-chin*). Although the rebellion was put down, and Chang Chüeh and his two brothers were executed, the Yellow Turbans for some considerable time remained a political power whose influence was by no means negligible.

Chang Chüeh announced the dawning of a new age and promised the people to establish a utopian order of the kind described in the *T'ai-p'ing ching*. This new age was to commence when the Blue Heaven (i.e., the rule of the Han Dynasty) was succeeded by the Yellow Heaven (i.e., the Way of Supreme Peace), which venerated → Huang-ti, the Yellow Emperor, as one of its founders. This was to happen in 184 C.E. The Rising of the Yellow Turbans was motivated by desire for equality, but in the end the followers of Chang Chüeh did not consider equality without peace worth fighting for.

T'ai-shan   the most important of China's sacred mountains. It is situated in Shantung Province in eastern China and for that reason also known as the Sacred Mountain in the East. From earliest times T'ai-shan has been a focal point of the religious life of the Chinese people; its deity, the Great Emperor of the Eastern Peak (→ T'ai-yüeh ta-ti) is one of the most famous Taoist gods. His daughter Sheng-mu, the Sacred Mother—patroness of women and children—also plays an important role in the faith of the people.

The Great Emperor of the Eastern Peak is generally believed to rule over Earth and mankind. He is subordinate only to the Jade Emperor (→ Yü-huang). His most important task is to determine the dates of a person's birth and death.

During the early centuries of our era T'ai-yüeh ta-ti was furthermore venerated as a deity of the dead; the soul of a person was believed to come from T'ai-shan and return there after that person's death. These souls were said to assemble on a hill at the foot of T'ai-shan, known as Hao-li-shan. Nevertheless, T'ai-shan's importance in the role of the Great Emperor of the Eastern Peak by far exceeded his significance as a deity of the dead, because the Jade Emperor had also entrusted him with the regulation of all worldly affairs.

Mount T'ai-shan is 1,545 meters high. Its top is reached via an ascending terrace of approximately 7,000 steps, known as the Stairway to Heaven. It is lined by temples dedicated to important Taoist deities; on its peak stands the temple of the Jade Emperor. Over the centuries, many artists have been drawn to this mountain and have left their inscriptions in the rock face at the side of the stairway. Last but not least, T'ai-shan is famous for its breathtakingly beautiful sunrise.

T'ai-shang kan-ying p'ien   Chin., lit. *"Treatise on Action and Recompense";* Taoist text from the time of the Sung Dynasty, mainly emphasizing the moral side of Taoism. Its central theme is the rewarding of good actions and the punishment of evil deeds by Heaven, on the basis of reports submitted by the three worms (→ *san-ch'ung*) and the Ruler of Fate (→ Ssu-ming). A person's life is shortened in proportion to the sins he or she has committed: a serious transgression costs 12 years, a lighter one 100 days. By performing 300 good deeds, a believer can become a terrestrial immortal (→ *hsien*), and after 1,300 good deeds, a celestial immortal.

The text lists a number of virtues that are not specifically Taoist and seems to have been influenced by Buddhist and Confucianist moral concepts.

Among the sins that are punished are contradicting your teacher, father, or older brother; refusing to obey an order; and slander. It is a woman's duty to obey and respect her husband. These demands show a strong Confucianist influence. In addition, a Taoist should not be dishonest, cruel, boastful, or false; he must not commit adultery and must always respect those older than him. Nor is he allowed to kill animals. These prohibitions reflect the Buddhist influence.

T'ai-shang lao-chün   Chin., lit. "Supreme Master Lao"; → Lao-chün

T'ai-shang tao-chün   Chin., lit. "Supreme Master of the → Tao," also called Ling-pao t'ien-tsun (lit. "Celestial Venerable of the Magic Jewel"); one of the highest deities in religious Taoism (→ *tao-chiao*). T'ai-shang tao-chün dwells in the Heaven of High Purity, one of the three pure heavens (→ *san-ch'ing*). He is also the patron of the second section (*tung*) of the Taoist canon (→ *Tao-tsang*).

Occasionally T'ai-shang tao-chün is identified with T'ai-shang lao-chün. Both are considered to be incarnations of the Taoist teachings—the Tao. Another such incarnation was → Lao-tzu, whose task it was to instruct mankind in the wisdom of the Tao.

T'ai-shan niang-niang   → Pi-hsia yüan-chün

T'ai-shih   Chin., 1. roughly "nourishing the embryo"; Taoist method of prolonging life; preliminary exercise for embryonic breathing (→ *t'ai-hsi*). When practicing *t'ai-shih* the Taoist adept, while inhaling, collects saliva (→ *yü-chiang*) in his mouth, by pressing his tongue against the palate. He then rolls back his head and swallows the accumulated saliva in three gulps, allowing it to ascend and feed the brain (→ *huan-ching pu-nao*) and to descend and moisten the five (internal) organs (→ *wu-tsang*).

2. lit. "great beginning"; the primordial beginning of the world—a state existing before form came into being (→ *Huai-nan-tzu*).

T'ai-yüeh ta-ti   Chin., lit. "Great Ruler of the Eastern Peak" (→ T'ai-shan); the most important and most popular of Taoist mountain deities. He is considered to be the ruler of Earth and mankind. His superior is the Jade Emperor (→ Yü-huang). His task consists in regulating human affairs and determining the time of a person's birth and death. In addition, he keeps a register of the lives and reincarnations of people and has the power to decide their social position, wealth, and progeny.

T'ai-yüeh ta-ti is usually portrayed in imperial dress. His facial expression is impersonal. In the houses of Taoist families, however, it is not his image that is venerated but his seal or amulets dedicated to him, which are said to have the power to dispel evil spirits.

To help him fulfill all these responsibilities, he has at his disposal an enormous administration that is a faithful copy of the actual administration of the state. There are separate departments to deal with various aspects of life: one for births, another for deaths, a third to determine a person's fate in the light of his good or bad deeds, etc. Additional offices are responsible for the various professions, natural phenomena, illnesses, and so on. The administrative staff is recruited from among the dead, but the performance of such functions may also be entrusted to living persons.

Ta-luo-t'ien   Chin. → t'ien

Tan   Chin., lit. "cinnabar"; the most important substance used in Taoist alchemy. The followers the Outer Alchemy (→ *wai-tan*) strive to produce purified cinnabar, the ingestion of which is said to have a life-prolonging effect. The most powerful type of cinnabar has been recycled nine times (*chiu-huan-tan*), because its life-prolonging power increases in proportion to the number of transformations it undergoes.

In his *Pao-p'u-tzu* the great Taoist alchemist → Ko Hung describes the properties of cinnabar as follows: "If a person ingests cinnabar that has been transformed once, it will take him three years to become an immortal (→ *hsien*). The same goal can be reached in two years by ingesting cinnabar that has been transformed twice and in one year if it has been transformed three times. Cinnabar of the fourth transformation allows the practitioner to become immortal within six months; and fifth-generation cinnabar, within a hundred days. Anyone who ingests cinnabar of the sixth transformation will become immortal after only forty days. In the case of cinnabar that has been transformed seven times, this process takes only thirty days, and a mere ten days if the practitioner ingests eight-fold purified cinnabar. The most powerful type of cinnabar, however, is one that has been transformed nine times: it renders a person immortal within three days. During these 'transformations' various other substances are added, which are difficult to obtain, especially in restless times such as these. In addition, it is necessary to tend the fire or furnace with extreme care in order to adjust its strength during the various phases of the operation."

In the symbolic language of the Inner Alchemy (→ *nei-tan*), cinnabar represents the energy of combined yin and yang (→ yin-yang) which is set alight in the lower cinnabar field (→ *tan-t'ien*) by means of various meditative breathing techniques. This practice ultimately results in the spiritual immortality of the Inner Alchemy practitioner.

Tan-t'ien Chin., lit. "cinnabar fields," elixir field; three regions of the human body through which the vital energy

(→ *ch'i*) flows: the upper cinnabar field is situated in the brain, the middle one near the heart, and the lower in the region of the navel.

Some Taoist schools believe that these three vital centers of the human body are inhabited by deities (→ Inner Deity Hygiene School, → *shen*) and harmful beings (→ *san-ch'ung*).

The lower cinnabar field—sometimes equated with the "ocean of breath" (→ *ch'i-hai*) is of particular significance in connection with various practices aimed at the prolongation of life, because it is the place where not only the → *ch'i* but also a man's semen (→ *ching*) and a woman's menstrual flow are accumulated (see also → *huan-ching*, → *nei-tan*, → *t'ai-hsi*, → *wai-tan*).

Each of the three cinnabar fields consists of nine compartments arranged in two rows (one of five and one of four). The only descriptions in existence refer to the various compartments of the upper cinnabar field. Among the most important of these is one referred to as government palace (*ming-t'ang-kung*), which, according to the teachings of the Inner Deity Hygiene School, is the dwelling place of → Huang-lao-chün and his retinue. In the central compartment—known as the palace of → *ni-huan* (or *ni-wan* after the Sanskrit Buddhist term *nirvana*)—resides the highest body deity, the → T'ai-i, or Supreme One.

Tao Chin., lit. "Way"; central concept of Taoism (→ *tao-chia*, → *tao-chiao*) and origin of its name. The Tao also is the central feature of the *Tao-te ching* and the → *Chuang-tzu*.

Although the original meaning of the pictogram for Tao is "Way," it can also denote "Teaching." From earliest

times the term has been used in the sense of human behavior and moral laws—the Way of man; this certainly
is its meaning in Confucianist texts. The *Tao-te ching*
of → Lao-tzu is the first text to ascribe a metaphysical
meaning to the term, in the sense that it is seen as the
all-embracing first principle, from which all appearances
arise. It is a reality that gives rise to the universe. Lao-
tzu referred to it as the Tao only because there was no
other adequate term available. In the translation of Chang
Chung-yuan (1963):

> There was something complete and nebulous
> Which existed before the Heaven and Earth,
> Silent, invisible,
> Unchanging, standing as One,
> Unceasing, ever-revolving,
> Able to be the Mother of the World.
> I do not know its name and call it Tao.

The Tao then is nameless, unnamable. Chapter 1 of the
Tao-te ching (Feng & English 1972) states:

> The Tao that can be told
> is not the eternal [→ *ch'ang*] Tao.
> The name that can be named
> is not the eternal name.

The Tao is the mother who gives birth to and nourishes
the ten thousand things (→ *wan-wu*). It is the primordial
source of all being. In Chapter 6 of the *Tao-te ching* it is
compared to a "mysterious female" whose gateway is the
root of Heaven and Earth. (During the later phases of Taoism this passage was frequently quoted by Taoist adepts to
justify certain sexual practices [→ *fang-chung shu*] as a
means of becoming one with the Tao.)

All things, furthermore, return to the Tao. This is a universal law. Enlightenment (→ *ming*) in a Taoist sense is the realization of this universal law of the return of all things to the Tao (→ *fu*). This return is something to which the Tao itself is subject: "Return is the movement of the Tao."

Chapter 14 of the *Tao-te ching* describes the Tao as invisible, inaudible, unfathomable, the form of the formless and eternal. The function of the Tao is being; its essence is nonbeing. It is the Great One, in which all opposites are canceled.

That which you look at but cannot see
Is called the Invisible.
That which you can listen to but cannot hear
Is called the Inaudible.
That which you grasp but cannot hold
Is called the Unfathomable.
None of these three can be inquired after,
Hence they blend into one.
Above no light can make it lighter,
Beneath no darkness can make it darker.
Unceasingly it continues
But it is impossible to be defined.
Again it returns to nothingness.
Thus it is described as the Form of the Formless,
The Image of the Imageless.
Hence it is called the Evasive.
It is met with but no one sees its face;
It is followed but no one sees its back.
To hold to the Tao of old,
To deal with the affairs at hand,
In order to understand the primordial beginnings,
That is called the rule of Tao.
(Chang Chung-yuan 1963)

The Tao acts spontaneously and in accordance with its nature (→ *tzu-jan*). Its effect and activity are without intent (→ *wu-wei*), yet there is nothing that remains undone. In the phenomenal world, the Tao manifests through its power, its "virtue" (→ *te*), which all things receive from the Tao and by which they become that which they are.

All Taoists strive to become one with the Tao. This cannot be achieved by trying to understand the Tao intellectually; the adept becomes one with the Tao by realizing within himself its unity, simplicity (→ *p'u*), and emptiness.

This requires intuitive understanding, which Book 22, Chapter 2 of the *Chuang-tzu* describes as follows: "*Tao* may be known by no thoughts, no reflections. It may be approached by resting in nothingness, by following nothing, pursuing nothing. . . . The Sage teaches a doctrine which does not find expression in words" (Chang Chung-yuan 1963). The Tao thus is realized by abiding in silence, and the way to silence is found by "letting go": "To search for knowledge means to acquire day after day; to seek the Tao means to let go day after day." In the *Tao-te ching* silence corresponds to the return to the source; by abiding in stillness all inner and outer activity comes to rest and all limitations and conditions fade away. This is when the celestial light shines forth, allowing us to behold our true selves and realize the absolute (*Chuang-tzu* 23.2).

This process of submerging oneself in stillness is also described in Chapter 16 of the *Tao-te ching* (Chang Chung-yuan 1963):

Devote yourself to the utmost Void;
Contemplate earnestly in Quiescence.
All things are together in action,

But I look into their non-action.
For things are continuously moving, restless,
Yet each is proceeding back to its origin.
Proceeding back to the origin means Quiescence.
To be in Quiescence is to see "being-for-itself."

Taoism has developed a number of practices to facilitate the realization of the Tao. Both the *Chuang-tzu* and the *Tao-te ching* contain guidelines for producing a state of meditative absorption. In this context breathing exercises are particularly important, either as a preliminary practice or as a means of enhancing the meditative process. They were developed by the School of the Inner Elixir (→ *nei-tan*).

Even in pre-Confucianist China the Tao was a symbol for human ideals, and a great variety of philosophical schools subsequently incorporated it into their system. In this context Chuang-tzu makes the following observation: "There are many masters in the school of philosophy in the world of today. Each of them claims to have found the correct answer. When we ask, 'Where is the philosophy of the ancient *Tao*?' we may answer, 'It is in every system'" (Chang Chung-yuan 1963).

The early Chinese Buddhists made use of Taoist terminology to express their ideas and saw the Tao as the Way to nirvāna. There is also a famous Zen saying, "The wondrous Tao consists in carrying water and chopping wood."

Tao-chia Chin., philosophical Taoism; one of two streams of Taoism, the other being religious Taoism (→ *tao-chiao*). Philosophical Taoism bases itself on the writings of → Lao-tzu (→ *Tao-te ching*) and → Chuang-tzu, who are considered to be its founders, → Lieh-tzu and → Yang Chu being their acknowledged successors.

Followers of philosophical Taoism strive to achieve mystical union with the → Tao by meditation and by following the nature of the Tao in thought and action. Unlike the adherents of religious Taoism, they are not interested in attaining physical immortality.

The term *tao-chia* was first used during the Han Dynasty and refers to the central meaning of Tao as the Way. The Tao is thus understood to be the all-embracing principle from which all things arise. The ideology of philosophical Taoism is strongly marked by political considerations. A central feature is the concept of *wu-wei*—spontaneous, unmotivated action—which philosophical Taoism emphasizes as a model for rulers. From an ethical point of view, philosophical Taoism is the opposite of → Confucianism, whose cardinal virtues of humanity (→ *jen*) and uprightness (→ *i*) it rejects, because they veil the true nature of man and impede the Tao.

The political ideas of philosophical Taoism soon were adopted by other philosophical schools, but during the Han Dynasty philosophical Taoism lost a great deal of influence when Emperor Wu-ti (156–87 B.C.E.) proclaimed Confucianism the official state religion. At the same time, however, the teachings of philosophical Taoism spread among the people and played a decisive role in the later development of religious Taoism, which venerates the deified Lao-tzu as its founder.

During the Wei and Chin dynasties the *tao-chia* experienced a revival in the form of neo-Taoism (→ *hsüan-hsüeh*), which combined Confucianist and Taoist ideas. In addition, philosophical Taoism played an important part in the establishment of Buddhism in China: it has been said that the Chinese form of Zen (Ch'an) could not have flowered if philosphical Taoism had not prepared the ground for it. The philosophical ideas of Lao-tzu and Chuang-tzu live on in the hearts and minds of the Chinese people and find their most immediate expression in Chinese painting and poetry.

Tao-chiao Chin., religious Taoism; one of the two streams of Taoism, the other being philosophical Taoism (→ *tao-chia*). The *tao-chiao* embraces all Taoist schools and movements whose aim consists in the attainment of immortality (→ *ch'ang-sheng pu-ssu*). The most important of these are: the → Inner Deity Hygiene School, Five-Pecks-of-Rice Taoism (→ *wu-tou-mi tao*), the Way of Supreme Peace (→ *t'ai-p'ing tao*), the School of the Magic Jewel (→ *ling-pao p'ai*), the Way of Right Unity (→ *cheng-i tao*), and the Way of the Realization of Truth (→ *ch'üan-chen tao*).

The methods employed to attain immortality range from meditation to alchemical practices, physical exercises, breathing exercises, and sexual practices.

Religious Taoism is the product of several philosophical and religious movements. The teachings of → Lao-tzu, → Chuang-tzu, and → Lieh-tzu (350–250 B.C.E.), which form the basis of philosophical Taoism, also left their mark on the *tao-chiao*. In addition, there already existed a hygiene school whose followers strove to lengthen their life by certain breathing practices (→ *hsing-ch'i*) and physical exercises (→ *tao-yin*). There also was the doctrine of the five elements (→ *wu-hsing*), formulated toward the end of the 4th century B.C.E. by → Tsou Yen, whose followers searched for the elixir of immortality (→ *wai-tan*, → *nei-tan*). Another influence was the search for the isles of the immortals (→ P'eng-lai, → Fang-chang, → Ying-chou), which were first mentioned in Lieh-tzu's writings.

Between ca. 220 and 120 B.C.E. the teachings of the various movements became intermingled. This development was prompted by the activities of the Taoist magicians (→ *fang-shih*) (also → Li Shao-chün). That also was the time when various deities began to be venerated within the *tao-chiao* (→ Tsao-chün, → T'ai-i, → *san-i*).

During the early centuries of our era, the Inner Deity Hygiene School and other religious mass movements came into being. Western scholars often refer to these as the Taoist church. In fact, they constitute the actual *tao-chiao*.

In the first half of the 2d century B.C.E. → Chang Tao-ling founded what became known as Five-Pecks-of-Rice Taoism. His followers venerated Lao-tzu as their founder and quoted the → *Tao-te ching* as a doctrinal source. Its leaders or patriarchs called themselves celestial masters (→ *t'ien-shih*). Not long after that → Chang Chüeh established the School of the Way of Supreme Peace, whose followers—the so-called Yellow Turbans—in 184 C.E. rebelled against the central government. Both these schools made use of talismans (→ *fu-lu*) and conducted mass fasting and healing ceremonies (→ *chai,* → *ho-ch'i*). This accounts for their extraordinary popularity.

In 140 C.E. → Wei P'o-yang wrote his celebrated *Chou-i ts'an-t'ung-ch'i,* considered to be the oldest alchemical text preserved for posterity. In publishing his encyclopedic *Pao-p'u-tzu,* → Ko Hung tried to unite the various streams of religious Taoism. The *Pao-p'u-tzu* is a systematically arranged compendium of methods and practices aimed at becoming an immortal (→ *hsien*). Around the same period the School of the Magic Jewel became established and, in the course of time, displaced the Inner Deity Hygiene movement.

In the 5th century C.E. → K'ou Ch'ien-chih strove to carry out a reform by ridding Taoism of the damaging influence of the Chang lineage (→ *t'ien-shih*) and proclaiming a number of moral rules. This led to the foundation of the Northern

Way of the Celestial Masters, while Lu Hsiu-ching, basing himself on the teachings of the Chang clan, founded the Southern Way of the Celestial Masters.

During the 6th century the alchemists abandoned their search for an outer elixir and turned toward the teachings on the inner elixir; this led to a gradual fusion of the practices of the followers of the inner elixir, the inner breath teachings (→ *nei-ch'i*), and Zen Buddhism. Later, → Chang Po-tuan became one of the most prominent proponents of this syncretist movement.

In the 7th century the Emperor T'ang Wu-tsung de facto proclaimed Taoism a state religion: each district had to have its own Taoist temple. The Taoist canon (→ *Tao-tsang*) was compiled—and first appeared in print—during the Sung Dynasty. Taoism reached its greatest flowering under this imperial protection.

Under the Yüan Dynasty the Southern and the Northern Way of the Celestial Masters and various other movements merged to form the Way of Right Unity. In 1167 C.E. → Wang Ch'un-yang founded the School for the Realization of Truth, which incorporated Buddhist teachings and elements of Confucianism.

Some smaller schools—such as the Way of the Supreme One (→ *t'ai-i tao*)—came into being during the transition period between the Chin and Yüan dynasties, but were very short-lived. The survivors were the two great movements of the *ch'üan-chen tao* and *cheng-i tao*. The main doctrines of religious Taoism are based on the → Tao, which is understood as emptiness and the primordial ground of all being. From it arise the cosmos, the five elements, → yin-yang, and the ten thousand things (→ *wan-wu*). Among its objects of veneration are the three pure ones (→ *san-ch'ing*), which are seen as personifications of the Tao, and the celestial venerables (→ *t'ien-tsun*), the most important of whom is Tao-te t'ien-tsun, i.e., Lao-tzu.

The followers of religious Taoism strive to attain physical immortality. Among the practices directed at realizing that aim are *tao-yin*, embryonic breathing (→ *t'ai-hsi*), *nei-tan* (inner elixir), *wai-tan* (outer elixir), *fu-lu* (talismans), → *pi-ku* (abstention from eating grain), and sexual practices (→ *fang-chung shu*). The most important ceremonies are communal fasts (→ *chai*), collective confession, and healing sessions and rituals for the veneration of deities.

T'ao Hung-ching 456–536 C.E.; Taoist scholar and physician; a follower of → Ko Hung. By applying the strict Confucianist hierarchy of the state to the world of the immortals (→ *hsien*) and deities (→ *shen*), T'ao Hung-ching was the first to classify the Taoist deities. In his writings he endeavored to establish a connection between Confucianism, Buddhism, and Taoism.

T'ao Hung-ching lived on Mount Mao, where he was taught the secret of talismans (→ *fu-lu*) and other magical practices. In his search for life-prolonging substances he visited all the famous Taoist mountains. He was well known for his profound knowledge in relation to the → yin-yang, astrology, and geomancy. His prophecies concerning future events of national importance frequently turned out to be correct, as a result of which the emperor invited him to court on several occasions, but T'ao refused to leave the mountains. However, the emperor's respect for him was so great that he sought him out in his hermitage to benefit from his counsel. Because of this role as imperial advisor T'ao became known as the "Prime Minister in the Mountains."

In addition, T'ao Hung-ching possessed great knowledge of medicinal herbs, which he classified systematically, thus making an important contribution to Chinese phamacology.

T'ao Hung-ching's hierarchy of the deities and immortals consisted of seven levels, each of them ruled by a main deity residing at the center of that particular level. There are numerous deities on each level, their importance diminishing proportionate to their distance from its center. Beyond the fifth level some of the figures have no specific location assigned to them.

Each level corresponds to a celestial palace, in which the deities and immortals of that particular level reside. The first level is that of pure jade; its central deity is the Celestial Venerable of the Primordial Beginning (→ Yüan-shih t'ien-tsun). On the third level we find the major figures of Chinese mythology, such as → Yao, → Shun, and Yü the Great (→ Ta-yü) but also such historical figures as Confucius (→ K'ung-tzu). Here → Lao-tzu ranks as an immortal of the left wing but—under another name—also holds the central place on the fourth level, with → Chang Tao-ling among those placed to his left.

Taoism   collective term used in the West for two essentially different movements of Chinese philosophy and religion, namely philosophical Taoism (→ *tao-chia*), whose most important representatives were → Lao-tzu and → Chuang-tzu, and religious Taoism (→ *tao-chiao*), which consisted of various schools. Philosophical Taoism is a mystical teaching about the → Tao, i.e., the Way, and → *wu-wei* (unmotivated action), whereas the main characteristic of the various streams of religious Taoism consists in their teachings on how to attain immortality (→ *ch'ang-sheng pu-ssu*).

(Also → *cheng-i tao,* → *ch'üan-chen tao,* → Lieh-tzu, → *nei-tan,* → *wai-tan,* → *wu-tou-mi tao.*)

Tao of the Celestial Masters   → *t'ein-shih*

Tao-shih   Chinese scholar(s) and priest(s) of religious Taoism (→ *tao-chiao*). From approximately the 4th century C.E., the *tao-shih* have been the leaders of Taoist congregations. Their office was passed on by inheritance. They were responsible for supervising all religious matters such as the various rituals and ceremonies (→ *chai*) and assisted members of their flock in times of difficulty by the use of talismans (→ *fu-lu*), spells to ward off demons and evil spirits, etc.

The *tao-shih* of the School of Right Unity (→ *cheng-i tao*) lived with their families near a monastery (→ *kuan*) and were ruled by a celestial master (→ *t'ien-shih*). Those of the School of the Realization of Truth (→ *ch'üan-chen tao*) lived in strict celibacy. The office and title of the *tao-shih* originated with a religious movement known as Five-Pecks-of-Rice Taoism (→ *wu-tou-mi tao*). *Tao-shih* usually wore a long gray or black gown with wide sleeves. They allowed their hair to grow and pinned it up in a knot. At ceremonies they wore a robe consisting of 240 segments arranged on 10 strips of material. This robe was gathered around the waist by a belt adorned with images of clouds. On their head they wore a five-pointed crown.

Tao-shih living in a monastery were subject to strict monastic discipline. They had to observe a large number of fast days, and their daily life was governed by five rules of behavior: they were not allowed to kill, had to abstain from eating meat and drinking alcohol, were forbidden to lie or steal, and could not marry or enter any other kind of sexual relationship.

Beyond this basic moral code, monastic Taoism had additional sets of ten, twenty-seven, or more rules. The School for the Realization of Truth divided these into three stages according to their difficulty: on the first stage the *tao-shih* had to obey rules relating to the "dawning of truth" (*ch'u-chen chieh*) and were referred to as "noble ones in transformation." The second stage contained three hundred rules relating to the intermediate goal (*chung-chi chieh*), and aspirants on this level were known as "noble persons of virtue." *Tao-shih* on the highest level had to observe the rules relating to a celestial immortal (*t'ien-hsien*) and were known as "noble persons in the → Tao." These rules and guidelines governed both the personal behavior of monks as well as the life of the monastic community as a whole. They related to dress, diet, the use of monastic facilities, the performance of religious practices, the relationship between teacher and student, ways of assisting people on their spiritual path toward enlightenment, etc. At the ordination of a *tao-shih* a certain number of fully ordained *tao-shih* had to be present. Analogous to Buddhist practice, *tao-shih* took refuge in the Tao, the Taoist scriptures (→ *Tao-tsang*), and the Taoist masters.

Tao-te ching Chin., lit. *"The Book of the Way and Its Power";* a work attributed to → Lao-tzu. It consists of five thousand pictograms and for that reason is often referred to by the Chinese as *Text of the Five Thousand Signs.* The *Tao-te ching* forms the basis of both philosophical Taoism (→ *tao-chia*) and religious Taoism (→ *tao-chiao*). According to tradition, it was written by Lao-tzu during the 6th century B.C.E., but scholars now take the general view that it cannot have come into existence before the 4th or 3d century B.C.E. The oldest existing copy dates from between 206 and 195 B.C.E.

According to legend the *Tao-te ching* was given by Lao-tzu to → Yin Hsi, the Guardian of the Mountain Pass, before continuing on his journey toward the West. It consists of eighty-one short chapters, the first thirty-seven of which form *The Book of the Way* (→ Tao), and the remaining forty-four the *Book of the → Te*. The reason for this somewhat arbitrary division is that Chapter 1 deals with the Tao and Chapter 38 with the *te*. The *Tao-te ching* contains, apart from Taoist ideas, teachings of other philosophical movements. Its central philosophy, however, revolves around two concepts: the Tao or (Way), and the *te* (virtue or power). Further central ideas of the *Tao-te ching* are → *wu-wei* (unmotivated action) and → *fu* (the return of all things to their origin or source).

The *Tao-te ching* sees the Tao as the all-embracing ultimate principle, which existed before Heaven and Earth. It is unnamable and cannot be described; it is the mother of all things; it causes everything to arise, yet acts not. Its power (*te*) is that which phenomena receive from the Tao and which makes them what they are.

The goal of philosophical Taoism consists in becoming one with the Tao by realizing within oneself the universal law of the return of everything to its source (→ *fu*). For this the aspirant must acquire the emptiness (→ *wu*) and simplicity (→ *p'u*) of the Tao and abide in nonaction (*wu-wei*). According to the *Tao-te ching*, the latter quality is also characteristic of the exemplary ruler, whose virtues it describes in some detail: the ideal ruler is one of whom the people are unaware, because he interferes as little as possible in the natural flow of things. He lays down the barest minimum of laws, whereby the number of transgressors is reduced, and attaches no value to the traditional Confucianist virtues of uprightness (→ *i*) and humanity (→ *jen*). He endeavors to diminish wishes and desires by reducing their objects, so that the hearts of the people may not be confused and simplicity—*p'u*—may be realized. Originally the *Tao-te ching* was known simply as the *Lao-tzu;* later it received its present title from an emperor of the Han Dynasty. By the designation *ching* it was raised to the same level as the Confucianist classics. More than fifty commentaries—reflecting a great variety of views—on the *Tao-te ching* have been preserved. It is quoted and referred to not only by Taoist movements but also by the Yin-Yang School (→ *yin-yang chia*), scholars of constitutional law, and followers of the → *I-ching*.

Religious Taoism (→ *tao-chiao*) venerates Lao-tzu, under his title of → Lao-chün, as its founder and bases its teaching on the main concept of the *Tao-te ching,* i.e., the Tao. For that reason, the followers of the *tao-chiao* consider it one of the sacred books: Chang Tao-ling and his descendants instructed their followers in its teaching and applied its principles. In addition, the basic text of the → *t'ai-p'ing tao,* the → *T'ai-p'ing ching,* refers to the *Book of the Way and Its Power* as its philosophical basis. Alchemists such as → Wei P'o-yang and → Chang Po-tuan quote the *Tao- te ching* in justification of their practices, and rulers like the Han emperor Wen-ti, the T'ang emperor Hsüan-tsung, and the Ming emperor T'ai-tzu made its doctrine the basis of their rulership.

Tao-tsang   Chin., Taoist canon; a collection of writings that form the basis of Taoist doctrine. The oldest sections of the *Tao-tsang* date from the 5th century C.E.; the present complete version of the canon stems from the time of the Ming Dynasty and consists of 1,476 works in 5,486 volumes. The individual works contained in it do not bear the names of their authors and are undated.

Apart from purely Taoist works dealing with all aspects of the doctrine, the *Tao-tsang* also contains texts on medicine, botany, astronomy, etc. According to tradition, most of the purely Taoist texts were revelations and thus represent a means of communication between the deities (→ *shen*) and mankind. This explains the belief that a proper understanding of the ancient Taoist texts makes it possible to penetrate the secrets of immortality.

Various works about Taoist deities and immortals (→ *hsien*) existed already at the beginning of the common era, and the catalogs of such writings compiled during the 5th and 6th centuries must be considered precursors of the *Tao-tsang,* the actual compilation of which began in the 8th century when—according to varying sources—3,744, 5,700, or even 7,300 volumes were compiled. This first canon achieved wide dissemination but was no longer extant by the end of the 10th century. In 1010 C.E. the then emperor entrusted a Taoist scholar with making a new compilation, which originally consisted of 4,359 volumes. A few years later this was expanded to 4,565 volumes, divided into three main sections and four subsections: the three main sections are known as *tung,* which, literally translated, means "grotto" (many of the texts were believed to have been concealed in grottos) but can also be understood as "penetrating a secret." Each *tung* is preceded by a text revealed by an important deity of the Taoist pantheon. The first section thus stands under the sign of the Celestial Venerable of the Primordial Beginning (→ Yüan-shih t'ien-tsun), the second under that of the Supreme Lord of the Tao (→ T'ai-shang tao-chün), and the third under the Supreme Master Lao (T'ai-shang lao-chün), i.e., Lao-tzu himself. In time, however, the view that all three sections were revealed by Lao-tzu gained ground and finally became firmly established.

Between 1111 and 1118 C.E. this last version was once again expanded and finally printed in 5,481 volumes. It has become the model on which all subsequent editions of the *Tao-tsang* were based. Due to the hostilities between the Taoists and Buddhists during the Yüan Dynasty, many Taoist scriptures were burned so that part of the canon was irretrievably lost.

Tao-yin   Chin., lit. "stretching and contracting [of the body]"; Taoist practice of guiding the breath, consisting of a combination of physical and breathing exercises that promote and facilitate the circulation of the breath within the body by resolving tensions and blockages. *Tao-yin* may also be practiced as simply a health exercise; according to the Taoist view it dispels illness as well as bad → *ch'i* and prolongs life. Taoist adepts practice it as a preliminary exercise for → *hsing-ch'i* ("letting the breath circulate").

The various sequences of performing *tao-yin* exercises are said to have originated with immortals (→ *hsien*) such as → P'eng-tzu or Lü Tung-pin (→ *pa-hsien*).

Nowadays it is usual to perform a sequence of eight exercises. During their performance it is essential that all physical movements as well as ways of relaxing and tensing and the actual flow of the breath itself are followed with wakeful attention. The eight exercises are as follows (cf. Pálos 1984, p. 175):

1. "Clapping the teeth together and drumming" (→ *k'ou-ch'ih*, → *t'ien-ku*).

2. "Turning to the left, looking to the right" and vice versa: the head and shoulders are moved in opposite directions to loosen and relax that region of the body.

3. "Stirring the ocean and swallowing the saliva": the tongue is rotated around the cavity of the mouth and then pressed against the palate, thereby promoting the production of saliva, which is then swallowed (→ *yü-chiang*).

4. "Massaging the area around the sacrum with both hands": after rubbing his hands to warm them, the practitioner massages the area on either side of the sacrum in a downward direction with both his hands. This exercise relieves back pain and menstrual difficulties.

5. "Stretching the arms": the hands are made into fists as the arms are extended sideways, then moved back in the direction of the body as if pulling something toward it. This exercise is beneficial for people who suffer from a warped spine.

6. "Double winds": the practitioner rotates shoulders and arms in forward and backward directions while his hands (made into fists) rest against his chest. This stimulates the organ of breathing.

7. "Raising the palms (of the hands)": both arms are extended to the front with the palms of the hands turned upward, then the forearms are angled so that the palms are opposite the face. This exercise harmonizes the activity of the stomach and intestines.

8. "Relaxed muscles, loose joints": the practitioner extends his legs from a sitting position, inclines his head forward, at the same time extending his arms to grab his toes. This exercise relaxes the body and stimulates the circulation.

Ta-tung chen-ching　Chin., lit. *"True Book of the Great Secret"*; a text of the → Inner Deity Hygiene School, dating from the 2d–4th centuries C.E. Its thirty-nine chapters— each of which was revealed by a different deity—describe in esoteric language and considerable detail the most important deities of the body, thus helping the practitioner to recognize them when he encounters them in his meditative visualizations. The highest such deity is the Supreme One (→ T'ai-i).

Ta-yü Chin., lit. "Yü the Great," also known as the "Master of the Way"; mythological founder of the Hsia Dynasty. Because he is said to have stopped a great deluge by making holes through the mountains and thus producing outlets through which the waters, which had already risen up to Heaven, could drain away, Ta-yü is sometimes referred to as the creator of the world. In addition it is believed that he traversed the nine provinces of the world (the figure nine is a symbol of wholeness) and made the land arable by regulating the course of the waters and connecting the nine provinces with each other. To this task he applied such energy that he began to walk with a limp. His limping gait became the model for the "step of Yü" (→ *Yü-pu*), a shamanic dance performed by Taoist masters.

According to legend, Great Yü received the river diagram (→ *Ho-t'u* and *Lo-shu*) from a turtle that emerged from the Yellow River.

Another tradition states that during his work Yü would turn himself into a bear. Every day his wife would bring him his food as soon as he beat his drum. One day he was breaking up rocks, the fragments of which crashed against each other, producing a sound like a drum. His wife came running with the food and fled again when she beheld a bear. Yü pursued her, but she ran on until she fell exhausted to the ground and turned to stone. As she was pregnant at the time, the stone continued to grow. At the end of the tenth month Yü opened her petrified body with a stroke of his sword and his son Ch'i (lit. "the Opener") was born.

Te Chin., lit. "virtue, power"; the energy of the → Tao; the inherent principle, i.e., the qualities or nature each thing receives from the Tao, making it what it is, and through which it manifests in the phenomenal world. In addition, *te* signifies the virtue attained by realizing the Tao.

The *Tao-te ching* accords to *te* the same attributes as to the Tao itself: it is deep, profound, mysterious; it enables man to return to childlike innocence, natural simplicity (→ *p'u*).

Confucius (→ K'ung-tzu) considers *te* to be a quality possessed by noble and civilized human beings and argues that a sage, because of his *te,* becomes a cultural ideal and a model for his fellowmen.

Concerning the Tao and *te,* Chapter 51 of the *Tao-te ching* (Feng & English 1972) states,

All things arise from Tao.

They are nourished by Virtue [*te*].

They are formed from matter.

They are shaped by environment.

Thus the ten thousand things all respect Tao and honor Virtue.

Respect of Tao and honor of Virtue are not demanded,

But they are in the nature of things.

Therefore all things arise from Tao.

By Virtue they are nourished,

Developed, cared for,

Sheltered, comforted,

Grown, and protected.

Creating without claiming,

Doing without taking credit,

Guiding without interfering,

This is the Primal Virtue.

Ten Wings   → *Shih-i*

Ti   Chin., lit. Lord, God, also known as Shang-ti (Supreme Lord); the oldest Chinese designation for a supreme being. In legend, Ti is the primordial ancestor of the people of Shang (2d millennium B.C.E.). The meaning of *Ti* in Taoist texts varies.

On the basis of oracular inscriptions, scholars have established that in ancient times Ti was considered one of the highest rulers and was credited with supernatural powers as well as the ability to influence natural phenomena such as rain, drought, the harvest, etc. He was furthermore thought to direct and determine the fate of people, but was not venerated as a lord of fate in religious rites. Later *Ti* became an honorary title for royal ancestors.

At the time of Confucius the terms *Ti* and *Shang-ti* had already been replaced by *t'ien* (Heaven). In the *Chuang-tzu*, *Ti* is used in the sense of "God"; for example, death is referred to as the "loosening of the bands by Ti." The *Tao-te ching* considers Ti to be subordinate to the → Tao. Other philosophers considered Ti to have been a personal god.

T'iao-ch'i   Chin., lit. "harmonizing the breaths"; Taoist breathing technique performed as a preliminary to other breathing exercises (→ *fu-ch'i*, → *hsing-ch'i*, → *lien-ch'i*).

The practitioner of *t'iao-ch'i* assumes the prescribed posture (usually the lotus position) and begins by inhaling and exhaling three times to dissolve any blockages. He then calms his mind and endeavors to forget his body. He continues to breathe calmly and deeply, exhaling the contaminated breath through his mouth and inhaling the pure breath through the nose. This cycle is repeated six or seven times.

T'ien Chin., lit. "Heaven"; religious Taoism (→ *tao-chiao*)—following the example of Buddhism—recognizes thirty-six heavens, arranged on six levels and inhabited by different deities.

The lowest level consists of the six heavens of desire. This is followed by the eighteen heavens of the world of forms. Above these are the four heavens of formlessness, followed by the four heavens of Brahma. On the penultimate level are the heavens of the three pure ones (→ *san-ch'ing*), which are inhabited by the celestial venerables (→ *t'ien-tsun*) and are the most important heavens in Taoism. The highest Taoist heaven is the *ta-luo-t'ien,* the Heaven of the Great Web. The descriptions of this supreme heaven in ancient texts vary considerably: some describe it as empty (uninhabited), others as the seat of the Celestial Venerable of the Primordial Beginning (→ Yüan-shih t'ien-tsun). This last and highest heaven separates the universe from the great darkness.

The *Tao-te ching* considers *t'ien* to be synonymous with the → Tao. The *Lu-shih ch'un-ch'iu* states, "Heaven is invisible and begets, Earth is visible and forms." In the *I-ching,* Heaven is symbolized by the hexagram *ch'ien* (→ *ch'ien* and *k'un*) and corresponds to pure yang (→ yin-yang). It represents the male principle, as opposed to Earth, which is yin and female.

T'ien already was a central concept in Chinese thought during the Chou Dynasty. It referred to a supreme being, which influenced man's destiny by virtue of a celestial mandate (→ *t'ien-ming*). Heaven preserved order and calm, but also caused catastrophes and punished human transgressions. This supreme being reveals itself only to those who cultivate their innermost self and their virtue. The *Shih-ching* (*"Book of Songs"*)—a Confucianist classic—states, "Heaven in producing mankind annexed its laws to every faculty and relationship. Man possessed of this nature should strive to develop its endowment to perfection" (Chang Chung-yuan 1963, p. 63).

In Confucianism, *t'ien* generally means "God" but can also refer to the material sky, to fate, or to nature. When *t'ien* designates an ethical principle, it is considered the highest such principle in the universe.

Heaven is also symbolically represented by the so-called Pi disc—a round disc, the outer rim of which is twice as wide as the diameter of the circular hole at its center.

Furthermore, the emperor is referred to as "Son of Heaven" (T'ien-tzu) and considered to be a mediator between Heaven and man, because he combines in himself both secular and sacred power. His sacred power he receives from Heaven in the form of his celestial mandate.

T'ien-i   Chin. → *san-i*

T'ien-ku   Chin., lit. "heavenly drum"; Taoist health exercise. To "beat the heavenly drum," the practitioner places the palms of his hands over his ears in such a way that the fingertips touch behind his head. He then presses upon the middle finger of his right hand with the index finger of his left and allows the latter to slide off the former, so that it knocks against the back of his head, producing a sound similar to that of a drum.

This exercise is performed before various breathing exercises and is said to prevent harmful influences.

T'ien-kuan   → *san-kuan*

T'ien-ming   Chin., lit. "celestial mandate"; the mandate by virtue of which the Son of Heaven, i.e., the Chinese emperor, rules. The notion of a celestial mandate has been traced back to the Yin and Chou dynasties. The ruler received his mandate directly from heaven, whereby his rule was legitimized and at the same time made subject to certain limitations. It was the task of the ruler to recognize the signs of heavenly wrath and heavenly approval and act accordingly. Abnormal or unusual natural phenomena were considered to be an indication of heavenly disapproval, which compelled the ruler to reexamine and correct his rulership so as to bring it once again into harmony with the will of heaven.

This understanding of the idea of a celestial mandate is also found in the philosophy of Confucius (→ K'ung-tzu). He took *t'ien-ming* to be the will of Heaven—a power directed at a specific aim. In *Analects* (*Lun-yü*) 2.4 we read, "At the age of fifty, I knew the will of Heaven."

T'ien-shih Chin., lit. "celestial master"; title borne by all Taoist masters who were genealogical descendants of → Chang Tao-ling. The *t'ien-shih* were the leaders of Five-Pecks-of-Rice Taoism (→ *wu-tou-mi tao*) and its successor, the School of Right Unity (→ *cheng-i tao*).

The title *celestial master* has been passed on within the Chang family to this day. Up to the time of the Communist takeover the *t'ien-shih* lived on → Lung-hu-shan in Kiangsi Province; the present holder of the title lives in Taiwan.

Western scholars often wrongly translate *t'ien-shih* as "Taoist pope." From its very beginnings, religious Taoism (→ *tao-chiao*) did not recognize a central authority in charge of all schools and factions. Instead, each monastery or congregation had its own hierarchical structure. In some cases, several monasteries (→ *kuan*) were ruled by the leader of the school to which they belonged, but in most cases the abbot, i.e., the → *tao-shih*, held the highest position in the hierarchy. The authority of a *t'ien-shih* was formal rather than factual. He issued two types of diplomas, which he awarded to *tao-shih* in recognition of their office. Thereafter, these *tao-shih* were able to settle with their families in a place of their choice and there performed their spiritual functions, which mainly consisted of casting out demons and warding off evil spirits.

T'ien-shu Chin., lit. "celestial writing"; Taoism distinguishes between two types of *t'ien-shu:* (1) natural *t'ien-shu* (Chinese pictograms that resemble clouds in the sky and can only be understood by those who have realized the → Tao) and (2) Taoist texts written in so-called cloud script (→ *yün-chuan*).

T'ien-ti Chin., lit. "Heaven and Earth"; conventional expression to designate the universe (→ *wan-wu*).

T'ien-tsun Chin., lit. "celestial venerable"; title accorded to the highest deities in religious Taoism (→ *tao-chiao*, → *shen*). The most important *t'ien-tsun* are the Celestial Venerable of the Primordial Beginning (→ Yüan-shih t'ien-tsun), the Celestial Venerable of the Magic Jewel (Ling-pao t'ien-tsun), and the Celestial Venerable of the Tao and the Te (Tao-te t'ien-tsun, → *san-ch'ing*). In addition, the Jade Emperor (→ Yü-huang) is venerated as a *t'ien-tsun*.

The celestial venerables of Taoism are modeled on the bodhisattvas of Mahayana Buddhism. The title *t'ien-tsun* began to be attached to Taoist deities around the 3d century C.E., at which time Buddhism became a growing influence in Chinese religion, so that Taoists felt impelled to create a counterpart to the Buddhist idea of a bodhisattva.

The celestial venerables—like bodhisattvas in popular belief—descend from Heaven to teach mankind or intimate their knowledge and wisdom to lower-ranking deities or immortals (→ *hsien*), who in turn explain them to ordinary humans. This is how man is believed to have come into possession of the sacred Taoist writings and of the prescriptions for attaining immortality. When Buddhism first came to China, the title *t'ien-tsun* became attached to the Buddha himself, but was later withdrawn in favor of *shih-tsun* ("terrestrial venerable") to avoid confusion.

Ti-i   Chin. → *san-i*

Ti-kuan   → *san-kuan*

Tou-mu   Chin., lit. "Mother of the Great Wagon"; Taoist deity. Tou-mu supervises a register in which the life and death of each person is recorded. She is venerated by all who hope for a long life and personifies compassion.

It is quite common for a whole hall of a Taoist temple to be dedicated to her. She is portrayed sitting on a lotus throne and has four heads, with three eyes in each, and eight arms—four on each side of her body. In her hands she holds various precious objects. Tou-mu is also venerated by Chinese Buddhists.

Ts'ai-shen   Chin.; a god of prosperity, one of the most important deities of religious Taoism (→ *tao-chiao*) and in the syncretist folk religion of China. In Taoism, the personality venerated as Ts'ai-shen traditionally is Chao Hsüan-t'an Yüan-shuai, i.e., General Chao of the Dark Terrace, who is said to have lived during the Ch'in Dynasty and allegedly attained enlightenment on top of a mountain. Legend further relates that → Chang Tao-ling, during his search for the life-prolonging elixir, asked for the assistance of a protective deity, whereupon the Jade Emperor (→ Yü-huang) sent him General Chao.

As a deity of prosperity, Ts'ai-shen has various magical powers: he is capable of riding a black tiger, warding off thunder and lightning, fighting illnesses, and ensuring profit from commercial transactions.

Ts'ai-shen is usually portrayed with a black face and a thick moustache. On his head he wears a cap made of iron and he holds a weapon, also of iron.

A great number of personalities, apart from General Chao, are venerated as *ts'ai-shen*. In fact, he holds a central position in popular faith and is venerated by most families, although no specific cult has formed around him. Poorer families content themselves with writing the two signs of his name on a piece of paper, which they affix to the door of the most important room in their house. Richer families may own a statue of him. On his birthday (the sixteenth day of the third month) it is customary to sacrifice a cockerel to him, the blood of which is smeared all over the doorstep of the house.

Sometimes two figures are venerated as *ts'ai-shen*—one military, the other civilian—whose roles may differ from one region of the country to the next.

Tsao-chün   Chin., lit. "Lord of the Hearth"; a Taoist hearth and kitchen deity, who, to this day, holds the most important place in Chinese folk religion. A picture of Tsao-chün is fixed above the hearth and venerated by the whole family on the days of the new and full moon.

From his place above the hearth Tsao-chün notes everything that happens in the house and reports on this to the Jade Emperor (→ Yü-huang) on each New Year's Day. For that reason it is customary to smear honey around the mouth of the deity on New Year's Eve, hoping that this will prompt him to submit a favorable report to Yü-huang.

On color prints Tsao-chün is usually surrounded by a host of children, because he also acts as protector of the family.

According to legend Tsao-chün was already venerated in the 2d century B.C.E. One tradition states that he granted eternal youth and freedom from want to the Taoist magician → Li Shao-chün, who promised to pass on these gifts to the Emperor Hsiao Wu-ti (140–86 B.C.E.) if he were to pass a law to protect the cult of the hearth deity. Li caused the deity to appear to the emperor at night, whereupon the emperor offered a sacrifice to Tsao-chün, hoping to gain possession of the pill of immortality and be initiated into the secret of turning base metal into gold. When the emperor's hopes were not fulfilled, Li Shao-chün tried another ruse: he wrote signs on a piece of silk, which he fed to an ox, and prophesied that when this ox was slaughtered a miraculous message would be found. The emperor, however, recognized Li's handwriting and had him punished. Nevertheless, the cult of Tsao-chün had already become established at court and has been part of Chinese folk religion ever since.

One legend still circulating among the people tells of a man called Chang Lang, who was married to a very virtuous woman, who brought good fortune and blessings upon his house: "One day he left her for the sake of a flighty young girl, and the rejected wife returned to her parents. From then on Chang Lang was plagued by bad luck. The young girl turned from him, he became blind and was forced to support himself by begging. One day, his search for alms brought him to the house of his former wife, but he was not aware of this. She, however, recognized him, invited him in, and served him his favorite dish. This reminded Chang of his lost happiness and, with tears running down his face, he related to her his sad tale. She ordered him to open his eyes and, as if by a miracle, he regained his eyesight and recognized her. Deeply ashamed at the way he had treated her, he was unable to remain in her presence and jumped into the hearth, not realizing that it was lit. The wife attempted to save him, but could only salvage one of his legs. Since then, the fire tong or poker is known in popular language as 'Chang Lang's leg.' Chang's wife mourned for him, fixed a small plaque above the hearth in which he lost his life, and made sacrifices to him. That was the beginning of his veneration as a hearth deity" (trans. from E. Unterrieder, *Glück ein ganzes Mondjahr lang* [Klagenfurt, 1984], 12).

Ts'ao Kuo-chiu   → *pa-hsien*

Tsou Yen   3d century B.C.E.; most famous representative of the Yin-Yang School (→ *yin-yang chia*). According to the great historian Ssu-ma Ch'ien, Tsou Yen's method consisted in first examining small things and then gradually widening his analysis to larger things until he reached the limitless. He applied the doctrine of the five elements (→ *wu-hsing*) to history and geography; classified the country's rivers, mountains, valleys, animals etc.; and maintained that the area of China accounted for less than one eightieth of the surface area of the world, which he described as consisting of nine continents surrounded by a large ocean.

Tsou Yen developed a new view of history, by relating political and social events to the sequence of the five elements: the Yellow Emperor (→ Huang-ti) had ruled under the element earth, which was conquered by the wood of the Hsia Dynasty. This in turn was vanquished by the element metal of the Shang Dynasty and that by the element of fire, under whose sign the Chou Dynasty ruled. The fire would—according to Tsou Yen—be succeeded by the water of the next dynasty, which would then be followed by another dynasty, once again ruled by the element earth.

Tsou Yen's philosophy of history is described in Book 13, Chapter 2 of the → *Lü-shih ch'un-ch'iu,* although his name as such is not specifically mentioned: "Whenever a ruler or king is about to appear, Heaven reveals this to mankind through happy omens. At the time of the coming of the Yellow Emperor, Heaven caused a large earthworm and a gigantic cricket to appear. The Yellow Emperor said, 'The might of earth is victorious.' Because of this, he chose yellow as his supreme color and took the earth as a model for his actions. At the time of Yü (→ Ta-yü) Heaven prevented grasses and trees from yellowing or shedding their leaves in autumn or winter. Thereupon Yü said, "The might of wood is victorious.' Because of this, Yü chose green as the ruling color and let wood be the example that determined his actions. At the time of T'ang (the founder of the Shang Dynasty) Heaven first caused a metal blade to appear in water, whereupon T'ang said, "The might of metal is victorious.' As a result of this, T'ang chose white as the superior color and made metal the guiding principle of his actions. At the time of King Wen (the founder of the Chou Dynasty) Heaven first caused a red crow to appear, which held a red envelope in its beak and settled on the earth altar of Chou. Thereupon King Wen said, 'The might of fire is victorious.' Because of this, he made red the superior color and in his actions followed the example of fire. One day, the rule of fire will surely be succeeded by the might of water. Before that happens, Heaven will reveal that the might of water is victorious. The future ruler will then choose black as the superior color and model his actions on the characteristics of water. When the might of water is manifest and the ruler and people fail to seize the fateful moment, might will pass to the element earth" (Wilhelm 1979, p. 160).

Tso-wang Chin., lit. "sitting [and] forgetting"; Taoist method of meditation descriptive of the highest stage of Taoist absorption. The practitioner of *tso-wang* does not meditate on an object, but rather allows his mind to float freely without intervening. In this way, he abides in nonaction (→ *wu-wei*) and becomes one with the → Tao. He leaves behind all forms and limitations and is free of wishes and desires.

The → *Chuang-tzu* (Book 6, Chapter 7) describes *tso-wang* as follows: "On a third occasion Wen Hui met Confucius and said, 'I am getting on.' 'How so?' asked the Sage. 'I have got rid of everything,' replied Wen Hui. 'Got rid of everything!' said Confucius eagerly. 'What do you mean by that?' 'I have freed myself from my body,' answered Wen Hui. 'I have discarded my reasoning powers. And by thus getting rid of body and mind, I have become One with the Infinite. This is what I mean by getting rid of everything.' 'If you have become one,' cried Confucius, 'there can be no room for bias. If you have passed into space, you are indeed without beginning or end. And if you have really attained to this, I trust to be allowed to follow in your steps'" (Giles 1961).

Ts'un-shen Chin. → Ts'un-ssu

Ts'un-ssu Chin., lit. "maintaining the thought [the attention]"; Taoist method of meditation, in which the practitioner contemplates a certain object. The most common objects of meditation are the three jewels (→ *san-pao*); the Tao, i.e., the Taoist writings—above all the writings on the Magic Jewel (→ *Ling-pao ching*)—and the Master (in this case, → Lao-chün). A variant of *ts'un-ssu* consists in trying to visualize the deities (→ *shen*) said to inhabit the body of each human being (→ Inner Deity Hygiene School). This method is known as *ts'un-shen* (lit. "maintaining the deities"; → *nei-kuan*). It specifically aims at attaining longevity by the production of pure energy.

T'u-ku na-hsin also called *t'u-na,* Chin., lit. "disposing of the old and acquiring the new"; Taoist breathing exercise, in which the stale breath is expelled as completely as possible through the mouth, whereupon the practitioner inhales fresh air through his nose, endeavoring to fill the lungs to their maximum capacity. This allows him to expel the dead breath (*ssu-ch'i,* → *ch'i*) and then absorb the living breath (*sheng-ch'i*)—an essential precondition for the attainment of immortality. *T'u-na* is one of several methods of nourishing the body, or life (→ *yang-hsing,* → *yang-sheng*). As he expels the stale air, the adept may produce six different sounds, each of which acts upon a particular internal organ and is said to have specific healing powers.

Exhaling and at the same time making the sound *ch'i* strengthens the lungs and can cure tuberculosis. The sound *ho* strengthens the heart and also is a cure for headaches. The sound *hsü* acts on the liver and dispels a phlegmatic temperament. *Hu* acts on the pancreas and lowers the temperature when the patient is suffering from a fever. *Ch'ui* acts on the kidneys and is a prophylactic against catching cold. *Hsi* influences the alimentary tract, the stomach, and the urogenital system and relieves rheumatic pain.

T'ung Chung-shu Chin. → Confucianism

T'un-t'o Chin. → *yü-chiang*

T'u-t'an-chai   Chin. → *chai*

T'u-ti   Chin.; deity subordinate to a city god (→ *ch'eng-huang*) and in charge of a specific district or building. Each area, street, temple, or public building of a Chinese town has its own protective deity. Sometimes the functions of a *t'u-ti* are delegated to famous historical personalities.

The responsibilities of the *t'u-ti* are the same as those of the *ch'eng-huang,* i.e., to keep a register on the lives and deaths of the inhabitants in the districts or area under their protection. For that reason they must be informed of all deaths; when someone dies, weeping women visit the temple or shrine of the deity and present incense and paper money. In addition, rich harvests depend on the good will of the *t'u-ti.*

Tzu   Chin., lit. "ancestor." The veneration of ancestors has a central role in Chinese religion. Ancestors continue to be part of each family in the form of ancestral plaques. They protect the members of the family and provide a link between the living and the higher worlds. On certain days sacrifices are made to them.

The ancestral plaques are kept in the family shrine. They are about four to five inches wide and twice as long, with the name and possibly the title—sometimes also the dates of birth and death of the departed—engraved on them. Rich families keep these plaques in a separate ancestral temple; families in more modest circumstances usually place them against the north wall of the house. They are surrounded by candles and incense.

The plaques are arranged according to the rank of the ancestors within the family hierarchy: by the side of the plaque of a male ancestor stands that of his main wife. The larger the number of plaques a family possesses, the greater its pride and prestige.

On the days of the new moon and full moon, the ancestors are venerated in small ceremonies, at which the head of the family lights candles and incense and bows to the ancestral plaques. There are other ceremonies of a more complex nature, which differ from one family to the next but are usually held on the birthday or date of death of the ancestor in question. On these occasions it is not at all uncommon to serve the departed ancestor a complete meal.

Tzu-jan Chin., lit. "being such of itself," natural, spontaneous; a concept of philosophical Taoism (→ *tao-chia*). Everything that is spontaneous and free of human intention or external influences is *tzu-jan*. It is something in harmony with itself. It denotes the highest realization of being and absolute loyalty to itself.

Tzu-jan is closely related to → *wu-wei*, unmotivated action, in that it could be said to be both its aim and norm.

Chapter 25 of the *Tao-te ching* defines *tzu-jan* as follows: "There are four great ones in the universe, and one of them is man. Man conforms to Earth, Earth to Heaven, Heaven to the → Tao and the Tao to nature [lit. 'suchness']."

According to the Japanese *Tao-te ching* scholar Akira Ōhama, *tzu-jan* is a spontaneous energy inherent in the Tao, and thus the self-unfoldment of its effect: "The Tao acts like an immanent energy, a mysterious presence within the world of the ten thousand things (→ *wan-wu*). Therefore the individual effects of the ten thousand things—if they are not prevented from following their own nature—are in accordance with the *tzu-jan* of the Tao. What matters, is not the self-conscious intentional striving for oneness with the Tao, but rather the fact that human action is identical with the Tao that is present and acting in man. That is *tzu-jan*" (Béky 1972, p. 126).

* * *

Wai-ch'i Chin., lit. "outer breath"; the air we inhale, as opposed to the inner breath (→ *nei-ch'i*) that corresponds to the cosmic primordial energy (→ *yüan-ch'i*) within the human body.

Up to the time of the T'ang Dynasty Taoists believed that in breathing exercises such as holding the breath (→ *pi-ch'i*) or circulating the breath (→ *hsing-ch'i*) it was the outer breath that was held or circulated. The practitioner would therefore endeavor to retain the inhaled air for as long as possible and/or make it circulate throughout the body. These practices were not exclusively Taoist in that they also played an important part in Chinese medicine.

During the middle T'ang Dynasty exercises such as *pi-ch'i* and *hsing-ch'i* were reinterpreted as a result of which it was accepted that it was not the outer but the inner breath that was held or made to flow through the body. The dangerous practice of holding the breath—at times for as long as two hundred heartbeats—thus became redundant. In addition, this new understanding of Taoist breathing exercises made it possible to distinguish them from the purely health-promoting exercises recommended by Chinese medicine.

Wai-tan Chin., lit. "outer cinnabar"; the "outer elixir," the "outer alchemy." One of two branches of Taoist alchemy, the other being → *nei-tan*, Inner Alchemy. *Wai-tan* practitioners strive to produce a pill of immortality (→ *ch'ang-sheng pu-ssu*) by the transformation of chemical substances. The most important ingredients during the working of the outer elixir are cinnabar (*tan*) and gold. The latter was used because of its durability, the former—red mercury ore—because of its color and chemical properties.

The followers of the Outer Alchemy believed that a person's life force was identical with the so-called primordial energy (→ *yüan-ch'i*) or cosmic energy. A reduction or loss of a person's *yüan-ch'i* would therefore result in illness or death. The *yüan-ch'i* itself was understood to be a special mixture of yin and yang (→ yin-yang). According to the doctrine of the Outer Alchemy, only cinnabar and gold were capable of restoring within the organism that primordial state in which yin and yang combine and thus become indistinguishable from each other.

The most important Taoist alchemists were → Wei P'o yang and → Ko Hung. As Taoism developed, the view that immortality could be attained by ingesting a pill or drug was gradually replaced by the doctrine and teachings of the Inner Elixir School.

The practitioner of the Outer Alchemy produces his elixir over a fire in a cauldron, by which method transformations normally occurring in nature are accelerated. A series of reductions and recyclings produces purified cinnabar, the efficiency of which increases proportionate to the number of such recyclings. The most powerful immortality drug is said to be cinnabar that has been purified nine times (*chiu-huan-tan*): anyone ingesting it is believed to be capable of ascending to Heaven in broad daylight (→ *fei-sheng*). Ko Hung describes the properties of gold and cinnabar as follows: "Cinnabar becomes transformed when heated. The longer the period it is heated, the more miraculous the transformation it undergoes. Gold, on the other hand, retains its nature even when placed into fire, melted a hundred times or buried in the

ground to the end of time. The ingestion of these two substances brings about a sublimation of the body. . . . Even the
cheapest and coarsest type of cinnabar is infinitely superior to
the most excellent medicinal plants. If you incinerate plants
they turn into ashes. Granules of cinnabar, on the other hand,
give rise to granules of mercury when heated; a further sublimation once again produces cinnabar" (chap. 4 of Ko Hung's
Pao-p'u-tzu; trans. from Kaltenmark, *Lao-tzu und der Taoismus;* see Kaltenmark 1969).

Wang Ch'un-yang   → *ch'üan-chen tao*

Wang Hsiao-yang   → *ch'üan-chen tao*

Wang Jung   → *chu-lin ch'i-hsien*

Wang Pi   226–49 C.E.; a representative of neo-Taoism (→
hsüan-hsüeh) and one of the most important commentators
on the *Tao-te ching* and the *Book of Change(s)* (→ *I-ching*).

Wang Pi's edition of the *Tao-te ching* has remained authoritative to this day. In his commentary he takes the
view that the → Tao is equivalent to emptiness (→ *wu*):
"Although we say of the Tao that it is nonbeing, we must
not forget that all things owe their perfection to the Tao.
The assumption that the Tao is being still does not permit
us to perceive its form."

Thus *wu* is considered to be the primordial ground of all
being: "All things in this world arise from being. But the origin of being is rooted in nonbeing. To realize true being it is
necessary to return to nonbeing."

Wang Pi's commentary on the *I-ching* describes it as a
book of wisdom rather than one of oracles, and thereby
cleanses it of the inflated interpretations of the Yin-Yang
School (→ *yin-yang chia*).

Wan-wu   Chin., lit. "ten thousand things or beings"; a conventional expression descriptive of the totality of phenomena within the universe. *Ten thousand* here simply means "innumerable" or "all."

Way of Supreme Peace   → *t'ai-p'ing tao*

Way of the Realization of Truth   → *ch'üan-chen tao*

Wei Ch'eng   Chin. → *men-shen*

Wei P'o-yang   2d century C.E.; one of the most important representatives of Taoist alchemy and author of the oldest known treatise on alchemy, the *Chou-i ts'an-t'ung-ch'i* (roughly "On the Uniting of Correspondences"), which deals with the production of the elixir of immortality (→ *ch'ang-sheng pu-ssu*). In this work Wei P'o-yang also makes reference to certain elements and concepts of the *Book of Change(s)* (→ *I-ching*). Its language is highly esoteric and allows a variety of interpretations. For that reason, it has come to be understood both as a recipe for producing the outer elixir and as a method of creating or developing the inner elixir. In the opinion of some Taoist practitioners it also contains references to certain sexual practices (→ *fang-chung shu*). In later Taoism, however, it is generally seen as a text of the Inner Alchemy. The *Chou-i ts'an-t'ung-ch'i* owes its fame in part to a commentary by the 12th-century neo-Taoist philosopher → Chu Hsi.

Another commentator (→ Yü Yen) sees its central notion as follows: Man makes use of the secret energies of Heaven and Earth to produce for himself the great elixir of the golden liquid and thus is part of Heaven and Earth from their very beginning. . . . Whenever Heaven combines with Earth man should strive to acquire and make use of the secret energies of the creative activities of yin and yang.

A well-known anecdote portrays Wei P'o-yang as a follower of the Outer Elixir School:

"One day Wei P'o-yang went into the mountains with three of his pupils in order to prepare the elixir. When it was ready they first fed it to a dog, which immediately fell dead to the ground. Wei P'o-yang then asked his pupils whether he, too, should ingest the elixir and follow the dog [into death]. His disciples turned the question back on him, and he replied, 'I have abandoned the ways of the world and my family and friends to go and live in the mountains. It would be shameful to return without having found the Tao of the sacred immortals (→ hsien). To die from the elixir can be no worse than to live without it. So I must partake of it.' He did so and fell dead to the ground. One of the three pupils followed his example but the other two went back into the world. When they had gone, Wei P'o-yang, his pupil, and the white dog came back to life and despatched a letter to the two that had left, thanking them for their kindness. When they received the message their hearts were filled with sadness and regret." (Trans. from Colgrave 1980.)

Wen-ch'ang Taoist god of literature. In reality, Wen-ch'ang is a constellation of six stars in the vicinity of the Great Bear. It is said that when these stars are bright, literature flourishes. However, the stellar deity Wen-ch'ang, according to legend, repeatedly descended to Earth and manifested himself in human form. Taoists texts mention seventeen separate existences of Wen-ch'ang on Earth. He is above all venerated by people who require help with their entrance examinations for an official career. Wen-ch'ang is believed to be the author of extensive literary works, which were revealed to man in various, miraculous ways.

Many educated Chinese put up a plaque—or, more rarely, a picture—showing Wen-ch'ang dressed as a mandarin and holding in his hand a wish-fulfilling scepter (→ *ju-i*). He is usually portrayed in the company of K'uei-hsing (also a stellar deity) and Chu-i, the Red-robed One. The former is responsible for issuing official testimonials, while the latter acts as the patron of ill-prepared candidates for official examinations.

Wu   Chin., lit. "nonbeing," emptiness; a basic concept in Taoist philosophy; the absence of qualities perceivable by the senses. *Wu* is the essential characteristic of the → Tao, but may also refer to a Taoist so imbued with the Tao that he has become free of all desires and passions, i.e., empty.

Chapter 11 of the *Tao-te ching* (Feng & English 1972) describes the nature of emptiness as follows:

Thirty spokes share the wheel's hub;
It is the centre hole that makes it useful.
Shape clay into a vessel;
It is the space within that makes it useful.
Cut doors and windows for a room;
It is the holes which make them useful.
Therefore profit comes from what is there;
Usefulness from what is not there.
Chapter 5 (ibid.) states:
The space between heaven and earth is like a bellows.
The shape changes but not the form;
The more it moves, the more it yields.

Wu-ch'ang   Chin., lit. "five constants"; the five cardinal virtues of Confucianism (→ K'ung-tzu), which regulate human behavior: → *jen* (humanity, fellow feeling), → *i* (uprightness), → *li* (rites and customs), *chih* (wisdom, insight) and *hsin* (trust). See also → *wu-lun*.

Wu-chen pien Chin., lit. *"Treatise on Awakening to the Truth"*; best-known work of the alchemist → Cheng Po-tuan (983–1082 C.E.), containing his interpretation of the doctrine of the inner elixir (→ *nei-tan*), which became the doctrinal basis of the later Southern School of → *ch'üan-chen tao*.

The hundred chapters of the *Wu-chen pien* are written in verse and describe the various methods for producing the inner elixir. Chang Po-tuan rejected the outer elixir (→ *wai-tan*). He was convinced that every human being contained it within himself, so that there was no need to collect medicinal herbs or perform hygiene exercises.

Chang Po-tuan taught that to produce the inner elixir, the practitioner must know the nature of true lead (yang) and true mercury (yin) (→ yin-yang). Yang must catch and absorb yin—a process described in the *Wu-chen pien* as the marriage of yin and yang. The alchemist adept, lying on his bed at midnight or at the time of the winter solstice, causes the two energies (yin and yang) to combine in his abdomen with the help of → *ch'i*, the vital energy, and thus produces an embryo (→ *sheng-t'ai*) that grows in proportion to the increase in yang. In this way the alchemist practitioner can become an immortal (→ *hsien*).

Wu-chi Chin., lit. "peak of nothingness"; the limitless, unconditioned, primordial, formless, and invisible, to which everything returns (→ *fu*). The Taoist philosopher Chou Tun-i considered *wu-chi* to be synonymous with the *t'ai-chi* (→ *t'ai-chi-t'u*).

Wu-ch'in-hsi   Chin. → Hua T'o

Wu-chi-t'u   Chin. → Ch'en T'uan

Wu-hsing   Chin., lit. "five movers," also known as *wu-te* (lit. "five virtues"); the five elements. Five phases of transformation, or five energies, that determine the course of natural phenomena. These five elements—water, fire, wood, metal, and earth—are not to be understood as real substances but rather as abstract forces and symbols for certain basic characteristics of matter: e.g., it lies in the nature of water to moisten and to flow downward; of fire to heat and to rise; of wood to bend and straighten again; of metal to be cast or hammered into various forms; and of earth to be fertile. At the time of the Warring States Period, the notion arose that the elements not only give rise to each other but also may help conquer or destroy each other (*hsiang-sheng hsiang-k'o*): wood can give rise to fire, fire to earth, earth to metal, metal to water, and water to wood. At the same time water will conquer fire, fire vanquishes metal, metal can destroy wood, wood can conquer the earth, and earth overcomes water. This theory, furthermore, is of relevance in Chinese medicine.

Within a more complicated system of correspondence, the five elements are related to the seasons of the year, the cardinal points, colors, flavors, numbers, internal organs, and other groupings.

During the 4th and 3d centuries B.C.E., the doctrine of the five elements constituted an independent school. The most important representative of this school was → Tsou Yen (3d century B.C.E.), who applied the theory of the five elements to the area of politics by relating the course of history to their interdependence and succession. At the time of the Han Dynasty the Five Elements School combined with the Yin-Yang School (→ *yin-yang chia*) and has since been considered part of the latter.

The succession of the four seasons is reflected by the interdependence of the five elements: in spring, wood is dominant and gives rise to fire, the element of summer. Fire gives rise to earth, which is characteristic of the center, i.e., the third month of summer. Earth, in turn, gives rise to metal which dominates autumn, and metal to the water of winter.

Furthermore, each element has its corresponding color, flavor, and cardinal point: the north and that which is black and salty correspond to water. Fire is related to the south, the color red, and to that which tastes bitter. The east, the color green, and that which tastes sour correspond to wood. The qualities of metal are related to the west, the color white, and that which tastes sharp; and water corresponds to the color yellow, that which tastes sweet, and to the center, which, in the Chinese view of the world, is the fifth cardinal point.

In the microcosmic realm, the five elements are connected with various organs of the body and with certain emotions. These correspondences are of great importance in Chinese medicine. Wood is related to the eyes, the sinews, the gall bladder, the liver, and anger; fire to the tongue, the blood vessels, the small intestine, the heart, and the feeling of joy; earth to the mouth, the muscles, the stomach, the pancreas, and worrying; metal to the nose, the hairs of the body, the large intestine, the lungs, and sadness; and water to the ears, the bones, the bladder, the kidneys, and fear.

In addition, the five elements are said to be connected with the planets Mercury, Venus, Mars, Jupiter, and Saturn as well as the signs of the Chinese lunar calendar.

The Yin-Yang School allocated numbers to the five elements: one and six to water, two and seven to fire, three and eight to wood, four and nine to metal, and five and ten to earth. Even numbers are said to be Earth numbers and odd numbers Heaven numbers. In this sense the odd numbers are characteristic of what gives rise to an element, and the even numbers of what brings it to fruition or perfection. These relationships are also of significance in connection with the *Book of Change(s)* (→ *I-ching*).

According to the historical view of Tsou Yen, the succession of the various dynasties imitates that of the elements: Earth, under whose sign the legendary Yellow Emperor (→ Huang-ti) ruled, was conquered by the wood of the Hsia Dynasty; this in turn was vanquished by the metal of the Shang Dynasty; and Tsou Yen was of the opinion that the fire of the Chou Dynasty, during which he lived, would be conquered by the water of the next dynasty and that by the earth of a further dynasty, thereby initiating a new cycle. Each ruler of a dynasty adopted the color of, and ruled in accordance with, the quality of its corresponding element and furthermore adapted the calendar, the color of fabrics, etc. to it.

Wu-lun Chin., lit. "five relationships"; five types of relationship—between (1) parent and child, (2) ruler and subject, (3) husband and wife, (4) older and younger brother, and (5) friend and friend—which, according to the Confucianist model of society, form the basis of human interaction (→ *wu-ch'ang*).

Wu-shih Chin., lit. "five corpses"; five types of contaminated (impure) energy found in the five internal organs of the human body (to which the colors red, green, white, yellow, and black are allocated). Because the presence of these impure energies within the body reduces a person's life span, a Taoist practitioner wishing to attain immortality must eliminate the five corpses by meditative practices and fasting.

Wu-shih ch'i-hou Chin., roughly "five periods and seven time spans"; various stages and phases on the meditative path of a Taoist practitioner, ranging from a simple pacifying of the mind to the highest state of spiritual realization.

They are, in summary, as follows:

1. The mind is moving, restless, and only rarely still.

2. The mind begins to be less restless.

3. Calm and movement hold each other in balance.

4. The mind is calm most of the time and only rarely moves, and the practitioner concentrates on an object of meditation.

5. The mind abides in pure stillness; it is no longer kept in motion by external impressions.

After these five *wu-shih* the practitioner passes through the following seven *ch'i-hou*:

1. Worry and sorrow subside, as do the passions and the practitioner realizes the → Tao.

2. The outer appearance of the adept becomes like that of a child, his body supple and his mind at peace, and the practitioner possesses supernatural powers.

3. The practitioner is assured of a long life and reaches the level of an immortal (→ *hsien*).

4. He purifies his body and perfects the energy (→ *ch'i*) and thus attains the level of the true man (→ *chen-jen*).

5. He purifies the energy and perfects the mind (spirit) (→ *shen*) and reaches the level of a saint (→ *shen-jen*).

6. He purifies the mind and brings it into harmony with all forms, thereby reaching the level of a perfected human being.

7. The adept has passed beyond all rites and rules and is free of all motivated action, the highest realization in Taoist practice.

Wu-te Chin. → *wu-hsing*

Wu-ti Chin., lit. "five emperors"; legendary emperors said to have ruled China between 2697 and 2205 B.C.E. or—according to an alternative calendrical calculation— 2674 and 2184 B.C.E. The five are the Yellow Emperor (→ Huang-ti), Chuan Hsü, Ku, → Yao, and → Shun. The belief in their existence is based on historical speculations dating back to the 2d and 1st centuries B.C.E.; Confucius—who lived earlier than that—only mentions Yao and Shun. Their grouping into five reflects the Chinese system of cosmological correspondences. Since the number five is also related to the five elements (→ *wu-hsing*), one element is allocated to each of the five emperors.

Wu-tou-mi tao Chin., lit. "Five-Pecks-of-Rice Taoism"; early Taoist school (→ *tao-chiao*), founded by → Chang Tao-ling between 126 and 144 C.E. in Szechwan in western China. It remained active up to the 15th century. The reason for the school's name stems from the practice that anyone wishing to join it had to make a payment of five pecks of rice to the → *tao-shih*. *Wu-tou-mi tao* is also known as the School of the Celestial Masters (→ *t'ien-shih*) because the heads of this school bore the title *celestial master.* Five-Pecks-of-Rice Taoism is based on the teachings of Lao-tzu, who is venerated by his followers as → T'ai-shang lao-chün. The root text of the school is the → *Tao-te ching,* which it interprets in a way specifically suited to its practices and requirements.

Like other Taoist movements of the period, Five-Pecks-of-Rice Taoism, in its religious rituals, placed particular emphasis on the healing of illnesses that it believed to be a consequence of evil deeds. In this context mass confessions at which believers recited a catalog of their transgressions to the three rulers (→ *san-kuan*)—Heaven, Earth, and Water—were of particular significance. Other practices of Five-Pecks-of-Rice Taoism were ritual fasts (→ *chai*), the use of talismans (→ *fu-lu*), orgiastic feasts (→ *ho-ch'i*), and ceremonies for the dead.

The followers of the *wu-tou-mi tao* were organized on a strictly hierarchical pattern. The bulk of the congregation was made up of so-called demon soldiers, who were led by the presenters of liquid sacrifices (Chin., *chi-chiu*), each of whom was in charge of a particular district. The top position in the hierarchy was held by the celestial master (*t'ien-shih*).

After the death of its founder, the leadership of the school passed to Chang Heng and from him, in turn, to → Chang Lu, who, toward the end of the Eastern Han Dynasty, established in the northern part of the country a state structure in which there was no separation between politics and religion. The religious hierarchy thus was at the same time a military one. This form of government continued until the year 215 C.E. During the subsequent centuries Five-Pecks-of-Rice Taoism spread among the peasantry and played an important part in several peasant uprisings at the time of the Chin Dynasty.

In the 5th century → K'ou Chien-chih, under whose influence Taoism was proclaimed a state religion, assumed the ancient title of *celestial master* and endeavored to liberate Taoism from the negative influences of → Chang Chüeh by introducing various Confucianist ideas, as a result of which good deeds and hygiene exercises became an integral aspect of *wu-tou-mi tao* practice. This new form of Five-Pecks-of-Rice Taoism is also known as the Northern Branch of the Tao of the Celestial Masters.

In the south of the country the most influential representative of Five-Pecks-of-Rice Taoism was Lu Hsiu-ching, who incorporated Buddhist ideas and rites and thus founded the southern branch of the school. He also established strict rules on how to conduct the various ceremonies. During the T'ang and Sung dynasties, the *wu-tou-mi tao* merged with other Taoist movements such as the School of the Magic Jewel (→ *ling-pao p'ai*) and later became absorbed by the Way of Right Unity (→ *cheng-i tao*), a movement embracing several schools.

Wu-tsang Chin., lit. "five [internal] organs." Taoist doctrine distinguishes between two groups of inter-nal organs, namely the six containers (→ *liu-fu*) and the five organs (lit. "entrails"), i.e., the lungs, the heart, the pancreas, the liver, and the kidneys. The Taoist system of correspondences between the microcosm and the macrocosm accords to these five organs corresponding phases of transformation (→ *wu-hsing*), colors, seasons, flavors, etc.

Wu-tsung 814–46 C.E.; T'ang Dynasty emperor, a fanatical supporter and champion of Taoism. He surrounded himself with Taoist priests (→ *tao-shih*) and alchemists, organized communal fasts (→ *chai*) and attempted to produce life-prolonging elixirs.

In 842 C.E. following the promptings of his Taoist advisors, he passed a series of laws to suppress Buddhism. This led to a persecution of Buddhists that reached its peak in 845 C.E.; no less than 260,000 Buddhist monks and nuns were forced to leave their monastic establishments. The art treasures of forty-six hundred monasteries were ipounded and even Buddhist families were forced to surrender statues of the Buddha and other ritual objects to imperial officials.

Wu-wei   Chin., lit. "nondoing"; unmotivated, unintentional action. A concept of the → *Tao-te ching,* designating nonintervention in the natural course of things; spontaneous action that, being completely devoid of premeditation and intention, is wholly appropriate to a given situation. *Wu-wei* is said to be the attitude of a Taoist saint.

In Chapter 48 of the *Tao-te ching* (Feng & English 1972), Lao-tzu describes *wu-wei* as follows:

In the pursuit of learning, every day something is acquired [as regards our efforts and expectations].

In the pursuit of Tao, every day something is dropped [as regards our business and desires].

Less and less is done

Until non-action is achieved.

When nothing is done, nothing is left undone.

The world is ruled by letting things take their course.

It cannot be ruled by interfering.

Wu-wei therefore does not denote absolute nonaction but rather a form of action that is free of any desires, intention, or motivation.

A Taoist adept, by following the ideal of *wu-wei,* imitates the Tao, the universal effectiveness of which is a consequence of *wu-wei:*

Tao abides in non-action,

Yet nothing is left undone. [Ibid.]

A Taoist therefore endeavors to imitate the Tao by not intervening in the course of things, thereby permitting all things to unfold in accordance with their own nature. *Wu-wei* may essentially be understood as action confined to what is natural and necessary.

The *Tao-te ching* furthermore applies the notion of *wu-wei* to the way a ruler acts. In this context, Lao-tzu illustrates the effectiveness of unmotivated action by the example of a ruler of whose existence the people, ideally, would not even be aware. Only by abiding in *wu-wei* is it possible for a ruler to have power and influence.

Chapter 37 of the *Tao-te ching* (ibid.) describes how someone following the ideal of unmotivated action would rule:

If kings and lords observed this, the ten thousand things [→ *wan-wu*] would develop naturally.

If they still desired to act, they would return to the simplicity of formless substance.

Without form there is no desire.

Without desire there is tranquility.

In this way all things would be at peace.

This view is also shared by Confucius. In the *Analects* (*Lun-yü*) 15.4 we read, "The Master said, 'If there was a ruler who achieved order without taking any action, it was, perhaps, (the legendary emperor) Shun. There was nothing for him to do but to hold himself in a respectful posture and face due south'" (Lau 1979).

In addition, the ideal of nonaction is a central characteristic of Chinese Zen (*Ch'an*) Buddhism.

✳   ✳   ✳

Yang Chu Taoist philosopher of the 4th/3d century B.C.E. His writings have not been preserved, but his basic teachings are contained in the → *Chuang-tzu,* the → *Lü-shih* *ch'un-ch'iu,* and various other works. There is a chapter devoted to him in the → *Lieh-tzu,* but its authenticity has not been established beyond doubt.

Yang Chu was an opponent of Confucianism (→ K'ung-tzu). His basic ideas are those of appreciating life and respecting the self. He considered it a primary duty to preserve and protect life so that its inherent truth might be nourished. External things, therefore, should not be allowed to corrupt life and the individual. It has been said of him that he would not sacrifice a single hair, even if thereby he could save the whole world. For that reason, his philosophy is sometimes described as extremely egotistical or hedonistic.

Yang Chu exclusively concentrates on man's life in this world and maintains that death constitutes the absolute end of this life. For that reason, he recognizes no ideals. In his view, any form of human ambition and striving—be it for fame or moral perfection—will only distract a person from life, which is the only boon and must be lived as fully as possible. Therefore an individual should unreservedly surrender himself to his natural impulses and inclinations and follow them without any thought of the consequences. Yang Chu categorically opposes any external intervention in human affairs. As a result, he rejects culture as such, and considers social standards as mere arbitrary conventions. His philosophy is thus diametrically opposed to that of Confucius.

Yang-hsing Chin., lit. "nourishing the life principle"; collective term for all Taoist exercises and practices aimed at prolonging life and attaining immortality. This includes all practices whose purpose it is to nourish the body (→ *yang-sheng*) or the mind (→ *yang-shen*).

Yang-shen Chin., lit. "nourishing the mind [or spirit]"; Taoist practice aimed at attaining immortality. The purpose of *yang-shen* consists in using meditation as a means of preventing the deities inhabiting the human body from leaving it (→ Inner Deity Hygiene School).

This method of Taoist meditation involves a concentration of the practitioner's attention on so-called body deities, thereby causing them to appear in great detail before the inner eye. In this way, these deities are guarded and prevented from leaving the body, so that it is impossible for death to occur. If *yang-shen* is practiced in combination with techniques aimed at nourishing the body (→ *yang-sheng*), immortality is attained. At first, the practitioner only perceives insignificant inner deities, but as he perseveres with his practice, he gradually succeeds in making contact with the highest deities of the upper cinnabar field (→ *tan-t'ien*) in the brain.

A more advanced stage of nourishing the mind is reached when the practitioner is able to keep the mind free of all attachments and external distractions. This is considered to be the right method of becoming one with the Tao. For anyone experiencing such indissoluble unity, physical immortality becomes a matter of minor importance. A practitioner at this level possesses supernatural powers, and his actions are devoid of all intention and motivation (→ *wu-wei*). This is the path pointed out by Lao-tzu and Chuang-tzu.

Sometimes other forms of meditation, such as → *tso-wang,* → *ts'un-ssu,* and → *shou-i* are considered forms of *yang-shen.*

Yang-sheng Chin., lit. "nourishing life," also "nourishing the body"; Taoist exercises aimed at attaining immortality. This includes the various breathing exercises such as "allowing the breath to circulate" (→ *hsing-ch'i*), "melting the breath" (→ *lien-ch'i*), "absorbing the breath" (→ *fu-ch'i*), "swallowing the breath" (→ *yen-ch'i*), "embryonic breathing" (→ *t'ai-hsi*), and an exercise known as "expelling the old and taking in the new" (→ *t'u-ku na-hsin*). In addition, abstention from eating grain (→ *pi-ku*) and various gymnastic exercises (→ *tao-yin*) as well as sexual practices (→ *fang-chung shu*) fall under the general heading of *yang-sheng*.

Many Taoists believe these exercises to be indispensable for prolonging life and attaining immortality. Philosophical Taoism (→ *tao-chia*), on the other hand, attaches only secondary importance to such practices, because it is of the opinion that the meditative technique known as "nourishing the mind" (→ *yang-shen*) alone is able to bring the practitioner to immortality.

Yao 2333–2234 B.C.E. or—according to an alternative calendrical calculation—2356–2255 B.C.E.; one of the legendary five emperors (→ *wu-ti*). Yao is said to have established the calendar and introduced official posts, the holders of which were responsible for making proper use of the four seasons of the year. Instead of his son he made → Shun his successor and subjected him to a series of severe tests, extending over a period of three years, before entrusting the rule of the country to him. According to legend, ten suns appeared in the sky and threatened to scorch the earth to a cinder when Shun seated himself on the throne after the death of Yao. However, Shen I, the heavenly archer, was able to shoot nine of them out of the sky with the help of his magic bow.

Tradition further relates that Yao, assisted by Shen I, restored order in the realm, after a monster had devastated the south of the country by violent storms. For that reason, he is known as the Tamer of the Winds. With the help of another mythological figure—i.e., Kun, the great-grandson of the Yellow Emperor (→ Huang-ti)—he fought to dam the floods of the Yellow River, which were threatening to reach Heaven.

Yellow Turbans   → *huang-chin*, → *t'ai-p'ing tao*

Yen-ch'i   Chin., lit. "swallowing the breath"; Taoist breathing exercise forming part of embryonic breathing (→ *t'ai-hsi*). The breath swallowed during this exercise is the inner *ch'i* (→ *nei-ch'i*), which, during exhalation, accompanies the outer *ch'i* (→ *wai-ch'i*) from the lower cinnabar field (→ *tan-t'ien*) as far as the throat. However, if damage to the practitioner's health is to be avoided, the inner *ch'i* must not be allowed to escape. For that reason, the practitioner—as the outer breath leaves through his throat—quickly closes his mouth, "beats the heavenly drum" (→ *t'ien-ku*), swallows the inner *ch'i* together with the accumulated saliva (→ *yü-chiang*), and directs it back to the "ocean of breath" (→ *ch'i-hai*). When the breath has been swallowed three times in succession, the *ch'i-hai* is full.

The purpose of this exercise therefore consists in preventing the inner *ch'i* from leaving the body and instead accumulating it in the "ocean of breath"—this being the only way of attaining immortality.

A particularly effective method is that of following the practice of *yen-ch'i* by an exercise known as "allowing the breath to circulate" (→ *hsing-ch'i*) or by "melting the breath" (→ *lien-ch'i*).

Ying-chou   Chin., lit. "world-ocean continent"; one of three islands in the East China Sea believed to be abodes of the immortals (→ *hsien*) and representative of the very epitome of bliss (→ P'eng-lai, → Fang-chang).

Yin Hsi   also known as Kuan-yin-tzu; the Guardian of the (Mountain) Pass encountered by Lao-tzu on his journey to the West. At Yin Hsi's request, Lao-tzu embodied his teachings in a written work consisting of five thousand pictograms and containing his thoughts on the Tao and its → *te*. This has become known as the *Tao-te ching*. Lao-tzu is said to have continued on his journey toward the West. Yin Hsi, as a result of his encounter with Lao-tzu, became an important figure in religious Taoism and was admitted to the Taoist pantheon as an immortal (→ *hsien*). He is furthermore credited with the authorship of the *Kuan-yin-tzu*, which describes and explains various Taoist techniques of meditation.

According to legend, Yin Hsi lived as a recluse. One of his practices consisted in absorbing the essences of the sun and moon (→ *fu jih-hsiang*). It is said that as Lao-tzu came toward him, Yin Hsi was able to tell by his → *ch'i* that he was a true man (→ *chen-jen*). Later he followed Lao-tzu to the West and—like him—disappeared without a trace.

Yin-yang   Chin.; two polar energies that, by their fluctuation and interaction, are the cause of the universe. Yin and yang are polar manifestations of the Tao of the supreme ultimate (→ *t'ai-chi*), their concrete manifestations being Earth and Heaven.

From the intermingling of yin and yang arise the five elements (→ *wu-hsing*); they in turn are the basis of the ten thousand things (→ *wan-wu*). This manifestation of all phenomena is seen as a cyclic process, an endless coming into being and passing away, as everything, upon reaching its extreme stage, transforms into its opposite. The underlying shared characteristic of yin and yang therefore consists in giving rise to this continuous change, which is said to be the movement of the Tao.

The composition of the hexagrams found in the *Book of Change(s)* (→ *I-ching*), from which the concept yin-yang stems, also reflects the view that all things and situations arise from a combination of yin and yang. The two hexagrams → *ch'ien* and *k'un* represent, respectively, pure yang and pure yin; all other hexagrams are combinations of these basic energies.

Originally the word *yin* designated the northern slope of a mountain, i.e., the side facing away from the sun—and was further associated with cold, turgid water and a cloud-covered sky. *Yang* denoted the mountain slope facing the sun and was associated with brightness and warmth.

The system of correspondences between the microcosm and the macrocosm attributes further properties and phenomenal associations to yin and yang: yin is the feminine, the passive, the receptive, the dark, the soft. Symbols of yin are the moon, water, clouds, the tiger, the turtle, the color black, the north, lead, and all even numbers.

Yang corresponds to what is masculine, active, creative, bright, and hard. Symbols of yang are the sun, fire, the dragon, the color red, the south, mercury, and all odd numbers. Yin and yang are represented by a well-known symbol.

The symbol stands for the universe composed of yin and yang, which form a whole only in combination. The two spots in the symbol indicate that each of the two energies—at the highest stage of its realization—already contains the seed of, and is about to transform into, its polar opposite.

Yin-yang symbol

The first known mention of yin-yang occurs in Chapter 5 of the *Hsi-tz'u* (→ *Shih-i*) of the *Book of Change(s)*, which states, "One yin, one yang, that is the Tao." In Book 5, Chapter 2 of the → *Lü-shih ch'un-ch'iu* (*Spring and Autumn Annals*) the arising of all things from yin and yang—the light and the dark—is described as follows: "The Great One produces the two poles [i.e., Heaven and Earth], which in turn give rise to the energies of the dark (yin) and the light (yang). These two energies then transform themselves, one rising upwards and the other descending downwards; they merge again and give rise to forms. They separate and merge again. When they are separate, they merge; when they are merged, they separate. That is the never-ending course of Heaven and Earth. Each end is followed by a beginning; each extreme by a transformation into its opposite. All things are attuned to each other. That from which all beings arise and from which they have their origin, is known as the Great One; that which gives them form and perfection, is the duality of darkness and light" (Wilhelm 1979).

The energies of yin and yang are furthermore of great importance in traditional Chinese medicine. The body is healthy only when yin and yang hold each other in balance. Too much yang causes heightened organic activity; too much yin, an inadequate functioning of the organs.

Yin-yang chia Chin., lit. "School of → Yin-Yang"; Chinese philosophical school that flourished at the end of the Warring States Period (3d century B.C.E.). Originally *yin-yang chia* referred only to teachings that were based on the premise that the universe arises from the interplay of yin and yang. During the Han Dynasty, the meaning of the concept was widened, when the followers of the *yin-yang chia* began to incorporate the teachings about the five elements (→ *wu-hsing*).

The theoretical basis of the Yin-Yang School is to be found in the commentaries on the *Book of Change(s)* (→ *I-ching*)—the so-called *Ten Wings* (→ *Shih-i*)—which tradition attributes to Confucius.

According to the *yin-yang chia,* the universe arises from the fusion of the masculine and the feminine—i.e., yang and yin—which in the *I-ching* are symbolized, respectively, by the trigrams *ch'ien* (Heaven) and *k'un* (Earth), from which all other trigrams arise. Each trigram corresponds to a particular natural energy (→ *pa-kua*).

Specifically, the doctrine of the *yin-yang chia* is based on the eight trigrams of the *I-ching,* which correspond to different natural phenomena and interhuman relationships:

Ch'ien is Heaven, the Ruler and Father, and representative of pure yang.

K'un is Earth, the Mother, and representative of pure yin.

219

Chen is Thunder, the eldest son.
Sun is Wind and Rain, the eldest daughter.
K'an is Water and Clouds, the second son.
Li is Fire and Lightning, the second daughter.
Ken is the Mountain, the youngest son.
Tui is the Lake, the youngest daughter.

The Yin-Yang School also tried to explain the mystery of the universe numerologically, allocating to Heaven (yang) the odd numbers 1, 3, 5, 7, and 9 and to Earth (yin) the even numbers 2, 4, 6, 8, and 10, which are said to complete each other. Later, the *yin-yang chia* made use of numbers to relate the energies of yin and yang to the five elements.

Yü → Ta-yü

Yüan-ch'i Chin., lit. "primordial breath"; the primordial energy in which yin and yang (→ yin-yang) are still closely intermingled and which gives rise to the whole universe— i.e., the multiplicity and variety of the ten thousand things (→ *wan-wu*).

The *yüan-ch'i* corresponds to the inner *ch'i* (→ *nei-ch'i*) found in the human body. The → *Yün-chi ch'i-ch'ien* states, "Before the breaths became separated in order to take on form, they were entangled and resembled an egg. They formed a perfect whole—the Great One [→ T'ai-i]. The *yüan-ch'i* [i.e., the egg-shaped energy forming a whole] ascended in a pure state and became Heaven; when it was already turbid it descended and became Earth."

In addition, the concept of *yüan-ch'i* is of great importance in traditional Chinese medicine.

According to traditional Chinese medicine, the *yüan-ch'i* is produced in the "portal of destiny" (→ *ming-men*) near the kidneys and accumulated in the lower cinnabar field (→ *tan-*

t'ien) or the Ocean of Breath (→ *ch'i-hai*). From there it follows the path of the threefold meridian and disperses to all parts of the body, ensuring the proper functioning of the five organs (→ *wu-tsang*) and the six containers (→ *liu-fu*). By absorbing the *yüan-ch'i* of the cosmos and strengthening it within the body, a person may considerably lengthen the life span.

Yüan-shih t'ien-tsun   Chin., lit. "Celestial Venerable of the Primordial Beginning"; one of the highest deities of religious Taoism (→ *tao-chiao*). Yüan-shih t'ien-tsun is one of the three pure ones (→ *san-ch'ing*) and resides in the Heaven of Jade Purity. He is believed to have come into being at the beginning of the universe as a result of the merging of the pure breaths. He then created Heaven and Earth.

At the beginning of each age or aeon he transmits the *Scriptures of the Magic Jewel* (→ *Ling-pao ching*) to subordinate deities, who in turn instruct mankind in the teachings of the Tao. He rescues souls caught in the various hells and sets them free. Originally, the Celestial Venerable of the Primordial Beginning headed the administration of Heaven but—like a wise ruler—entrusted that task to his assistant, the Jade Emperor (→ *Yü-huang*), whose importance later came to exceed that of Yüan-shih t'ien-tsun.

The earliest mention of Yüan-shih t'ein-tsun occurs in the writings of the alchemist → Ko Hung. Gradually, he came to take the place of → Huang-lao-chün, the most important deity of early Taoism, who now occupies a subordinate place in the celestial hierarchy.

Yüan-shih t'ien-tsun is said to be without beginning and the most supreme of all beings, in fact, representative of the principle of all being. From him all things arose. He is eternal, invisible, and limitless. He is the source of all truths contained in the *Scriptures of the Magic Jewel*. An alternative description of the celestial hierarchy states that the Celestial Venerable of the Primordial Beginning resides in the *ta-luo-t'ien* (→ *t'ien*) above the heavens of the three pure ones.

Yü Chi   also known as Kan Chi, d. 197 C.E.; Taoist scholar, well versed in the teaching on the five elements (→ *wu-hsing*), magic, and medicine. Yü Chi worked as a miracle healer in eastern China, effecting cures by the use of incense and holy water.

Around 145 C.E. he wrote the *T'ai-p'ing ch'ing-ling shu* (*The Book of Supreme Peace and Purity*, → *T'ai-p'ing ching*) which became the doctrinal basis of the School of Supreme Peace (→ *t'ai-p'ing tao*). According to legend, Yü Chi is not the actual author of this work, but is said to have come into its possession in a miraculous manner. In 197 C.E. he was murdered by his relatives.

Yü-chiang   Chin., lit. "jade liquid"; euphemism for saliva. In Taoist health exercises saliva is considered to be an important substance that has to be carefully preserved within the body, because its loss—e.g., by spitting—can result in a dangerous reduction of vitality. For that reason a practice known as *t'un-t'o* ("swallowing the saliva") frequently forms part of Taoist breathing exercises. When the practitioner has swallowed the accumulated saliva in small quantities, it ascends to nourish the brain and then descends to moisten the five organs (→ *wu-tsang*). In Taoist terminology this process is known as "feeding the embryo" (→ *t'ai-shih*). By swallowing his saliva, a practitioner may also succeed in expelling the three worms (→ *san-ch'ung*). Furthermore, the practice is said to strengthen the teeth, the growth of hair, and general resistance to illness.

Swallowing the saliva—which, according to the Taoist view, is produced in two containers below the tongue—is best practiced at dawn. The practitioner adopts a sitting position, closes his eyes, dispels all disturbing thoughts, and claps his teeth together twenty-seven times (→ *k'ou-ch'ih*), causing the cavity of the mouth to fill with saliva. He rinses his teeth with it and, after swallowing it, guides it—by the power of the mind—first to the brain and then downward to the "ocean of breath" (→ *ch'i-hai*). In this way the "three foundations" (→ *san-yüan*) are nourished.

Yü-ch'ing   Chin. → *san-ch'ing*

Yü-huang   Chin., lit. "Jade Emperor"; one of the most important deities in Chinese folk religion and religious Taoism (→ *tao-chiao*); one of the three pure ones (→ *san-ch'ing*). Yü-huang personally determines all that happens in Heaven and on Earth. For this purpose he has at his disposal an enormous celestial administration, which is a faithful replica of the terrestrial administration of the Chinese Empire. Each deity has a clearly defined responsibility. At the beginning of each year all the deities report to the Jade Emperor after ascending to his palace, which is situated in the highest of all the heavens. Depending on how well the deities have lived up to their responsibilities, the Jade Emperor may promote them to higher positions or transfer them to other departments.

The Jade Emperor's earthly representatives are the deity of Mount T'ai (→ T'ai-yüeh ta'ti), the city deities (→ *ch'eng-huang*), the hearth deity (→ Tsao-chün), and the local deities (→ *t'u-ti*). Yü-huang is usually portrayed sitting on a throne, dressed in the ceremonial robes of an emperor, which are embroidered with dragons. On his head he wears the imperial headdress, from the front and back of which dangle thirteen strings of pearls. In his hand he holds a ceremonial plaque. His stern facial expression is meant to express calm and dignity. In the Taoist celestial hierarchy Yü-huang originally was the assistant of the Celestial Venerable of the Primordial Beginning (→ Yüan-shih t'ien-tsun), who later resigned from his post in favor of the Jade Emperor, thereby making him the most important deity in the Taoist pantheon.

According to legend, Yü-huang was the son of a king. Before he was born, his mother had a dream in which → Lao-chün handed her a child. After the death of his father the young prince ascended to the throne but abdicated his office after only a few days to withdraw to the mountains and study the Tao. Upon attaining perfection, he devoted the remainder of his life to the sick and poor, instructing them in the Tao. After 3,200 world periods he became a golden immortal and after a further hundred million aeons, the Jade Emperor.

The cult of Yü-huang began in the 11th century C.E. In the year 1005 C.E. the then emperor—Sung Chen-tsung—was forced to conclude a humiliating treaty with a foreign power and thus was in danger of losing the support of the people. To pacify them, the emperor posed as a visionary and claimed to be in direct communication with Heaven. He further stated that an immortal (→ *hsien*) had appeared to him in a dream, handing him a letter from Yü-huang, who promised that the founder of the dynasty would appear to him. With the fulfillment of this promise began the veneration of the Jade Emperor, to whom Sung Hui-tsung, in 1115 C.E., erected the first temple, and on whom he bestowed the title *Shang-ti* (God).

Yü-huang's palace is situated in the highest Taoist heaven, known as *ta-luo-t'ien* (→ *t'ien*). From there he rules the whole of the universe, i.e., the subordinate heavens, the Earth, and the lower regions. His palace is guarded by a figure known as the Transcendental Official (*Ling-kuan*), who was so widely venerated during the 15th century that a separate temple was dedicated to him in Peking.

Yü-huang had a large family: one of his sisters was the mother of Erh-lang, who dispels evil spirits by setting the Hounds of Heaven (*t'ien-kou*) on them; one of his wives is the so-called horse-headed deity, who rules over silkworms; and one of his daughters, known as the "Seventh Lady" (Ch'i ku-niang), is venerated by all girls wanting to know whom they will marry.

The immeasurably vast administration of the Jade Emperor contains ministries responsible for various natural phenomena and aspects of human existence, such as thunder, wind, water, fire, time, sacred mountains, war, literature, wealth, medicine, epidemics, etc. Each of these ministries is run by a president with a large number of subordinates. However, only very few of these have become significant in the religious life of the Chinese people.

These divine officials look after the spiritual and material welfare of mankind and are punished by Yü-huang if they neglect their duties. In reality, however, all these tasks were the responsibility of the terrestrial administration under the emperor. In other words: if the deity responsible for rain neglected its duties, it was "warned" by an imperial official, who would try to persuade it by logical arguments to live up to its responsibilities. If this intervention did not bring the desired result, the deity would be threatened with the loss of its rank. As a last resort, its noble title would be withdrawn by imperial decree. These changes in the celestial hierarchy and the appointment of new deities were confirmed by Taoist priests (→ *tao-shih*) at special religious ceremonies.

Yü-jen Chin., lit. "feather man"; alternative designation for a Taoist priest (→ *tao-shih*). Originally, feather men were flying immortals (→ *hsien*), whose bodies were covered with a coat of feathers. As a result of the Taoist belief that *tao-shih*, after attaining immortality (→ *ch'ang-sheng pu-ssu*), ascend to Heaven in broad daylight (→ *fei-sheng*), they also came to be referred to as *yü-jen*.

Yün-chi ch'i-ch'ien Chin., lit. *"Cloud Book Cassette and Seven Strips of Bamboo";* an 11th-century Taoist encyclopedia consisting of 122 volumes. The special containers of Taoist scriptures are known as "cloud book cassettes"; the seven strips of bamboo refer to the four main parts and seven subsections of the Taoist canon (→ *Tao-tsang*). The *Yün-chi ch'i-ch'ien* contains a complete survey of Taoist exercises aimed at prolonging life and of meditation practices up to the time of the Sung Dynasty.

It is an extremely extensive work, providing additional information on all aspects of religious Taoism, such as biographies of immortals (→ *hsien*), instructions for hygiene and breathing exercises, descriptions of the methods of the Inner and Outer Elixir Schools (→ *nei-tan*, → *wai-tan*), sexual techniques (→ *fang-chung shu*), magical practices (→ *fang-shih*), fasting ceremonies, etc. A further aspect of the *Yün-chi ch'i-ch'ien*'s importance for Taoist scholars is that it contains passages or chapters of Taoist works that are no longer extant.

Yün-chuan Chin., lit. "cloud writing"; a style of writing used in religious Taoism (→ *tao-chiao*). *Yüan-chuan* resembles a script known as seal script. Its curved lines are an imitation of cirrus clouds, hence its name.

Cloud writing is difficult to read and can only be understood by initiates. It is often found on talismans and amulets (→ *fu-lu*) and is said to be imbued with miraculous properties, such as the power to cure sickness and ward off evil spirits and demons.

Yü-pu Chin., lit. "step of Yü" (→ Ta-yü); magic Taoist dance said to have originated with Great Yü, the founder of the Hsia Dynasty and Master of the Waves. The dance is performed by Taoist masters (→ *tao-shih*), often in a state of trance. It enables them to get in touch with supernatural forces and thus serves to dispel evil spirits and demons. The "step of Yü" is considered to be the most ancient form of Taoist magic.

The legends about the origin of *Yü-pu* vary; one states that Yü observed this manner of walking in birds who were trying to crack open pebbles. According to another, Great Yü overexerted himself when he was taming the waves and thereafter walked with a limp. The dance is thought to be an imitation of his limping gait. Yet other traditions state that Yü was taught this sequence of steps by the heavenly spirits to give him power over the forces of nature.

Yü Yen 1258–1314 C.E.; Taoist scholar famous for his interpretation of the *Book of Change(s)* (→ *I-ching*) and an expert in alchemy. In his writings, Yü Yen combines Taoist and neo-Confucianist ideas. He is the author of commentaries on the *I-ching,* the *Chou-i ts'an-t'ung-ch'i* of → Wei P'o-yang, and other texts.

Bibliography

Primary Sources

Blofeld, John (trans.). 1965. *I Ching: The Book of Change.* London.

Chai, Ch'u, and Chai, Winberg. 1965. *The Sacred Books of Confucius, and Other Confucian Classics* (6 vols.). New Hyde Park, N.Y.

Chang Chung-yuan (trans.). 1975. *Tao: A New Way of Thinking. A Translation of the Tao Te Ching.* New York.

Chia Yü. See Wilhelm 1981*a*.

Chuang-tzu. See H. A. Giles 1961, Graham 1981, Legge 1962, Watson 1968.

Confucius (Konfutse). *See Chia Yü, Lun Yü, Shih Ching, Shu Ching.*

Feng, Gia-fu, and English, Jane. 1972. *Tao Te Ching.* New York. (London, 1973.)

Giles, Herbert A. (trans.). 1961. *Chuang Tzu: Taoist Philosopher and Chinese Mystic.* London.

Giles, Lionel (trans.). 1910. *Sun Tzu: The Art of War.* London.

_____.1912. *Taoist Teachings from the Book of Lieh Tzu.* London.

Graham, A. C. (trans.). 1978. *Later Mohist Logic, Ethics, and Science.* London & Hong Kong.

_____.1981. *Chuang Tzu: The Inner Chapters.* London.

Huang Ti Nei Ching Su Wen. See Veith 1966.

I Ching. See Blofeld 1965, Legge 1964, Wilhelm 1967.

K'ung Tzu. *See* Confucius.

Lao-tzu. *See Tao Te Ching.*

Lau, D. C. (trans.). 1963. *Lao Tzu: Tao Te Ching.* London.

_____.1979. *The Analects (Lun Yü).* New York.

Legge, James (trans.). 1861–1872. *The Chinese Classics.* Hong Kong; London 1875–1876.

_____.1962. *The Texts of Taoism* (2 vols.). New York.

_____.1964. *The Sacred Books of China* (6 vols.). Delhi. (Orig. pub. Oxford 1879–1885)

Li-chi. See Chai & Chai 1965, Legge 1964.

Lieh-tzu. See L. Giles 1912, Wilhelm 1981*b.*

Lin Yutang (trans.). 1948. *The Wisdom of Laotse.* New York.

_____.1949. *The Wisdom of China.* London.

Lun-yü. See Lau 1979; Legge 1861–1872, 1964; Waley 1938; Ware 1950.

Lü Shih Ch'un Ch'iu. See Wilhelm 1979.

Mei, Yi-Pao (trans.). 1929. *The Ethical and Political Works of Motse.* London.

Meng-tzu. See Legge 1861–1872, 1964.

Miyuki, Mokusen (trans.). 1984. *Die Erfahrung der goldenen Blüte* [The Secret of the Golden Flower]. Bern.

Mo Ti. *See* Graham 1978, Mei 1929, Watson 1967.

Shih Ching. See Legge 1861–1872, 1964.

Shu Ching. See Legge 1861–1872, 1964.

Sun Tzu. See L. Giles 1910.

T'ai Hsüan Ching. See Walters 1983.

T'ai I Chin Hua Tsung Chih. See Wilhelm 1938.

T'ai Shang Kan Ying P'ien Ku. See Legge 1962.

Tao-te Ching. See Chang 1975; Feng and English 1972; Lau 1963; Legge 1962, 1964; Lin 1948; Waley 1958; Wei 1982; Wing 1986.

Veith, Ilza (trans.). 1966. *The Yellow Emperor's Classic of Internal Medicine*. Berkeley.

Waley, Arthur (trans.). 1938. *The Analects of Confucius*. London & New York.

_____.1958. *The Way and Its Power: A Study of the Tao Te Ching and Its Place in Chinese Thought*. New York.

Walters, Derek (trans.). 1983. *The T'ai Hsüan Ching: The Hidden Classic. A Lost Companion of the I Ching*. Wellingborough, England.

Ware, James R. (trans.). 1950 *The Best of Confucius*. Garden City, N.Y.

Watson, Burton (trans.). 1967. *Basic Writings of Mo Tzu, Hsün Tzu, and Han Fei Tzu*. New York.

_____.1968. *The Complete Works of Chuang Tzu*. New York.

Wei, Henry. 1982. *The Guiding Light of Lao-tzu*. London.

Wilhelm, Richard (trans.). 1938 (repub. 1975). *The Secret of the Golden Flower*, trans. Cary F. Baynes. New York. (London, 1962)

_____.1967. *The I Ching, or, Book of Changes*, trans. Cary F. Baynes. Princeton, N.J.

_____.1969. *Dschuang Dsi: Das wahre Buch vom südlichen Blütenland*. Düsseldorf and Cologne.

_____.1979. *Frühling und Herbst des Lü Bu We*. Düsseldorf & Cologne.

_____.1981*a*. *Kungfutse: Schulgespräche (Gia Yü)*. Düsseldorf and Cologne.

_____.1981*b*. *Liä Dsi: Das wahre Buch vom quellenden Urgrund*. Düsseldorf and Cologne.

_____.1982. *Mong Dsi: Die Lehrgespräche des Meisters Meng K'o*. Düsseldorf and Cologne.

Wing, R. L. (trans.). 1986. *The Tao of Power*. Wellingborough, England.

Secondary Sources

Bauer, Wolfgang. 1974. *China und die Hoffnung auf Glück.* Munich.

Béky, Gellért. 1972. *Die Welt des Tao.* Freiburg & Munich.

Blofeld, John. 1973. *The Secret and the Sublime: Taoist Mysteries and Magic.* London.

_____.1974. *Beyond the Gods: Taoist and Buddhist Mysticism.* London.

_____.1978. *Taoism: The Road to Immortality.* Boulder, Colo.

_____.1979. *Taoism: The Quest for Immortality.* London.

_____.1983. *Selbstheilung durch die Kraft der Stille.* Bern.

Carus, Paul. 1907. *Chinese Thought.* La Salle, Ill.

Chan, Wing-tsit. 1979. *Commentary on Lao-Tzu.* Honolulu.

Chang Chung-yuan. 1963. *Creativity and Taoism.* New York.

Christie, Anthony. 1968. *Chinesische Mythologie.* Wiesbaden.

Colegrave, Sukie. 1980. *Yin und Yang* (German translation of *The Spirit in the Valley*). Bern.

Cooper, J. C. 1977. *Der Weg des Tao.* Bern.

_____.1981. *Yin & Yang: The Taoist Harmony of Opposites.* Wellingborough, England.

_____.1984. *Chinese Alchemy.* Wellingborough, England.

Delius, Rudolf von. 1930. *Kungfutse: Seine Persönlichkeit und seine Lehre.* Leipzig.

Diederichs, Ulf (ed.). 1984. *Erfahrungen mit dem I Ging.* Cologne.

Doré, Henri. 1911–1938. *Recherches sur les superstitions en Chine* (18 parts). Shanghai.

Durdin-Robertson, Lawrence. 1976. *The Goddesses of India, Tibet, China and Japan.* Clonegal.

Eberhard, Wolfram. 1986. *A Dictionary of Chinese Symbols.* London & New York.

Eisenberg, David. 1985. *Encounters with Qi: Exploring Chinese Medicine*. New York.

Fung Yu-lan. 1953. *A History of Chinese Philosophy*. Princeton, N.J.

Granet, Marcel. 1934. *La pensée chinoise*. Paris.

_____.1950. *Chinese Civilisation*. London.

_____.1975. *The Religion of the Chinese People*. New York.

Gulik, Robert van. 1961. *Sexual Life in Ancient China*. Leiden.

Homann, Rolf. 1971. *Die wichtigsten Körpergottheiten des Huang-t'ing-ching*. Göppingen.

Hook, Diana Farington. 1980. *The I Ching and Its Associations*. London & Boston.

Jaspers, Karl. 1966. *Anaximander, Heraclitus, Paramenides, Plotinus, Lao-tzu, Nagarjuna*. New York.

Jou, Tsung Hwa. 1980. *The Tao of Tai-chi Chuan*. Piscataway, N.J.

_____.1983. *The Tao of Meditation*. Piscataway, N.J.

Kaltenmark, Max. 1969. *Lao Tzu and Taoism*. Stanford.

Kielce, Anton. 1985. *Taoismus*. Munich.

Lai, T. C. 1972. *The Eight Immortals*. Hong Kong.

Legeza, Laszlo. 1975. *Tao Magic*. London.

Li, Dun Jen. 1975. *The Civilization of China*. New York.

Lu K'uan Yü (Charles Luk). 1969. *Secrets of Chinese Meditation*. London. (New York, 1964)

Malek, Roman. 1985. *Das Chai-chieh lu: Materialien zur Liturgie im Taoismus*. Frankfurt & New York.

Maspéro, Henri. 1981. *Taoism and Chinese Religion*. Amherst, Mass.

Needham, Joseph. 1954–1965. *Science and Civilization in China* (5 vols.). Cambridge, England.

_____.1977. *Wissenschaftlicher Universalismus: Über Bedeutung und Besonderheit der chinesischen Wissenschaft*. Frankfurt.

Opitz, Peter J. (ed.). 1968. *Chinesisches Alterum und konfuzianische Klassik*. Munich.

Pálos, Stephan. 1980. *Atem und Meditation*. Bern.

_____.1984. *Chinesische Heilkunst*. Bern.

Porkert, Manfred. 1978. *China: Konstanten im Wandel*. Stuttgart.

Rawson, Philip, and Legeza, Laszlo. 1973. *Tao: The Eastern Philosophy of Time and Change*. Farnborough, Hampshire, England.

Robinet, Isabelle. 1979. *Méditation taoiste*. Paris.

Rossbach, Sarah. 1983. *Feng Shui: The Chinese Art of Placement*. New York.

Saso, Michael. 1968. *The Teachings of Taoist Master Chuang*. New Haven.

Schipper, Kristof. 1982. *Le corps taoiste*. Paris.

Schluchter, Wolfgang (ed.). 1982. *Max Webers Studien über Konfuzianismus und Taoismus*. Frankfurt.

Sherrill, Wallace A., and Wen Kuan Chu. 1977. *An Anthology of I Ching*. London.

_____.1976. *The Astrology of the I Ching*. New York & London.

Simbriger, Heinrich. 1961. *Geheimnis der Mitte: Aus dem geistigen Vermächtnis des alten China*. Düsseldorf & Cologne.

Siu, R. G. H. 1974. *A Neo-Taoist Approach to Life*. Cambridge, Mass.

Sivin, Nathan. 1968. *Chinese Alchemy: Preliminary Studies*. Cambridge, Mass.

Skinner, Stephen. 1982. *The Living Earth Manual of Feng Shui: Chinese Geomancy*. London & Boston.

Smith, D. Howard. 1974. *Confucius*. Frogmore, England.

Twam, Kim. 1982. *Geheime Übungen taoistischer Mönche*. Freiburg.

Unterreider, Else. 1984. *Glück ein ganzes Mondjahr lang.* Klagenfurt.

Watts, Alan. 1975. *Tao: The Watercourse Way.* New York.

Welch, Holmes. 1957. *The Parting of the Way.* London.

Werner, E. T. C. 1961. *A Dictionary of Chinese Mythology.* New York.

Wilhelm, Hellmut. 1960. *Change: Eight Lectures on the I Ching.* New York.

_____.1972. *Sinn des I-Ging.* Düsseldorf & Cologne.

Wing. R. L. 1979. *The I Ching Workbook.* New York.

Zenker, E. V. 1941. *Der Taoismus der Frühzeit.* Vienna.

Zöller, Josephine. 1984. *Das Tao der Selbstheilung.* Bern.